JX   Clemens, Walter C.
1974
C4845   The superpowers and
        arms control: from
        cold war to
        interdependence

             23427 -2

DATE			

© THE BAKER & TAYLOR CO.

The Superpowers and Arms Control

The Superpowers and Arms Control

From Cold War to Interdependence

Walter C. Clemens, Jr.
Boston University and
Russian Research Center,
Harvard University

Lexington Books
D.C. Heath and Company
Lexington, Massachusetts
Toronto   London

Library of Congress Cataloging in Publication Data

Clemens, Walter C. Jr.
    The superpowers and arms control.

    1. Disarmament. 2. United States—Foreign relations—Russia. 3. Russia—
Foreign relations—United States. I. Title.
JX1974.C4845   327'.174   73-11657
ISBN 0-669-85480-8

Published simultaneously in Canada.

Printed in the United States of America.

International Standard Book Number: 0-669-85480-8

Library of Congress Catalog Card Number: 73-11657

For Diane

"Iz Rossii s liubov'iu"

677358

Contents

viii

List of Figures and Tables

Preface

"My topic," gentlemen, "is what the Russians are doing; why they behave that way; and what we ought to do about it." The meeting was not a convention of the Birch Society and the speaker was not a local Minuteman. Rather, it was a gathering of people from the business and policy-making establishment, and the speaker was a leading U.S. arms negotiator and defense planner—of liberal stripe. Given the premises implicit in his first words, it was not surprising that some distortion clouded his presentation. What this negotiator and many other thoughtful persons have neglected is the impact of the West upon Soviet policy.

The present study also originated in efforts to learn what the Soviet leaders were doing—and why—so that Westerners could better decide what to do about it. As such studies go, they are perhaps necessary but not entirely adequate for comprehending the USSR or knowing "what to do" about Soviet policy. To grasp the dynamics of Kremlin politics is in any case very difficult, but the task will not be made easier if the USSR is looked upon as an object and the United States as a subject. Because of the bipolar power structure that has persisted for most of the time since World War II, the moves of both superpowers must be seen as a dyadic pattern in which interaction is a key ingredient. To be sure, many U.S. and Soviet moves are also generated without much regard for what the other superpower is doing or how it may respond. It is very difficult to sort out the policy influences that come from domestic sources, from the availability of certain technologies, and from external stimuli. To minimize the role of stimulus and response, however, is surely to miss seeing ourselves as others see us, and to fail in our efforts to understand why others "behave that way."

Soviet ideas and actions—no less than the West's—have been based on perceptions and experiences that reflect international as well as domestic and ideological inputs, sparked often by the "mad momentum" of modern technology. The present book concludes that there has not been (nor should there be) any automatic tendency for the two rivals to maintain perfect symmetry in their power structures and mutual relations. Nonetheless the explanation for each escalation (or de-escalation) of the cold war and arms race must be looked for, at least partially, in the actions—some conciliatory, some refractory—of the other side.

If a Western reader picks up a Soviet text on East-West relations, the limitations of a one-side focus will seem most blatant. "True," this reader might say, "the West embarked on the Truman Doctrine, on NATO, on deployment of tactical nuclears in Europe, and so on, just as this Soviet book says. But its analysis leaves out the vital point that these were all *defensive* actions, responses to Soviet moves threatening the West." Scholars under less pressure to justify the moves of their own government, however, should strive for higher standards of objectivity.

Many readers will also put down with impatience the Western court histories that portray the policies of Washington and its allies as purely defensive moves in the struggle to defend "freedom." Many readers will also be offended by the extreme attacks on self-righteous orthodoxy which suggest that, if the West can do no good, the East can do no evil. A content analysis of both schools' footnotes suggests, on the whole, that few in either camp have read Soviet sources. And those that do read Russian rarely examine Western policy-making with as much care as they do the interstices of the Kremlin and its official publications.[a]

Pairs of Scylla and Charybdis dangers confront the student of the cold war and arms race at every turn. Even a centrist approach will have great difficulty in following the actual course of human history, replete with discontinuous zigs and zags as well as partial continuities. The present book attempts to steer clear of some of these perils by examining the problems of East-West relations from the standpoint of each superpower *and* from an overview of their dyadic relationship. It seeks to employ both history and social science to understand the evolution of these problems, and to answer such policy-oriented questions as: Can the USSR live with stability? Can U.S. interests be maintained with a strategic posture of "sufficiency"? What are the obstacles and the conditions for controlling the arms race? How effective has arms control proved as a way to peace? What principles should guide future efforts at war prevention and arms control? And finally, how can the cold war relationship be converted into one that benefits from and enlarges the domain of U.S.-Soviet interdependence?

Like other books, this one may say as much (or more) about its author as its intended subjects. Where objectivity is difficult, due in part to the political sensitivity of the material, it may be especially important to be explicit about the author's own values. An interest in reducing East-West misunderstandings developed during a sophomore year in Austria, still under four-power rule in 1952-53, when the author saw first hand not only some remnants of World War II (one-legged skiers as well as damaged buildings) and the potential for another

[a]Few observers of East-West relations have had the compassion and and historical sensitivity for the problems of all sides which the late Philip E. Mosely, for example, gathered from experience working on archives in Moscow in the grim years of 1930-32; doing ethnographic work in the Balkans in the late 1930s; and sitting on the councils that planned the postwar world. Such a man could advise his government during the Potsdam Conference that if Washington continued its position on reparations, Moscow might gain the impression that the United States sympathized more with the German than with the Soviet people. Mosely could also reflect: "Soviet acceptance, without bargaining, of a zone of slightly more than one third of Germany, appeared a moderate and conciliatory approach to the problem of how to deal with postwar Germany." In terms of "war effort and war-inflicted sufferings, the Soviet Union might have claimed a larger share." (See *The Foreign Relations of the United States: The Conference of Berlin [The Potsdam Conference], 1945* [2 vols.; Washington, D.C.: U.S. Government Printing Office, 1960], II, 850; and Philip E. Mosely, *The Kremlin and World Politics* [New York: Vintage Books, 1960], p. 156.) As U.S.-Soviet relations grew more strained and as Mosely became further removed from direct dealings with Russian scholars and diplomats, however, some of his work—like that of most Western writers—reflected the abstractions of the cold war *Zeitgeist* and official orthodoxy.

war (e.g., in the clumsy dealings which Americans and Russians had with each other in occupied Vienna). Five years after some disarming experiences in Vienna, the author came to know and like many Russians and aspects of Russian culture during an exchange year at Moscow University. Living in a country enables one to appreciate not only its positive but also its negative aspects (especially where intellectual freedoms are curtailed). These were vividly recalled again when field research on the Czechoslovak Springtime was interrupted by the military intervention directed from Moscow. If one could stand apart from these experiences, however, the role of misunderstanding in world affairs—even in relations between Czechs and Soviets in 1968—remains quite ˙salient.

And if a scholar is critical toward other governments, should he not be still more concerned about his own, for which he bears more responsibility? To be sure, the burden of a heavy defense effort weighs heavily on Russia and her neighbors—as it has for over a thousand years. But as Henry Steele Commager has pointed out, many of America's crises have been self-generated through a paranoia about security threats from outside and from within. These anxieties have helped produce policies that have wasted the resources not only of America but of her adversaries, and kept them from helping their own peoples and others even less fortunate in Asia, Africa and Latin America.

Some of the conflicts which have troubled U.S.-Soviet relations since 1945 were likely, owing to the objective realities of the times. But many of them have been virtually self-imposed—by both sides. Enlightened self-interest would have led each party to policies from which both might have gained.

Is it futile to analyze the ways in which policies could be made more "rational," more in accord with the values they are supposed to promote? Perhaps, for one generation rarely benefits from the negative lessons of another. There are also the ironies of history: That which we intend may produce quite different results. Nonetheless, as Marshall D. Shulman has noted, the superpowers may be on an upward learning curve. Both scholars and statesmen should do what they can to sustain that momentum.

Walden Pond
July 4, 1973

Acknowledgments

Many scholars, friends, and family have contributed to this work directly or indirectly: providing moral support; reading the manuscript; making bibliographical suggestions; generating inspiration from afar. These have included Lincoln P. Bloomfield, Diane Shaver Clemens, Alexander Dallin, Sergei Fedorenko, Raymond L. Garthoff, William E. Griffith, Franklyn Griffiths, Thomas Karas, Stephen F. Kenney, Roman Kolkowicz, Joseph Kruzel, Philip E. Mosely, Fred Warner Neal, Valerii Riabskii, Robin A. Remington, Steven Rosen, Carol A. Sakoian, Marshall D. Shulman, Boris E. Shtein, and Jerome B. Wiesner. They have included also many members of the Harvard-M.I.T. Arms Control Seminar, the Russian Research Center, and the Harvard Centers for International Affairs and for West European Studies; also a number of U.S. and Soviet officials; diplomats and scholars from other countries; and the 151 respondents to the Expert Survey Panel data file; and—in their own ways—Lani, Ellen, and W.C. Clemens, Sr.

Support for various components of the research has been received from the Ford Foundation, Inter-University Travel Grant Committee, the Stanley Foundation, the M.I.T. Center for Space Research, the Boston University Graduate School, and the *War/Peace Report*. Much of the work has grown out of earlier research sponsored by the U.S. Arms Control and Disarmament Agency and conducted with other scholars from Columbia and Harvard Universities, the M.I.T. Center for International Studies, and the Institute for Defense Analyses. Parts of Chapters 1, 2 and 4 were first published in *Worldview Magazine*, XVI, No. 2 (February 1973), pp. 40-47, *International Affairs* (London), IL, No. 3 (July 1973), pp. 385-401, and *World Affairs*, CXXXV, No. 3 (Winter 1972), pp. 197-219.

Introduction: Were/Are the Cold War and Arms Race Inevitable?

Many—probably most—writers, both "East" and "West," have contended that both the cold war and the arms race have been virtually inevitable because of one or more components in the post-World War confrontation: the geopolitics of divided Europe and Asia; the economic and political systems of the Soviet and Western "camps"; their different stages of growth and internal needs; the dynamics of military and other technologies; the psychology and ideology of the ruling elites in Moscow and in the West.[1] These analysts have disagreed on the weight to be assigned to particular factors, but they concur with Louis Halle that the superpowers' struggle was no less inexorable than that of a scorpion and a tarantula locked together in a bottle, their self-preservation instincts impelling them to fight one another to the death. While most writers share Halle's contention that the struggle was an "irreducible dilemma," many dispute his view that this was "not fundamentally a case of the wicked against the virtuous." Indeed, many historians have been concerned to assign major responsibility for the conflict to one side or the other. Some also disagree with Halle that, "For the moment, at least, no understanding between [the two sides] is possible," the "realist" school holding that the antagonists fought because they *correctly* assessed each other.[2] Internal contradictions are not unknown in the cold war studies: Thus, we find leading authorities holding on one page that it is futile to look for causes or assign responsibility for the conflict; on another berating the United States for overestimating Soviet power; and on a third noting that Washington missed many of Stalin's "cues." John G. Stoessinger and others, however, have explicitly noted the role of subjective factors such as misperception exacerbated by cultural divergencies, memories of past hurts, and inadequate communications systems.[3]

The arms race, most analysts also concur, was a natural consequence of the cold war and, in turn, a propelling agent.[4] A model of "multiple symmetry" has been advanced to explain this aspect of the rivalry: Each rival in such a competition must endeavor to match every asset of the adversary, both in degree and in kind. If he fails to do so, he will inexorably suffer in the overall competition, for the cold war entails intense rivalry on every plane, including the military. If the Americans have one or one thousand atomic bombs, Moscow must have the same. If Soviet espionage provides strategic intelligence and carries out subversive operations, it must be matched if not surpassed by American analogues. If the "free world" powers have multilateral economic and military alliances, so must the Soviet bloc.[5]

If the deterministic arguments of the cold war theorists are accepted, there is no basis for believing that the cold war can be tamed, unless the necessary and sufficient causes of the competition have been removed or transformed. But two of the major offending agents of various theorists, the capitalist economic system and the Soviet one-party regime, are still very much intact. If either of these is the *bête noire* of a particular world view, its proponents must argue that any apparent improvement in East-West relations is a snare and illusion. If the fundamental causes of communist-capitalist rivalry remain, the compulsion to match or exceed the foe militarily will persist both in Moscow and Washington. Since the profound roots of the arms race remain, military and political planning should assume the worst case, i.e., the most destructive capacity and most hostile intentions should be attributed to the adversary. Security should then be sought in superiority, not in will-o'-the-wisp agreements to stabilize the competition. Arms control should be seen as a form of gamesmanship or psychological warfare, an instrument for pursuing the revolution (or counterrevolution) by "other" means.[a]

The fact is that science cannot demonstrate and history does not support the contention that the cold war and/or arms race were unavoidable. Strictly speaking, no event in the life of individuals or collectivities is "necessary" until it actually occurs. Claims that the cold war and arms race were foreordained are overwhelmed by a series of epistemological objections: Are cold war theorists talking about tangible phenomena or mental constructs? There is not even a commonly accepted definition of the concepts at issue; no consensus on the dependent and independent variables entailed; no accord on when the subjects of analysis began (1917? 1945? 1948?) or when they ended (1953? 1963? 1973?)—if they ever did. What were the necessary and sufficient causes for these competitive relationships? What factors made them "necessary" and not just likely? Why did they spread across so many dimensions of East-West relations? Why did they not escalate into hot war? Why, if these conflicts have abated, did they wither at one point in time rather than another? Why could they not have been curtailed in scope or intensity at some earlier period?[6]

The logical spectrum along which East-West relations may proceed can be defined both quantitatively and qualitatively, as suggested in Figure 1-1. Cold war, for example, is characterized by intense conflict (short of overt warfare) along many dimensions—military, economic, cultural, etc. If the conflict diminishes in intensity and exists on fewer planes, there is movement toward "relaxation of tensions." Should this de-escalation continue, there may be "détente" (of short or long duration). With further improvement in relations, there may be "rapprochement" and even a working understanding or "entente" and collaboration on certain problems. If relations develop in the opposite direction, the movement is toward war: local, limited, conventional, thermonuclear. Interdependence is a fact of life all along the spectrum, but is more likely to be recognized as tensions decrease. Arms controls may benefit both

---

[a]For a more adequate definition of "arms control," and a comparison with "disarmament," see below, Chapter 4.

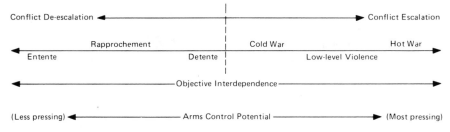

Figure I-1. Spectrum of East-West Relations

sides anywhere on the spectrum, even if these powers are engaged in overt warfare; if the parties move away from conflict, arms control becomes more feasible but also less pressing, as the sources of arms competition diminish.[b]

The assumption that "what was" equalled "what had to be" is a common historical fallacy. We simply do not know and cannot know what forces, what acts, what decisions pushed the superpowers over the brink toward cold war in the years 1945-48, and what developments might have held back this movement and instead perpetuated or intensified the collaborative relationships worked out in the anti-Fascist coalition. Rather than a scorpion and a tarantula, the superpowers often resembled half-blind giants, unsure whether to shake hands or attempt to throw the other to the floor. When one extended his hand, the other felt it sweep by his elbow; by the time the second giant put forward his own hand, the other was ready with a shoulder lock. In 1945-47, for example, American diplomats advocated a four-power security pact to suppress any threat from a resurgent Germany or Japan.[7] By the time Moscow responded with a counter-plan of its own, however, the containment policy had been adopted by Washington.[8] We cannot be sure that the positions of both sides on such issues would have ever been harmonized. Perhaps they were deliberately out-of-phase for purposes of psychological warfare. We cannot know with certainty that mutual accommodation was possible unless a specific agreement was reached and observed. But neither can we be sure that meaningful accords were fatalistically precluded.

The record does show that individuals and their decisions were able to affect the rise and fall of the cold war. President Eisenhower, for example, overruled his Secretary of State to pursue summit politics with Khrushchev and Bulganin in 1955. Indeed, after suffering a heart attack, Eisenhower had to correct a Dulles draft letter to Bulganin from a Denver hospital bed because "inadver-

[b]Marshall D. Shulman has drawn a careful distinction between an "atmosphere of détente" and a "rapprochement or real stabilization." "To wish to operate in a climate of reduced tension does not necessarily imply a desire for political settlements. . . ." What distinguishes a relaxation of tensions from real stabilization "is the fact that fundamental purposes are far from harmonized." See his *Beyond the Cold War* (New Haven: Yale University Press, 1966), p. 58.

tently [*sic*] Foster had omitted" the fundamental *quid pro quo* which Ike extended to the Russians in return for acceptance of his open skies plan.[9] At the October Foreign Ministers Conference, however, both Dulles and Molotov acted in concert to scuttle whatever movement toward detente had flowed from the summit. What if, instead of placing a "reservation" on all American "pre-summit" disarmament positions in September 1955, U.S. diplomacy had carefully explored the grounds for mutual agreement when Moscow accepted the basic principles of the Western position on May 10?[10]

Had Kennedy and Khrushchev allowed their governments to come to blows in 1962, had they not concluded arms control and other accords in 1962-63, historians might well have concluded that the weight of objective forces made detente impossible at that time. The partial ban on nuclear testing signed in 1963 could easily have *looked* unattainable had the U.S. President and Soviet party chief not played their cards close to their vest, signalling one another of a serious interest in an accommodation and bypassing internal opposition to the accord.[11] Similarly, the accords reached by Nixon and Brezhnev in 1972-73 could easily have been derailed. The bombing and mining of North Vietnam could have "precluded" the Moscow Summit as effectively as the U-2 incident subverted the Paris meeting in 1960. The objective challenges to detente were severe in all these cases; what differed was the willingness and ability of the governments on both sides to overcome them.

How valid is the multiple symmetry model of the cold war competition and the arms race? It is suggestive of the way that nations in conflict react to one another, often misperceiving and exaggerating threats from the other side. But the model is much too simplistic to fit the facts. There are many occasions when Moscow or the Western powers chose *not* to match the other side in numbers or types of weaponry. The Warsaw Pact, if an answer to NATO, came six years too late. Its purposes were rather to constitute a formal response to West Germany's entry to NATO. Events (Poland, Hungary, later Czechoslovakia) helped turn the Pact into an instrument for control within Eastern Europe. Only in the early 1960s did the Pact commence multilateral maneuvers and other procedures long characteristic of the Western alliance. Similarly, the COMECON was for years only a formal response to the European Recovery Program. If we look at specific weapons systems, we find that each side often did "its own thing," capitalizing on whatever strengths were available, e.g., Soviet deployment of hundreds of medium and intermediate range missiles targeted on hostage Europe, combined with elaborate efforts to bluff the existence of large ICBM forces as America started up a massive Minuteman and Polaris deployment program.

Multiple symmetry is inadequate to explain the restraint that has occasionally characterized both Soviet and U.S. decisions on weaponry. It also fails to explain other moves fueled by domestic pressures or the seductive temptation to exploit available technology to the hilt, regardless of external threat.

Multiple symmetry is also weak as a prescriptive principle, since it would be undesirable and unnecessary for two rivals to attempt matching each other in every dimension of power. Each side, after all, has unique advantages to exploit and vulnerabilities to defend. Both geography and history have made the USSR more "defense-minded" than the United States. It was natural (if not strictly rational) for the USSR to put more resources into air and missile defenses than the United States. It was fortunate that Washington did not automatically follow the Soviet example, for this gave both powers a chance to deliberate whether mutual forbearance in ABM defenses would not benefit both sides. If accepted as a prescriptive principle, multiple symmetry would imply that arms control can be neither feasible nor desirable.

It seems clear that, given a cold war mentality, competition in arms was highly probable, particularly during the time when the United States had a commanding lead in the most lethal of weapons and the USSR had no persuasive deterrent of her own. Even with high levels of tension, however, both sides might have found some accords that enhanced their common interest in survival and other basic values. Indeed, the record shows that conflict and cooperation often coexisted in counterpoint. In the 1950s, for example, crises over Hungary, Suez, the Taiwan Straits, and Berlin alternated with agreements on the Austrian State Treaty; the establishment of the International Atomic Energy Agency; a moratorium on nuclear testing; the demilitarization of Antarctica; and summit negotiations in Geneva and Camp David. There were many other occasions on which significant agreements seemed close, but slipped from grasp.

Despite the persistence of East-West crises and unsettling developments in technology and alliance patterns, the Soviet and American governments succeeded in widening the sphere of their agreements on arms control, moving from peripheral to central issues from the late 1950s to early 1970s. Had they failed in these efforts, historians might have concluded that arms control was impossible. Since these efforts have brought some positive results, we conclude that cold war tensions need not blind adversaries to a joint stake in war prevention and arms control.

If the superpowers were able to curb their arms competition despite persistent cold war tensions, could not other aspects of their conflict also have been ameliorated? If military buildups could be checked by mutual agreement, less sensitive domains should have been equally or more amenable to reciprocal limitation. Instead of focusing on the great issues most vital to national security, they might have worked at cultivating positive experiences in less sensitive domains. Occasional proposals urging "small steps" have often been spurned—in Moscow as well as in Washington—as a Trojan Horse that could subvert the home front. "Free World" leaders—from Eisenhower and Adenauer to Park Chung Hee—have demanded as conditions for serious negotiations that their Communist rivals perform "acts" demonstrating their willingness to change their evil ways. Communists, for their part, have generally viewed Western proposals for "free informational flows" as part of a Trojan cavalry. More attention to "fractionating" conflict and to building the moral-material foundations of interdependence might have eroded the cold war more efficaciously than concentration on the more glamorous but less tractable problems of arms control.

The evidence is conclusive: The cold war and arms race were not ineluctably beyond human control. The domestic and external environments of U.S. and Soviet policy making were surely conducive to competitive relationships and mutual distrust, but the objective realities left more room for free will than the retrospective prophets of determinism would allow. Once in motion, of course, the cold war and arms race fueled one another, producing a vicious spiral difficult to reverse. That they developed and have persisted with such intensity, however, represented what one analyst has correctly termed "a disastrous failure of statecraft."[1][2]

If the cold war and arms race were not and are not inevitable, why have they endured for decades? If both sides might gain from their abatement, why have governments in Washington and Moscow not acted with greater vigor and prescience? Why has there been this failure of statecraft?

The answers to these questions must be sought on many levels of world politics. The fact that leaders on both sides have doubted the feasibility of arms control has made it more likely that the arms race would continue. The very essence of Soviet and American politics, analysts on both sides have contended, condemn them to a protracted conflict which one or the other must lose. Policies based on such assumptions naturally lead to actions which help to confirm the darkest prophecies and fears of the adversary. The USSR, many Westerners continue to argue, is inherently expansionist. Since the West seeks to defend the status quo, it needs overwhelming military superiority to discourage the Soviet challenge. If the Soviet Union agrees to a Western proposal or advances one of her own that seems to enhance mutual interests, some joker must lie hidden in the deck.

That such views continue to guide Western policy represents a failure not only of statecraft but of scholarship. The historical record analyzed in Chapter 1 indicates that the long-term trends of Soviet external behavior have been compatible with measures to contain the arms race and, by extension, the cold war. Military superiority of the Western alliance is not a *sine qua non* for such controls, but may have made them more difficult to obtain from 1945 until the late 1960s because the Kremlin leaders have placed a high priority on "equal security."

Contrary to assertions that the 1972 SALT agreements conceded too much to the USSR, a balanced assessment indicates that they furthered the security and political interests of both sides, with no harm to third parties. Though the USSR has drawn alongside or surpassed the United States in some dimensions of strategic weaponry, the overall balance of power through the 1970s continues to favor Washington and its non-Communist allies. To borrow a phrase from Chairman Khrushchev, "the shrimp may first learn to whistle" if arms controls are delayed until perfect multiple symmetry has been achieved or one super-power acquiesces in the other's hegemony.

Completely "rational" thinking on arms and arms control is extremely difficult, for governments as well as for scholars. Each individual carries with him a cultural background and political-ideological orientation that confound his efforts accurately to perceive and understand the actions of other governments—*a fortiori* if they appear threatening. Even if top leaders in either superpower see a joint interest in arms and conflict control with the adversary, they may be unwilling or unable to implement this insight due to domestic opposition, whether organized loosely or in formal bureaucratic structures; uncertainties about military technology and the shifting balance of power; and/or lack of reciprocity by the other side.

Such obstacles to strategic rationality can be documented in the records of Russian and other participants in international conferences on arms control throughout this century (and earlier). Chapter 2, however, contends that the superpowers have increasingly viewed arms control in pragmatic terms, con-sciously or unconsciously reducing the impact on their decisions of ideology and national sentiment. The weight of bureaucratic routine and political bargaining within each country continues to leave its mark, but both Soviet as well as U.S. decision-making on arms control has come increasingly to reflect the imperatives of strategic logic and positive sum concepts about the superpower relationship. As Marshall D. Shulman has suggested, both countries seem to be "on a learning curve, in which the implications of their security interests are becoming increasingly apparent."[13]

For arms control to be politically feasible as well as strategically expedient, a variety of underlying factors must jell in the proper mold. The conditions essential for arms control are analyzed in Chapter 3 on the basis of agreements signed and not signed since the Cuban missile crisis. Even though the minimum *necessary* requirements for accords have been present on various occasions, these conditions are by no means *sufficient* to compel an agreement. Opportunities may arise, and be lost, never to recur.

Arms control, though more feasible than disarmament and more desirable than unlimited cold or hot war, is no panacea for the world's ills. The very fact of negotiations has led to the acceleration of certain weapons programs on the ground that they will serve as useful bargaining chips in SALT. Even when some aspects of the arms race are constrained, the development, procurement, and use of still more destructive and expensive armaments may continue. "Small wars" may persist, with superpower support or participation, even while Washington and Moscow perform a minuet around weapons that could be used only on doomsday. The costs and the gains of the arms control approach to peace are assessed in Chapter 4.

The network of positive ties between the United States and USSR has grown over the years, and it promises to expand further through the 1970s, overshadowing in many respects those aspects of the relationship in which tension predominates. As the quantity and quality of symbiotic relationships mount, cold war can give way to predominately cooperative transactions.

Just as cold war conflict did not proceed inexorably in a straight line, so movement toward de-escalation has often proved short-lived. The thaws in U.S.-Soviet relations in 1955, 1959, 1963 and 1968 lasted less than two years each. Though much time and energy are needed to bring governments to cross the threshold from hot or cold war toward negotiation, the movement toward tension reduction can be readily halted or even killed by a variety of forces. Some of these forces may be beyond the immediate control of the two sides, such as the Hungarian and Suez crises of 1956 or the Eisenhower heart attack and Kennedy assassination of 1955 and 1963. Other challenges may be more directly controlled, but may rank higher as policy priorities than detente, e.g., the Vietnamese war and Czechoslovak "Springtime" of the late 1960s. Pride and prestige may also complicate the handling of a crisis, as occurred when a U.S. U-2 plane was downed in 1960. Difficult to cultivate, complicated to nurture, detente is a fragile flower easy to trample.

To sustain the momentum toward beneficent U.S.-Soviet symbiosis, statecraft should work unremittingly to build on the positive aspects of the relationship. Deterrence, as Fred Iklé and others have warned, presumes that the balance of terror will prevent a rational leader on either side from launching a global war.[14] War prevention would rest on much safer foundations if perceived interdependence supplanted strategic deterrence; if gas lines and electric grids took the place of rockets. Until that time, survival continues to depend on the absence of nuclear accidents and the presence of cool rationality on all sides.

On balance, Chapters 4 and 5 conclude, arms control has been and can be a useful instrument for containing the arms race and for reversing the thrust of cold war competition. Arms control can be important not only for war prevention, but for economic development. In the long run, these goals may prove essential for the realization of other values such as social justice and ecological balance.

A "modernist approach" to arms control is advocated in Chapter 5, focusing on principles such as positive sum[15] concepts of interdependence; timely measures to prevent the development and procurement of new weapons systems; revised conceptions of the wealth and responsibility of nations; and the need for long-term holistic planning. Many of these principles have already been reflected in the words and deeds of U.S., Soviet, and other statesmen. Unless they are widely accepted, however, not only by top leaders but by policy-attentive elites and citizens, we are likely to face many more "disastrous failures of statecraft."

The cold war and arms race have entailed a tragic loss of time and energy for both superpowers. Tragedy, in Hegel's view, may be understood either in a Greek or a Christian sense. The first type of tragedy is fatalistically predetermined; the second is the result of free choices by human agents. Intense conflict or war between the superpowers was not and is not inevitable, and cooperation is not impossible. The Greek and Christian interpretations should be joined in a new synthesis: Many factors have impelled the superpowers toward competition. Despite the limitations of the human condition, there are behavior patterns to choose from that can minimize conflict and increase cooperation.

To make the most of the opportunities and avoid the momentous dangers that lie ahead, statecraft must apply the modernist principles first of all to the task of containing the arms race. To shift the superpower confrontation from cold war to interdependence, however, these principles must be applied broadly to the entire spectrum of U.S.-Soviet relations. This is no plea for superpower condominium or other policies aimed at hurting third parties. Mutual aid, rather than myopic attempts at one-sided exploitation, would benefit not only the superpowers but all peoples willing to join in the modernist approach needed for coping with the problems and opportunities of global interdependence.

Are there some limits that should govern the extent to which either superpower cooperates with the other? Should these be based, at least in part, on the impact that the external environment has upon domestic political affairs (and *vice versa*)? George F. Kennan, at the outset of the cold war, argued that the primary concern of the United States with the Soviet political system was that a centralized, totalitarian system might *require* external tension for its own survival. A somewhat different concern was expressed to Western newsmen on August 20, 1973, by Soviet physicist Andrei D. Sakharov, who warned that unqualified American willingness to improve relations with the USSR could "mean cultivating a country where anything that happens may be shielded from outside eyes—a masked country that hides its real face. No one should ever be expected to live next to such a neighbor, especially if it is armed to the teeth." The minimum condition for easing the terms of East-West trade, Sakharov declared, should be unrestricted emigration from the Soviet Union. Though the domestic consequences of détente appear to be quite different in the two countries, and while Sakharov warned of an external as well as an internal threat arising from U.S.-Soviet cooperation,[c] Americans concerned for their own country might also object to unqualified Soviet backing for the U.S. President in the Watergate and related affairs. Unfortunately, foreign successes may make it possible for any government to tighten its repressive machinery at home, at least for the short run. Neither superpower, however, can predicate its foreign policies on the second- and third-order consequences of its actions in the domestic sphere of the other. In the long run, hopefully, the quality of life within both countries (and others as well) will benefit from a curbing of the arms race and international tension.

---

[c]As Gregory Grossman has cautioned (*The New Republic*, June 16, 1973), however, there may be economic and foreign policy reasons to limit an unrestrained transfer of Western technology to the USSR if it were to be paid for basically by future deliveries of natural gas and other raw materials.)

Ideally, as Aleksandr I. Solzhenitsyn put it in his September 1973 statement nominating Sakharov for the Nobel Peace Prize: "Coexistence on this tightly knit earth should be viewed as an existence not only without wars—that is not enough—but without violence, or anyone's telling us how to live, what to say, what to think, what to know and what not to know." For the foreseeable future, however, it would be no mean accomplishment if mankind's physical survival—the *sine qua non* for other hopes—could be assured.

1 Can the USSR Live With Stability?; The United States with "Sufficiency"?

Can the Soviet Union survive "stability"? Can U.S. interests be maintained by a strategic posture of "sufficiency"? These questions are basic to judgments about the feasibility and utility of superpower arms control.

Some commentators hold that the Soviet Government is unwilling—indeed, unable—to engage in long-term undertakings to control the arms race. In part, they contend, this is due to the Kremlin's need for an external bogey to justify a system of economic sacrifice and political repression. It is also due, the argument runs, to the external dynamism of Soviet foreign policy. Given this threat from the USSR, the United States needs a strategic position of manifest superiority. The doctrine of "sufficiency," formally espoused early in the first Nixon Administration, is itself insufficient if it denotes mere equality or parity between the superpowers. Only by retaining a clear superiority can the United States prevent Soviet expansion and Western retreat.[a]

Versions of this argument have appeared and reappeared in the West since the onset of the cold war. They have recurred in response to the SALT accords of 1972. Senator Henry M. Jackson and other critics of SALT I have charged that the 1972 agreements amount to American capitulation and acquiescence to Soviet superiority. The U.S. Congress went on record in 1972 declaring its hope that any follow-on SALT agreements "would not limit the United States to levels of intercontinental forces inferior to the limits provided for the Soviet Union."

The rationale for the Senate position was provided in part by testimony such as that offered by Dr. William R. Van Cleave, a Defense Department representa-

---

[a]President Nixon has stated that the doctrine of "strategic sufficiency" takes into account a broader set of political and military factors than did the earlier "assured destruction" concept. Strategic sufficiency, he asserted, "means enough force to inflict a level of damage on a potential aggressor sufficient to deter him from attacking. . . . to prevent us and our allies from being coerced. . . . to maintain a stable strategic balance despite technological change. . . . to make it clear that even an all-out surprise attack on the United States by the USSR would not cripple our capability to retaliate." U.S. "forces must also be capable of flexible application." See *U.S. Foreign Policy for the 1970s: The Emerging Structure of Peace, A Report to the Congress by Richard Nixon, February 9, 1972* (Washington, D.C.: U.S. Government Printing Office, 1972), pp. 157-158. The 1972 report omitted the criterion of defending against damage from small attacks or accidental launches put forth in earlier years when the White House was still campaigning for a significant ABM defense. This omission and the failure to give more attention to "crisis stability" as a standard of "sufficiency" are among the points discussed by William R. Van Cleave, "Implications of Success or Failure of SALT," in William R. Kintner and Robert L. Pfaltzgraff, Jr., eds., *SALT: Implications for Arms Control in the 1970s* Pittsburgh: University of Pittsburgh Press, 1973), pp. 330-331.

tive serving with the SALT delegation 1969-71. Both he and Senator Jackson concurred that the SALT I agreements might leave the United States unable to protect her land-based missiles and bombers from a disarming first-strike by the offensive forces permitted the Soviet Union by the accords. Dr. Van Cleave was asked by Senator Jackson, "What impact will this knowledge have on Soviet diplomatic, military, and political behavior in the world?"

Dr. Van Cleave replied: "I would expect to be faced with a Soviet Union that is more adventuresome and willing to take risks than anything that we have had in the past." Since Moscow engaged in considerable risk-taking and intransigence even when the United States had a 5 to 1 strategic lead (in 1962), Dr. Van Cleave could "not imagine what it is going to be like with the [strategic] situation that these [1972] agreements seem to freeze."[1]

Senator Jackson and Dr. Van Cleave agreed that the notion of "overkill" is a fallacy; that the USSR might acquire a "first-strike disarming capability"; that the ABM system permitted Washington under the 1972 treaties bore no resemblance to the offensive threat which the treaties permitted to remain. Van Cleave contended that "there is a growing recognition that the Soviets would realize and exploit a political advantage from some form of strategic superiority, or from the stalemate of U.S. strategic power." He contended that Soviet objectives and strategic doctrine remain unknown, despite the long hours of negotiation. Moscow simply held out through the SALT I negotiations while the Washington bureaucracy negotiated with itself and finally dropped the U.S. guard so that—instead of freezing a U.S. lead of 1969—the agreements ratified a series of Soviet advantages in missile numbers, quality and throw-weight. SALT I gave up too much and only aggravated the U.S. strategic problems which the White House had hoped it would ameliorate.

The political dynamism of the Soviet Union has also been contrasted with the flagging "imperial will" of the United States.[b] RAND Corporation sovietologist Thomas W. Wolfe, for example, has written that:

---

[b]The appeals of Russian Communism to the naive and forlorn intelligentsia of the capitalist and underdeveloped worlds have been framed in terms similar to those by which Edward Gibbon looked for the "secondary" causes of the Christianity's "remarkable . . . victory over the established religions of the earth" (the first cause being the doctrine itself and the providence of its Author). "The rapid growth" of Communism, like that of the Christian church, might be attributed to five factors: "I. The inflexible, and, if we may use the expression, the intolerant zeal of the [Communists], derived, it is true, from [Russian Messianism], but purified from the narrow and unsocial spirit which, instead of inviting, had deterred [outsiders from accepting it]. II. The doctrine of a future [victory], improved by every additional circumstance which could give weight and efficacy to that important truth. III. The miraculous powers ascribed to the primitive [Soviet state (cf. the many Fabian idolators)]. IV. The pure and austere morals of the [early Bolsheviks]. V. The union and discipline of the [Soviet] republic, which gradually formed an independent and increasing state in the heart of [Eurasia, encircled by hostile capitalist states]." Cf. *The Decline and Fall of the Roman Empire*, Chapter XV. (New York: Capricorn Books abridgment, 1969), p. 131.

an energy and enthusiasm for playing the role of a great power in world affairs is not wanting in the Soviet case. Indeed, the dynamic and rather self-righteous quality that animates the Soviet world outlook and behavior appears not yet to have peaked. . . . Moreover, the rise of Soviet power comes at a juncture when the Soviet Union's principal post-war rival appears unsure of itself and disposed to cut back its own global commitments.

Wolfe adds that "the asymmetry between the expansion of Soviet military power and the Soviet system's declining appeal as an example of modern societal growth and progress may [also] tend to push the leadership in this outward direction during the next decade."[2]

Contrary to the arguments of these critics, we will contend that—at least since Stalin's death—the record of Soviet external behavior suggests an orientation that *is* compatible with durable arms control and other accords designed to stabilize East-West relations. To be sure, extrapolations from history give no guaranteed indicators of future behavior: underlying conditions as well as political actors may change. Despite the "worst case" analyses of Senator Jackson, however, the U.S.-Soviet military balance permitted under SALT I is more than adequate to maintain Washington's foreign policy objectives. Though each superpower has its particular strengths, the overall balance of power— military, political, economic, technological, societal—continues to afford the United States a commanding lead through the 1970s. If the weight of each superpower's allies is put on the scales, the advantages favoring the West are more marked still. Whether the U.S. Government and its allies have the moral resources, political wisdom, and diplomatic skill to employ their strengths to advance their objectives is, of course, much more difficult to predict.

The major characteristics of Soviet foreign policy relevant to controlling the arms race may be summed up in six propositions. These propositions suggest a less aggressive interpretation of Soviet behavior than is found in many of the leading works by American sovietologists, a point discussed below in Appendix A. And yet the interpretation indicates a much less roseate view of the Kremlin than that taken by many revisionist historians who place the major responsibility for the cold war squarely on U.S. and British shoulders. But the thrust of the propositions does seem to harmonize with the findings of an Expert Survey Panel in 1973[c] and with the earlier conclusion of Triska and Finley that most Western

[c]Expert Survey Panel ("ESP data"), based on questionnaires filled in by 151 authorities at major centers of international studies and in government or foundation service, indicated a wide consensus (as of early 1973) that the USSR ranked second, well below the United States as a country whose problems and policies constituted the greatest threat to world peace in 1969-72. These rankings were reversed for the next four years, a plurality of 45 respondents forecasting the USSR would be most dangerous in 1973-77, followed by the United States (32 votes); then Israel (about 20); and various Arab countries (also about 20), with China, South Africa, Portugal, India, Pakistan, and North Vietnam each receiving a few votes. Did respondents expect the USSR to take up in the next four years the role occupied

analysts see the Soviet risk-taking propensity as "low and the Soviet attitude toward risk-taking as conservative, defensive, and cautious."[3]

Three additional propositions in this chapter deal with U.S. attitudes toward containing the arms race; the balance of power in the 1970s; and the impact of SALT I on both U.S. and Soviet interests.

Proposition I:

Despite the clash of conflicting viewpoints and interest groups within the USSR, and despite some fluctuation between "leftist" and "rightist" orientations, *Soviet external behavior, at least since Stalin's death in 1953, has generally been consonant with an identifiable hierarchy of values.* These goals seem to be scaled in the following rank order:

1. The security of the ruling elite(s) within the USSR and the legitimization of their regime and ideology;
2. The security of the Soviet state;
3. Maintenance and strengthening of Soviet influence in areas of Eastern Europe and Outer Mongolia that have come under partial or complete Soviet control;
4. Rapid industrialization of the Soviet economy and improvement over time in the living standards of the Soviet people;

by the U.S. in the past, e.g., in Southeast Asia? The survey revealed a relatively low expectation of Soviet actions damaging to peace in specific situations, implying that the USSR's top ranking might have resulted in part from: (1) a high assessment of Moscow's military potential as distinguished from actual intentions; (2) some hangover of cold war thinking (respondents over age 40 were much more likely to assign the most dangerous role to the USSR; and (3) a mere redistribution of "first place" votes in the wake of America's reduced involvement in Indochina. Thus, two out of three respondents expected "the most likely scenario for U.S.-Soviet relations in the next four years" to be "a mounting sense of interdependence" between the superpowers. No respondents expected "reversion to unrelieved periods of cold war conflict" or "hot war," but one-fifth of them forecast an alteration between periods of cooperation and of tension. Will there be a "general strengthening of the Soviet potential for fighting limited or localized wars in far flung places?" 47 percent replied that this was probable and 24 percent thought it to be 50-50. Only 4 percent considered a Soviet-U.S. confrontation probable somewhere in the third world. Even in the area judged most explosive, the Middle East, most respondents (78) expected the Soviet military presence to remain about the same; 36 said it would be basically dependent on the character of the U.S. presence.

Only two respondents looked for a "serious attempt to establish bases [in Cuba] to service Soviet nuclear delivery systems." And very few anticipated Soviet assisted *coups d'état* in the third world or Soviet military-pressures on Western Europe (even if troop reductions occurred there). Ninety percent of respondents thought a Sino-Soviet nuclear war improbable; and even a major conventional war between Moscow and Peking was considered likely by only 3 percent. Only one respondent looked for the USSR to take the place of the United States in Indochina.

The ESP data are available under the title "The Prospects for Peace, 1963-1967," at the Inter-University Consortium on Political Research, University of Michigan. The findings are summarized in the "War/Peace Outlook, 1973-77: What the Experts Think," by Walter C. Clemens, Jr. in *War/Peace Report*, July/August 1973.

5. Less tangible and much less important than the first four goals, maintenance and strengthening of Soviet influence in the international Communist movement and the Third World.

In pursuit of these objectives, a number of subordinate goals have also been sought. These lesser goals are ends in themselves, but they are also instruments by which to achieve the more important and enduring priorities: first, strengthening of the Soviet armed forces to deter external attack and to intervene in East Europe or elsewhere abroad if necessary to maintain and support Soviet interests; second, developing the Soviet economy—particularly heavy industry—to serve the military requirements of the state and to contribute to a stronger base for production of consumer goods; third, maintenance of stable relations with the United States so as to reduce the chances of major war and to temper the thrust of the arms race; fourth, the prevention of political or military developments in Western Europe, Japan, or China likely to pose an active threat to Soviet security; fifth, the cultivation of Communist and revolutionary activities abroad so as to enhance Moscow's position in world communism without undue risk to other Soviet objectives; sixth, where possible at low cost, the weakening of Western ("imperialist") influences in the Third World and their replacement or countervailing by Soviet power.

While Soviet behavior has generally conformed to this set of priorities, at least since 1953, we must underscore that many Soviet actions cannot be explained in terms of strict logical analysis conducted within the Kremlin walls. Russia's foreign policy, like that of other countries, often seems to represent a continuation of historic and cultural traditions from decades or centuries past. Some of these continuities will be discussed in subsequent chapters. We will only note here the continued presence of historic patterns, some dating from Tsarist times, such as sinophobia and—as Molotov put it to Berlin in 1940—aspirations in the general direction of the Persian Gulf. Despite efforts to build a "new Soviet man," qualities known to "Russian" character before 1917 continue to surface: messianism, great power chauvinism, and so forth. The presence of a "warrior class" and other bureaucratic pressures may also skew Soviet behavior away from what Chapter 2 terms "strategic logic." These and many other factors will affect the perception and the response of Soviet decisionmakers to opportunities and threats in the world around them.[d]

---

[d]William Zimmerman points out in a recent article that the priorities of the Soviet leaders and the manner in which they seek to operationalize them will depend upon "the context, international and domestic, in which decisions in Moscow are taken at a particular time." To speak of *a* single policy may be impossible, owing to the number of competing forces which shape the formulation and execution of policy in the USSR. Sizing up the likely contours of the 1970s, however, both Zimmerman and Alexander Dallin make forecasts that accord with the thrust of this book and with the ESP estimates. Both contend that Soviet decision-makers in the mid-1970s are likely to focus on proximate, realizable goals such as improving Soviet living standards rather than on distant objectives flowing from abstract ideology. So long as external security can be maintained by negotiation, Soviet priorities are

Proposition II:

Despite the commitment (part feigned, part genuine) of the Soviet leadership to world revolution,[4] Soviet military actions have generally been defensive in character. Partial exceptions include the Bolsheviks' efforts to consolidate their rule in the border republics formerly part of the Tsarist empire (as in the Caucasus), and instances when the USSR has repulsed an attacker back into his own camp.[5] The following cases illustrate this proposition:

1. Even in the years of War Communism (1918-1921), the Soviet leaders put a higher premium on the security of their regime and on *raison d'état* than on revolution abroad, a point established as early as 1918 in the implementation of Lenin's policy rather than Trotsky's (or Bukharin's) in negotiating with Germany at Brest-Litovsk.

2. The Red Army's drive toward the gates of Warsaw in 1920 came after the scales had been tilted in a war initiated by Poland.

3. Soviet aggression against the Baltic countries, Finland, and eastern Poland in 1939-40 enlarged the "socialist fatherland" and was rationalized ideologically after the fact. It also settled old scores and regained some Tsarist partrimony. The immediate incentive, however, was probably defensive, since Soviet expansion would put additional territory between Hitler and Russia, even though Soviet policies in the occupied countries did little to prepare for the German onslaught and alienated the local population.

4. Soviet efforts after World War II to remain in control or to seize new territories in Eastern Europe, the Near and Middle East (Turkey and Iran), and in the Far East followed in the wake of a war not initiated by Russia, but which Moscow utilized to strengthen and consolidate its sphere of influence or control, particularly along the periphery. Many of these areas had belonged to the Tsarist empire; historical experience indicated that most were important to Soviet security; some were necessary to maintain communications with Soviet occupation forces in defeated Germany and Austria. Soviet behavior in Azerbaijan deviated most sharply from these defensive standards (though it could be rationalized by references to the 1921 Soviet-Iranian Treaty; to Caucasian oil interests; or to the right of the Azerbaijanese people to national self-determination).[6] The Soviet Union, of course, was not the only member of the wartime coalition to use force to reestablish an empire (*cf.* Indochina; Taiwan; Malaya) or to set up friendly governments (*cf.* Italy; Greece). In any case, a policy that seeks to *hold* the spoils of victory from a war commenced by another party is still consonant with a basically defensive orientation.

likely to focus on domestic concerns. In Dallin's words: Moscow's achievement of global military capabilities was intended either "to enable the Soviet Union to avoid backing down from unfought confrontations (à la Cuba) or else to prepare for possible future conflicts whose risks Moscow continues to find forbiddingly high and whose occurrence is rendered even less likely precisely because of the Soviet acquisition of gross strategic parity." See *Survey*, XIX, No. 2 (Spring 1973), pp. 197-200. Other authorities offer sharply conflicting views in the same issue (see, e.g., Richard Pipes at p. 61).

5. Moscow's role in fomenting the Korean War in 1950 has not been established, though Soviet equipment was used by the North Koreans.[7] (There is also an argument that South Korea initiated the war,[8] though this does not seem plausible or persuasive to the present author.)

6. Moscow threatened but did not use major military force to bring Yugoslavia into line in 1948-53. The use of such force to intervene in the internal politics of Eastern Europe (e.g., in 1953, 1956, and 1968) and contradicted all standards of national self-determination, even as expressed on occasion by Soviet leaders. Nevertheless, these interventions have represented efforts to *maintain* Soviet interests rather than expand them by force. These interests had more to do with Soviet security (internal as well as external) than with ideology, though an East European defection from the socialist camp would surely have been a serious blow to the image of Communist unity.

7. Soviet pressures on Western Europe since World War II have contributed significantly to East-West tensions and the arms race. But the entire process of escalating tensions and demands in the early cold war years must be seen as one of interaction, in which each side saw its actions as provoked by hostile initiatives and bad faith by the other. The most belligerent Soviet pressures occurred in 1958-62, when Moscow's bargaining advantages were at a temporary peak, due in part to talk of a missile gap. These and other pressures were, however, also a reflection of present and anticipated weaknesses, as seen by the perceived need to construct the Berlin Wall in 1961.

Some Soviet initiatives may also have been aimed at obtaining a negotiated settlement. Thus, Khrushchev's hard-line address on the German problem of November 10, 1958, was preceded by a second, rather conciliatory version of the Rapacki Plan for East Central Europe on November 4. It also came in the wake of less belligerent Soviet initiatives on which Secretary of State Dulles had thrown cold water. In any event, Soviet probes stopped far short of war when confronted by Western firmness, from the 1948 Berlin blockade to the Khrushchev's quasi-ultimata of 1958-61. Whether the Soviet leaders ever intended to resort to coercion to expand their influence in Western Europe cannot be proved on the basis of available documentation.

8. Advanced Soviet military equipment has been deployed abroad, manned sometimes by Soviet personnel—as in Cuba, North Vietnam, and Egypt. These and other arms shipments have been used as a means of securing political influence, an approach used also by Western governments (and by Peking). The Cuban missile buildup aimed primarily at redressing the global balance of power, while the impetus for sending military personnel and anti-aircraft missiles to Vietnam and Egypt was to protect those countries from air attacks by the United States and Israel. In each case, the West had provided some provocation, beginning in 1954-55 with the Dulles policy of closing the circle around Russia by means of the Baghdad Pact,[9] and continuing through air strikes deep in friendly territory that raised questions (even in Eastern Europe) about Moscow's reliability as an ally. When compelled by circumstance to station Soviet troops in

combat zones abroad, Moscow has generally sought to minimize news of their activities, sometimes withdrawing them to avoid escalation.[10]

Proposition III:

The historical record suggests that most Soviet actions threatening to world peace have resulted from a perceived sense of military inferiority rather than parity or superiority.

This proposition is implicit in many of the cases cited to illustrate proposition II; weakness vis-à-vis Hitler's *Drang nach Osten* seemingly countenanced by Britain and France; determination not to suffer such an attack again after World War II; determination to obtain resources from the defeated countries to rebuild the Soviet economy. Pressures to alter the status of Berlin came in part from the fact that the city was, as Khrushchev put it, a bone in his throat, unsettling to the status quo in Eastern Europe. (It was also a vulnerable extension of the Western camp which could be squeezed whenever Khrushchev wished to discomfit the NATO powers.) The Soviet decisions to resume nuclear testing in 1961 (after a three-year moratorium) and to attempt a quick-fix in Cuba were probably motivated primarily by a concern to compensate for the rapid buildup of Minuteman and Polaris missiles begun under the Kennedy-McNamara administration (whose spokesmen sometimes hinted that they would consider a counterforce pre-emptive strike[11]). Soviet weaknesses at this time were known not only through the U-2 flights and later satellite reconnaissance, but also through the Penkovskiy revelations.[12] The domestic repercussions of this whole situation meant that Khrushchev felt compelled to take strong positions in foreign policy after the revelation that Eisenhower had let him down by taking responsibility for the Powers U-2 flight in 1960.

It is not clear from the historical record to what extent the USSR would use a position of military superiority to wage an aggressive war or diplomatic campaign. This is so first of all because the Soviet Union has generally been inferior to the Western nations in strategic weaponry, even though Soviet and East European conventional forces have long been superior in some respects in the European theatre. Only toward the end of the 1960s did the Soviet Union establish herself as the rough equal of the United States in strategic weapons. What is clear is that the Soviet leaders have often utilized their *local* advantages to gain or to maintain control in areas along the Soviet periphery (in 1918-21, 1939-41, after World War II, and against East European revolts), i.e., in conditions where the Kremlin believed it could operate without interference from superior strategic forces of a distant foe. It also appears that Khrushchev attempted to exploit the alleged "bomber gap" and "missile gap" to buttress Soviet foreign policy, even though these gaps proved to be largely mythical. On the other hand, Khrushchev's policies were much less aggressive than those deemed feasible by Mao Tse-tung, who thought that the first sputnik and Soviet ICBM test in 1957 meant that the east wind could actively prevail over the west.

The objective character of the East-West balance as it is likely to unfold in the 1970s is discussed in more detail later in this chapter. Suffice it to say here that a general Soviet superiority over the United States is not foreseeable in the decade. Though Moscow enjoys superiority in some domains, as in numbers of strategic delivery vehicles, these particular advantages would hardly assure the Kremlin that the United States would be unable to respond lethally to a Soviet first-strike. The historical record suggests no proclivity in Moscow for advancing either the power or the ideological interests of the Soviet regime by means of direct military attacks upon major opponents, particularly if they are located far from Soviet borders.

Proposition IV:

Moscow's proposals to control the arms race (like those of the West) have generally been much more consonant with its military-strategic interests than with ideological or cultural imperatives. When the USSR has been weak in some respect, she has proposed measures that would tend to redress the balance in her favor. When Moscow has been strong in some domain, the Soviet leaders have advocated measures that would tend to perpetuate that advantage.

This kind of behavior is typical of the *Realpolitik* approach characteristic of the traditional nation-state. It implies that ideological or cultural factors are less important than material ones in shaping this facet of Soviet policy. To that extent, it also implies that—if the material environment offers incentives to both sides to freeze the arms race or to reduce force levels—some agreement may be struck, regardless of the parties' divergent world views. Soviet arms control proposals have often reflected the premises of Communist ideology, but ideology has over time been adapted to reflect the imperatives of the military and economic conditions facing the Soviet state.

The major obstacles to arms control may be catalogued as "objective" (e.g., great asymmetries in the force structures of the superpowers) and as "voluntarist" (*cf.* the long history of mutual distrust and lack of deep commitment to negotiated settlements on the part of the elites in either country).

The style and substance of *some* Soviet arms control proposals have been conducive to agreement in the sense that they balanced the interests of the negotiating parties. Other proposals had little chance of acceptance because they would favor Soviet interests while prejudicing those of the other side. Thus, the criterion of "sincerity" is not very illuminating, since both kinds of measures could be "sincerely" welcomed by the Kremlin.

Proposition V:

As Soviet and U.S. force structures have become more symmetrical, it has become more feasible for Moscow and Washington to put forward arms control proposals that would take into account the needs of one another. Since the mid-1950s, each superpower has offered a number of arms control schemes that were basically negotiable. Even though objective conditions often favored such accords, political conditions in Moscow or in Washington (or in their alliance systems) often did not. The superpowers have often been out of phase. When one side has been ready for an accord, the other has not been. Here the question of lag time has often been crucial. The closer the two sides move to parity, the more conducive the material environment to an agreement—assuming some technological breakthrough is not expected that would restore major advantages to one of the parties. The more that military-technical factors assure the second-strike deterrence systems of each party, the greater are the material incentives and potentialities for a political commitment to containing the arms race through explicit or tacit agreement. These and other "conditions for arms control" will be discussed in greater detail in Chapter 3.

Proposition VI:

Soviet foreign policy—both in word and in deed—has often contributed to the climate of suspicion and diffidence that complicates efforts to contain the arms race. Moscow has often subordinated arms control efforts to an instrumental role within a larger strategy that appears to assume a long-term, zero-sum struggle between the USSR and the West.

1. From 1917 to the present, Soviet ideological pronouncements have generated a self-fulfilling prophecy: Predicting "capitalist" intervention, and promising the victory of socialism, these statements have increased the probability of Western hostility to the Soviet regime. Even after world revolution has ceased to be an urgent goal for the Kremlin, the rhetoric of May 1 and November 7 ceremonies, the theses of Soviet Communist programs, the shrill polemics of Radio Moscow vs. Radios Peking and Tirana in the third world, the intermittent hawkish statements of Soviet military leaders and some politicians— all these aspects of Soviet declaratory policy have made Western statesmen ponder the ultimate objectives of the Kremlin leaders (forgetting of course the occasional July 4 oratory, the "rollback" and "captive nations" slogans of the U.S. government, and the press releases from the Pentagon).

2. The Soviet approach to arms control has typically been more "political" and less technical than that of the West. To be sure, both sides have on occasion inserted "jokers" in their disarmament schemes, i.e., proposals that would greatly favor their own interests if not rejected by the other party.[13] But Soviet

leaders have generally looked beyond the narrow issues under negotiation to consider how arms control talks may affect the broader aims of Soviet foreign and domestic policy. It was the wider issues at stake that led Lenin to denounce disarmament talks as counterrevolutionary before he came to power, and later to view them as useful for manipulating contradictions between the Western governments and their peoples; between one Western government and another; and between factions within Western elites that took a hostile or a conciliatory view toward relations with the Soviet Government.[14]

Given the political climate of the early 1920s or, say, the cold war tensions of the late 1940s, such tactics were not so surprising, nor did they greatly heighten international tensions *per se*. That the West was less alert to the possibility of using disarmament talks in this way is a commentary on the greater commitment and skill of the Bolsheviks in exploiting the new and open diplomacy which Lenin (and Wilson) helped to introduce.

To use arms control negotiations for ulterior motives—even aggressive motives—at a time when peace seems to depend upon a balance of terror or an entente between superpowers is highly deleterious for international stability. In Lenin's time there was little good faith and little prospect of East-West arms controls. The situation then was quite different from that which has prevailed since the mid-1950s, when each superpower has tried to persuade the other of its fundamental devotion to war prevention. Despite the fragile character of the new world situation, Moscow has continued to use arms control as part of a general political offensive. Thus Soviet Ambassador Vinogradov privately conveyed Moscow's acceptance of the Anglo-French memorandum as the basis for negotiations on force levels in 1954 just prior to the critical vote in the French Assembly on the European Defense Community.[15]

The detente that Moscow fostered in 1955, partly through arms control concessions, helped to camouflage the beginning of Soviet penetration of Egypt and the Middle East. Soviet proposals in the 1950s and 1960s seemed calculated to put pressure on West Germany (constraints on deployment of tactical nuclear weapons or multilateral nuclear sharing) and to appeal to Gaullist separatism (e.g., by Moscow's 1960 proposal to eliminate *all* strategic delivery vehicles in the first stage of general disarmament.[16]

But much higher stakes were involved in 1962, as the Soviet Union embarked on her plan to deploy nuclear missiles in Cuba. In July a World Congress for General Disarmament and Peace was held in Moscow, with non-Communist Americans allowed to speak their minds in the Kremlin. In September, weeks before the missile deployment would have been complete, Khrushchev himself made potentially important concessions in the Soviet posture on a nuclear test ban.[17] Khrushchev was joined by Gromyko and Ambassador Dobrynin in affirmations that no offensive weapons were being emplaced in Cuba.[18] The test ban and other arms control moves were apparently part of a larger strategy aimed at inducing Washington to engage in wishful thinking as evidence increased of an arms buildup in Cuba. It is also conceivable that Khrushchev meant to use concessions on arms control as a *quid pro quo* for Kennedy's tolerating a major breach in the Monroe Doctrine.

A second matter of great importance, it is conceivable that the Kremlin exploited the "Spirit of Moscow" following the 1963 test ban treaty to restrain an American arms program while laying the ground for a renewed Soviet effort to reach parity or to overtake the United States. Given the lead time required to move from the drawing board and test site to mass production, the missile program which brought the USSR toward parity with the United States by the end of the 1960s must have commenced either in the last year of Khrushchev's reign (1963-64) or shortly thereafter.[e]

A third serious case concerns the Soviet position on arms control just prior to the Warsaw Pact intervention in Czechoslovakia. As the Nonproliferation Treaty was signed in Moscow, Washington, and London, on July 1, 1968, the USSR announced a renewed and expanded Soviet commitment to a nine-point program of arms control.[20] Plans to commence strategic arms talks were also agreed to by Washington and Moscow. On August 19—as Soviet planes and armies were moving toward Czechoslovakia—Ambassador Anatoly F. Dobrynin sent a handwritten invitation to President Johnson to visit the Soviet Union.[21] Moscow played effectively on the President's emotions, and he is reported to have seriously considered the trip even after the invasion of Czechoslovakia. His trip as well as the onset of SALT were eventually cancelled, the latter being delayed by over a year.

The reasons why such behavior is dangerous to the success of arms control negotiations are obvious. Soviet negotiating behavior in SALT I was consistent with many hypotheses, one of them being that Moscow was stalling to gain time while the Soviet defense program attempted to catch up with the United States in numbers of land-based and sea-based missiles, in silo hardening, and in multiple warhead technology. As William Welch has demonstrated, Soviet treaty observance has been much more faithful than portrayed in some Western studies,[22] but Moscow's management of arms control concessions at crucial moments as in 1962 and 1968 suggests that the Kremlin's perception of its self-interest may have been quite different from the common cause sometimes supposed in the West. Though arms control accords are held to depend upon

---

[e]Official Soviet budget figures show defense spending as follows (in $ millions and at 1960 exchange rates):[19]

1960	1961	1962	1963	1964	1965
22,143	27,619	30,238	33,095	31,667	30,476

1966	1967	1968	1969	1970	1971	1972
31,905	34,450	39,780	42,143	42,619	42,619	42,619

These figures do not necessarily confirm or refute the hypothesis, since the official data probably exclude covert spending for some (or all) years. It might also be that the years 1964-1966 showed relatively low expenditures because of an emphasis at that time on R&D, assembly line production and associated costs coming only in the late 1960s.

mutual interest for their durability, even the act of entering into the negotiating process requires a modicum of trust on each side.

Every country's performance record lives on in the memories of other governments and colors their perceptions of its subsequent moves. Though the Soviet position on the problems of the Middle East was on balance conducive to a political settlement in 1970 (see *Mizan*, XII, No. 1, pp. 1-6), suspicions from the past affected Israeli and Western readings of Moscow's behavior. Thus, when Kremlin-supplied SAMs with Soviet personnel were deployed in the Suez Canal truce zone in August 1970, some commentators recalled the denials of Gromyko and Dobrynin in 1962 that the USSR had stationed anything but "defensive" weapons in Cuba. The words which Soviet diplomats had uttered eight years before were cited to cast doubt on the self-righteous claims of *Izvestiia* and *Krasnaia Zvezda* that mere "shifts" and "replacements" of missiles within the zone were permitted under the ceasefire agreement.

World confidence in the USSR has not been strengthened by Moscow's dealing with its putative allies. Thus Peking has complained about the continuation under the Soviet regime of unequal treaties imposed on China in Tsarist days. Nor was Stalin beneath imposing his own unequal treaty arrangements on Communist China, arrangements which were annulled in 1954. Peking has also declared (in the Sino-Soviet polemics of 1963) that the USSR did not stand by China in the Taiwan Straits crises of the 1950s. More to the point here, Peking also accused the USSR of unilaterally abrogating in 1959 the treaty on a new defense technology concluded in 1957. Though the evidence is not conclusive, it can be argued that Moscow played a double game with China in the late 1950s, extending limited nuclear assistance (perhaps stalling on delivery), while working simultaneously for a nuclear test ban with the Western governments. If the test ban could be achieved, it might serve as a pretext for discontinuing nuclear assistance to China. Though the test ban treaty was not signed until 1963, Moscow broke off aid to China in 1959-1960 as a result of a general deterioration in Sino-Soviet relations. This inconsistent and vacillating Soviet policy may also have been the result of Khrushchev's famous "subjectivism," reflected in this case by a determination to win Chinese support at the November 1957 Communist meeting in Moscow (if necessary by a "new technology" treaty), while deferring the question of how to implement Soviet commitments to Peking.[2 3]

The experiences of Moscow's Warsaw Pact allies have been no more encouraging. As early as 1956 the Soviet armies showed that they could virtually withdraw from Hungary only to return suddenly and with great force. The preparations for the invasion of Czechoslovakia in 1968 seem to have been still more elaborate and calculated. The attack did not come when political tensions were high in midsummer. It came rather after the accords of the Cierna Conference had been endorsed by the multilateral Bratislava Conference, which resulted in a widespread sense of relief in Czechoslovakia (and also in Western

Europe, where vacations in August are *de rigueur* for many government leaders as well as for the public). This was the moment—orchestrated with plans for SALT and a Johnson visit to Moscow—that Soviet and other Warsaw Pact forces descended, spearheaded by surprise takeovers of airports in Prague and other Czechoslovak cities.

As argued in the next chapter, we must refrain from assuming that all Soviet moves on the diplomatic and military chessboard are part of a master plan, consummately planned and executed by a unified Rational Actor in the Kremlin. The timing (or lack of timing) in Soviet actions can also be due to political differences within Soviet bureaucracies, long-established habits and routines, incomplete or faulty information and other influences such as *fortuna.* The Soviet leaders may well have wanted SALT to commence in 1968, and hoped that their actions in Czechoslovakia would not preclude strategic arms negotiations. Indeed, U.S. leaders had given them little reason to fear a strongly negative American reaction to the Warsaw Pact intervention.

Though the Soviet leadership (like that of other countries) has often subordinated arms control to other objectives, the historical record summarized in these six propositions suggests a secular trend in Moscow's foreign policy toward actions based on the premise that balanced arms control agreements with the West are both feasible and useful for Soviet interests in many fields.

What has been the role of the United States in strengthening or undermining these trends in Soviet policy? Many Soviet actions have been taken for reasons basically endogenous to the USSR and what used to be called the "Soviet bloc," but others were taken at least partly in response to or in interaction with moves by the other superpower. Many of Washington's actions have been enlightened and far-sighted. Even while spending almost half the world's arms budget, the United States has seriously explored the possibilities for arms control. As the next two propositions suggest, however, U.S. policies could have done much more to restrain the arms race and to make arms limitation more feasible.

Proposition VII:

The Western powers, led by the United States, have often conducted their policies to the Soviet Union in ways that perpetuate the vicious cycles of distrust and arms competition.

As George F. Kennan once put it:

The nature of Soviet power is something we influence by the way we conduct ourselves, and by the manner in which we speak of it and to it, even by the measures we take to protect ourselves against it. One's adversaries have a tendency to correspond, with time, to the pattern of the fears and expectations with which one views them. If we insist on viewing the Soviet leaders as wholly inhuman, and act on this hypothesis, make no mistake about it: We shall have them precisely that in the end—we shall leave them no other choice.[24]

1. Western policies on arms and arms control have often functioned to vindicate the darkest prophecies of Leninism on the irreconcilability of "socialist" and "capitalist" systems. One root of this behavior is the self-righteousness and intolerance of a Puritan outlook that feels justice and goodness are its virtual monopoly. This was the view which could contend self-righteously that armed intervention in Soviet Russia in 1918 was merely aimed at protecting depots of Western arms or at inhibiting Japanese aggression; that treated the Soviet Government as immoral and as temporary for over a decade, responding to its overtures regarding the Washington Naval Conference by asserting that the United States would look after the interests of the Russian people; that later contended America should retain her atomic monopoly as the custodian for all mankind until Washington was satisfied that international controls of atomic energy had become effective.

One aspect of Western policy is the mirror image of a vital facet in Soviet outlook as well: a profound distrust in the other side as a reliable negotiating partner. Western policy-makers have considered the Soviet regime to be unstable, immoral or amoral, unable to maintain itself except by force, and prone to cheating or violence to achieve its foreign objectives. One negative result of this outlook has been to look with extreme skepticism at any Soviet proposal, expecting that it must be loaded to favor only one side.[25]

Western diplomacy, led by the United States, has often reneged on its own initiatives when they were accepted, at least partially, by the Soviet Union. This occurred most dramatically in 1955 when Harold E. Stassen announced that Washington was placing a "reservation" on all its pre-Geneva Summit positions.[26] In 1958 the West turned down a revised version of the Rapacki Plan for disengagement, even though the revisions responded to many of the criticisms made by Western governments concerning the initial version of Eden Plans.[27] The Rapacki Plan is an especially poignant example of the West's at times almost pathological rejection of any "Communist" initiative on the assumption that if it comes from the East, it must be bad for the West, even if it looks good. The Polish Foreign Ministry's efforts to create conditions in which Poland would enjoy greater independence (as a result of partial disengagement) were condemned in advance by the West's tendency to assume some dark Soviet plot behind the scenes.

In the realm of strategic arms controls, Moscow may well have perceived a lack of good faith when—following an accord on the technical requirements for a nuclear test ban in 1958—further investigation by the RAND Corporation led the United States to call for more intensive inspection procedures in 1959.[28] Moscow would also note President Eisenhower's caveat on December 29, 1959, that the United States considered herself free to resume nuclear weapons testing, but that she would not do so without announcing this intention in advance—a point often ignored by Westerners who denounce Moscow's resumption of testing in September 1961.[29] Khrushchev also gained the impression that his willingness to accept up to three on-site inspections to police a test ban met minimum Western requirements, only to find Washington raising its minimum to eight.[30] Soviet negotiators may have been surprised by the somewhat critical Western response to Gromyko's calls for a nuclear umbrella (a minimum deterrent force) in 1962-63, considering that this modification of the Soviet plan for general disarmament seemed to meet the suggestions made by U.S. science advisers at the 1960 Pugwash Conference. Still later, Soviet negotiators at the SALT negotiations had reason for being puzzled by Washington's refusal in 1970 to negotiate on defensive arms alone, considering that the United States had earlier expressed particular concern about limiting ABM before massive deployments could begin. At least twice in SALT I, Washington seemed to renege on important issues. Offered a choice between zero-ABM and limiting ABM to the National Command Authority (NCA), the Soviet government reflected and instructed its diplomats to choose the latter, only to find the White House now contending that the United States should have four ABM sites to Moscow's one. On another occasion Dr. Kissinger suggested a freeze on land-based ICBMs to Ambassador Dobrynin. When the Soviet representative asked about SLBMs (submarine-launched ballistic missiles), he was told they would be "no problem." Later, however, when the Soviet delegation endorsed the idea of an ICBM freeze, its members were vexed to hear that the United States insisted on including SLBMs in the deal. To be sure, some of these inconsistencies could be partly explained as faulty communication. Others could have been due in part to changes in the objective military balance in the interval between U.S. initiative and Soviet response, but the Kremlin could hardly fail to ask whether such behavior did not confirm Lenin's original skepticism about the willingness of capitalist regimes to agree to meaningful limitations on armaments. (Such doubts would be reinforced by many White House statements on the Indochina war, which produced a credibility gap at home as well as abroad, leading Prime Minister Harold Wilson as well as Premier Kosygin in 1967 to question the good faith of the American President.)[31] This same type of conduct was suggested in 1971 by the go-slow response of the NATO governments after Moscow responded positively to Western calls for negotiations on mutual balanced force reductions (MBFR), proposals by which the West had sought to test (and impugn) Soviet goodwill and sincerity for several years.

Passing over other incidents of this kind, we come to the response in 1971 of two U.S. officials to the Soviet draft treaty on cooperation on the moon: "There's not one thing of any importance in it." "The Russians have never wanted to be held responsible for anything and they are trying to fuzz the thing [the negotiations] in Geneva."[32] Even if these officials were partially correct in matters of detail, it was significant that they could be so self-righteous (considering that the U.S. draft space treaty in 1966 was much narrower than the Soviet draft, which ultimately provided more of the content for the 1967 treaty), or that they could be so oblivious to the larger motives that may have inspired the 1971 Soviet proposal (which came on the heels of Soviet concessions on the issues of a separate treaty for biological weapons and MBFR negotiations).

In Washington no less than in Moscow, a semi-official line has stressed the country's steady dedication to the quest for peace and arms limitation, the United States citing the Washington Naval Conference of 1921-22 and the magnanimity of the Baruch proposals for the international control of atomic energy in 1946, just as the Soviet Union refers to her disarmament campaign in 1922; her "principled stand" at the League of Nations; and her efforts to "ban the bomb" after World War II. What most officials and citizens of each country have often failed to do is to consider their own policies as others perceive them. The self-righteousness of Washington and Moscow has been compounded as the two superpowers retain or increase their own arms while pressuring Israel, India, Japan, and other countries to forswear the nuclear option.

American self-righteousness was again manifested in Washington's self-serving interpretations of a series of "understandings" used (or asserted) where more formal agreements seemed unattainable in the early 1970s. Interpreting an agreement to favor one's own side is not new in bargaining among nations or other adversaries. Both Moscow and Washington had already registered their divergent readings of many written agreements such as those reached at Yalta, San Francisco, and Potsdam in 1945. In 1970-71, however, Washington began to justify its policies on the basis of alleged "understandings," even though the full text often remained unpublished and some of the alleged parties never admitted their agreement to the accord. None of these cases bore directly on SALT; Moscow's association in two of the cases was tangential; but Washington's words and deeds in each instance contributed to a climate of American opinion dubious about the feasibility of trusting the USSR or her allies in serious negotiations. The Soviet leaders, for their part, might also have become more doubtful about accords with the Americans.

It appears that there was only limited *mutual* understanding in any of these cases. At most there was an understanding by one side or another (though sometimes there was also misunderstanding *within* a particular government on the terms of an alleged accord). If differences cannot be resolved, it would be preferable to make unilateral declarations of intent rather than posit joint understandings which do not exist. The SALT I agreements, for example, were accompanied by a series of unilateral as well as joint statements indicating the manner in which they were officially interpreted by Moscow and Washington.

One set of understandings pertained to Indochina, where the Nixon Administration sought to legitimize stepped-up bombings of North Vietnam in March, May, and November 1970 on the ground that Hanoi had fired on unarmed American reconnaissance flights allegedly permitted under the October 1968 "understanding" by which Washington agreed to cease bombing the North. Hanoi, for its part, published excerpts of a record purporting to show that "no conditions" had been attached to the bomb halt.[33]

Lyndon Johnson's memoirs asserted that the aerial reconnaissance "condition" was cleared first with his own Joint Chiefs of Staff; that North Vietnam had originally balked at it because the October 1968 understanding was to stop "all acts of war," but that Hanoi finally acquiesced in the U.S. formulation to end "acts involving the use of force"—language that would permit continuation of unarmed reconnaissance flights. (Johnson makes no claim, however, that Hanoi also pledged not to shoot at such flights, flights which would countervene accepted principles of international law.) Johnson also indicates that he sought and received a general Soviet blessing of the October 1968 Paris accord, which he hoped would raise the chances of Soviet pressure on Hanoi to ensure compliance.[34]

Since the verbatim transcript of the 1968 negotiations has not been published, no final assessment of these arguments is possible. One State Department official has said that we simply took Hanoi's silence on certain matters as agreement: "We said what was our understanding, and they didn't object." He justified this stratagem as one that helped end the bombing, if only for a time, thereby keeping the nation from further falling apart, without any really pernicious results. W. Averell Harriman (the chief U.S. negotiator in 1968) indicated in 1972, however, that the 1968 understanding had already been subverted by Saigon and repudiated by Washington, and hence could not serve as a justification for further strikes on the north.[35] Still other critics opined that Nixon had simply become more dependent on air power to support "Vietnamization" once U.S. troops were withdrawing in large numbers.

Though scores of small U.S. strikes had been carried out against North Vietnam's surface-to-air missiles prior to March 1970, the "reinforced protective reaction strikes" were on a much larger scale, involving more than 500 aircraft in early May 1970. By September 1971 one Pentagon official explained: "Essentially, we're hitting targets of opportunity as they present themselves with an eye toward stopping any major build-up for an enemy offensive."[36] By 1972 the Pentagon had resumed intensive bombing of the North, no longer referring to its raids as "protective reaction" or "intensive duration" but simply as "strikes." Though many of them came close to China, Washington was sure that Peking "understood" they represented no threat to the People's Republic.

A second set of understandings pertained to the Middle East, where an American "initiative" led to a standstill ceasefire agreement between Egypt, Jordan and Israel which officially began on August 7, 1970. The outline of the accord had been communicated by Washington to Egypt, Israel, Jordan, the USSR, Britain and France on June 19. It was immediately rejected by Cairo and other Arab regimes, as well as by the USSR, which introduced her own proposal for the Middle East focusing on Israeli withdrawal from captured territories. After President Nasser's prolonged visit to Moscow, and as Soviet-built SAM-2 and SAM-3 defenses continued to down more Israeli planes, Cairo unconditionally accepted the U.S. plan on July 23, a move followed by Jordan on July 26 and reluctantly by Israel on July 28-31.[37]

This much of the record is fairly clear, but the timing and even the language of the agreement seem to have evolved over time, perhaps in response to Israeli demands for "clarification" from Washington. Egyptian sources claim that the United States sent Cairo an ultimatum demanding that the ceasefire begin within twenty-four hours on August 7 and that no part of the U.S.-proposed language could be altered. Egyptian officials indicated that they would need at least forty-eight hours before they could accept the "standstill" features of the accord. (On July 31, President Nixon had spelled out that "neither side [may] use the ceasefire period to improve its military position" along the truce lines.) Pressed, the Egyptian Foreign Ministry finally indicated that Washington could *state* that the accord was going into effect at the deadline proposed, but that several days would in fact be needed for Egypt to complete her hardware operations in the ceasefire/standstill zone. This approach seems to have been accepted by U.S. officials who may have assumed it would in any case require several days to establish verification procedures. Their attitude and public statements made later by Defense Secretary Laird, however, may have given Cairo the impression that strict compliance was not expected.

According to U.S. government statements issued in September and October, both Israel and Egypt violated the ceasefire/standstill from the outset. Israel's actions included aerial reconnaissance flights over the prohibited zone, the strengthening of fortifications, and road building in the zone. Egypt's actions, while they did not fundamentally alter the balance of power, were more serious, entailing the construction and movement of SAM defenses within the zone. U.S. Ambassador Charles Yost told the U.N. General Assembly on October 30 that "there can be no doubt that the country from which these highly advanced missiles came, as well as the government on whose territory they were placed, is responsible for these developments." He cited excerpts from the text of the agreement, parts of which had earlier been disclosed on August 13 by Israeli Defense Minister Moshe Dayan: "Both sides will refrain from changing the military status quo within zones [as defined] . . . . Neither side will introduce or construct any new military installations in these zones." Yost said that his government "had the concurrence of the parties and the major powers concerned that military standstill was an acceptable part of the ceasefire. . . . That is why we have stressed the need for rectification of the situation resulting from violations of the standstill." Earlier in October Joseph J. Sisco, Assistant Secretary of State for Near Eastern and South Asian Affairs, had stated in a television interview that the USSR had accepted the U.S. plan in writing, and that Ambassador Anatoly Dobrynin had indicated acceptance of the terms in a meeting with Secretary of State Rogers.

While it seems clear that U.S. and Soviet officials had discussed the Rogers initiative for some months, the details of the accord were presented by U.S. Ambassador Jacob Beam to Soviet Deputy Foreign Minister Kuznetsov only a short time before the ceasefire was to begin. "Are you asking for our concurrence?" Kuznetsov asked. Beam replied in the negative, saying that he was merely informing Kuznetov of the plan.

A similar conversation took place between Soviet Ambassador Dobrynin and Secretary of State William P. Rogers, in which Dobrynin did not challenge Roger's contention that the ceasefire also included a standstill. After talk of "violations" began, however, both Dobrynin and his deputy, Yuli Vorontsov, repeatedly denied to State Department officials that the USSR had been a party to the accord. Moscow, they later said, could not understand Egypt's concern with the Suez Canal, but the USSR would not infringe on Egyptian sovereignty. Vorontsov urged that Washington forget about "rectification," lest that issue impede progress when Gromyko arrived in Washington later in 1970 for high-level negotiations. Vorontsov also denied that the Egyptian moves had much bearing on the actual balance of power, a point supported by evidence that Egyptian SAMs were already taking a heavy toll of Israeli planes before the ceasefire.

Secretary Rogers probably read the silence of Dobrynin and other Soviet officials as constituting their affirmation of the understanding—American style. Rogers' subsequent anger was therefore "sincere" if misplaced. The Secretary's frustration was the greater since the Middle East ceasefire was one accomplishment which Rogers hoped his Department (rather than Dr. Kissinger) could claim.

While the Rogers plan was idealistically conceived, its execution left much to be desired. Washington stated that its reconnaissance planes were not deployed to verify the initial days of the ceasefire, which meant that the United States had to rely upon Israeli intelligence data that left it uncertain whether the first Egyptian SAM deployments occurred just before or just after the ceasefire was to commence. (Why reconnaissance satellites could not provide this information was not explained—strengthening the belief of many observers that Washington initially sought to minimize the significance of any possible violations. By late August, however, U.S. reconnaissance showed continued violations by Israel as well as Egypt. As foreign and domestic critics noted the shortcomings and contradictions in U.S. policy, Washington demanded "rectification" of the violations (though without any credible proposal for how this could be accomplished) and promised to sell more advanced military hardware to Israel to compensate for Egyptian gains. (Such sales, *Al-Ahram* charged on September 4, were prohibited for the initial ninety-day truce period, and hence would violate the accord.)

Though the verbatim records of these transactions remain unpublished, the self-righteousness of Israel and Egypt in these matters certainly matched that of Washington. Israel, for its part, seemed to believe that overflights of Cairo and other Egyptian cities in early 1970 would be a useful show of force. Egypt, like Israel, was surprised that its major foe had agreed to the U.S. initiative and tried to make the most of the time remaining before the ceasefire began. Israel insisted that it begin within a very short time, thereby cutting into the time in which Egypt could complete the deployment of new SAMs. Egypt could "agree," but with strong reservations. Under the circumstances, Cairo probably believed that the deployment of newly arrived SAMs should be continued. The ceasefire would assure that no more Egyptian lives were lost due to Israeli air attacks on the SAM sites. If there were later charges of "violations," this would be a small price to pay for acquisition of effective air defenses. Israel, after all, could also be accused of violations. By 1971-72, however, Egyptian leaders and especially the editor of *Al-Ahram* were denouncing the ceasefire as a U.S.-Israeli plot (supported tacitly by Moscow) to maintain a state of "no war, no peace" that benefited the Zionist cause.

Though President Anwar el-Sadat charged intermittently that he had been "misled" by "Bill Rogers" and let down by Mr. Nixon's failure to pressure Israel (as he had been let down by Moscow's refusal to deliver advanced arms), the fact was that Israeli planes ceased to fly over Egypt in 1971-73, and that conditions for a compromise peace improved, only to be repeatedly derailed by the terrorist acts of "Black September."

Though the USSR did not prevent Egypt from erecting the new SAMs in the standstill zone, and Soviet personnel helped in the operation, it is a gross oversimplification to accuse the Soviet leaders (as Hans J. Morgenthau did in *Foreign Affairs*) of "agreeing to a ceasefire for the Middle East and violating the agreement at the very moment of its coming into operation."[38] It is conceivable that the USSR was again engaged in a double game or that the diplomatic and military arms were not fully coordinated. But it is also noteworthy that the Soviet press took the lead (during Nasser's visit to Moscow) in suggesting the positive aspects of the Rogers initiative. The timing of the ceasefire, coming just as the new missiles were being deployed forward in the Canal Zone, may have caught the Russians as well as the Egyptians off guard. The Soviet press defended the ceasefire against the criticism of "extremists" in Iraq, Syria, the Palestinian commando groups and in Peking. Secretary Brezhnev declared (*Pravda* August 29, 1970) that "what is needed now is not new provocations and subterfuges aimed at bypassing or violating the ceasefire agreement, but honest observance and genuine steps in favor of peace."

A third "understanding" concerned Cuba, where the Nixon Administration challenged Soviet naval movements on the basis of President Kennedy's statement in 1962 that peace would be assured only "if all offensive missiles are removed from Cuba and kept out of the Hemisphere in the future." A September 1970 statement from the White House warned against servicing Soviet submarines from a base in Cuba. As in 1962, whatever understanding existed was acknowledged only obliquely by Moscow in 1970. The terms were broadened further by President Nixon on January 4, 1971, as he declared on television: "Now, in the event that nuclear submarines were serviced either in Cuba or from Cuba, that would be a violation of the understanding." The U.S. position, as George Quester has pointed out, puts a somewhat self-serving interpretation on the 1962 understanding, broadening it from "offensive missiles" (presumed emphasis on land-based missiles) to "nuclear submarines" (which might be nuclear-powered without carrying nuclear weapons) and their tenders. Thus, the redefined U.S. position—apart from legalities—also runs counter to Washington's expressed confidence in the principle of stabilized deterrence, a condition increasingly dependent upon sea-based missiles in the age of MIRV.[39] Here, as in the other alleged understandings, the United States seemed to presume that her interpretation (adjusted *ad hoc* to fit her needs) should be accepted by others.

Many of these manifestations of American self-righteousness had their root in a sense that it is both necessary and feasible for the United States to maintain a posture of strategic superiority. No matter what the accomplishments or challenges of the Communist bloc, they could and should be countervailed and surpassed by exerting the West's economic and technological prowess. As the British Navy was once pledged to superiority over any two competing fleets, Washington endeavored in the 1960s to sustain nuclear and general purpose forces capable of fighting two and one-half major wars. Any arms control system that threatened American hegemony was therefore regarded as undesirable if not immoral. Since our cause is just, treaties and understandings with the other side should be interpreted in a manner that squares with our military and political needs. As the British naval sights were lowered, however, so under President Nixon the United States sought a posture of "realistic deterrence" and strategic sufficiency, requiring an ability to fight only one and one-half major wars simultaneously.

The pressure of circumstances was compelling official Washington to concede that, in Marshall Shulman's words, "elements of political myth cling to the supposed advantages of superiority." American political ideas as well as Soviet ideology have been adjusted gradually to the realities of the nuclear-missile age. It took Soviet doctrine from 1954 to 1963 to accept fully that the character of nuclear war was beyond the laws of the class struggle as laid down by Marx and Lenin. It has taken from 1949 until the early 1970s for a series of Democratic and Republican presidents to alter or forgo political beliefs such as the notions that:

1. America's nuclear monopoly could be long-lived;
2. Russia (and China) were fated to be technologically backward for a long time;
3. American technology could overcome most political problems, from organizing nuclear sharing in Europe (the MLF) to defeating insurgents in Asian rice paddies;
4. the American economy could afford both guns and butter—no matter how expensive the former;
5. America could maintain effective superiority over the USSR in strategic weapons;
6. the United States could maintain forces adequate to fight two and one-half major wars simultaneously;

7. the United States could establish defenses that would guard most civilian targets from foreign air or missile attack;
8. U.S. society would support the Executive branch in virtually any foreign engagement with alleged Communist aggression.

Proposition VIII:

Despite all claims to the contrary, the United States has enjoyed a position of clear strategic superiority from the end of World War II until the late 1960s. Despite Soviet acquisition of relative strategic parity in the late 1960s, and despite the force ceilings permitted under the SALT I agreements, the overall balance of power seems destined to favor the United States and her allies throughout the 1970s.

American depictions of the Communist threat have often been exaggerated, sometimes from fear; sometimes from lack of accurate information; but sometimes in order to justify larger defense budgets or military intervention abroad. This kind of propaganda has been used to magnify the image of a monolithic Communist movement threatening many outposts of the Free World, and to justify corresponding actions by the West in support of the cause of freedom in such diverse places as Greece and Turkey (1947), Lebanon (1958), the Dominican Republic (1965), and—for over a decade—South Vietnam.

With respect to the East-West arms race, the United States has often magnified the military threat posed by the USSR. Much of this problem may be traced to Soviet secrecy, which creates real uncertainties about Soviet intentions as well as capabilities; to Russia's long-standing sense of inferiority and actual weapons inferiority vis-à-vis the United States—which made it expedient for Moscow to mask its real weaknesses; and—not least—to Khrushchev's boasts which naturally excited Western concerns about a possible gap in bombers, missiles, and ABM systems.

Given these problems, the impression remains that the Pentagon has often produced scare analyses on the eve of Congressional action on defense appropriations. The studies of the Stockholm International Peace Research Institute (based primarily on official U.S. data) suggest that, at the very moment in the early 1970s when the Nixon Administration warned about being overtaken and surpassed by the USSR, the United States had a commanding lead over Russia (approximately 2:1 or more in many cases) in:

1. Numbers of nuclear tests carried out both before and after the Moscow Treaty;
2. Deliverable nuclear and thermonuclear warheads;
3. Numbers of strategic delivery vehicles;
4. Available megatonnage (deliverable on *aircraft* as well as land- and sea-based missiles);

5. Quality of strategic delivery vehicles (hardening, accuracy, multiple warheads, etc.);
6. Numbers and quality of ships at sea and sea bases;
7. Arms shipments to other countries;
8. Defense spending.[40]

To be sure, some asymmetries in the strategic and conventional balance favored the USSR, but these were generally more than compensated by Western advantages. It seemed inappropriate, as SALT I got underway, for Washington to belabor Soviet deployment of FOBS (fractional orbital bombardment systems) or SS-9 missiles (large, liquid fueled) which Washington had already considered and opted not to deploy or to discontinue because more modern and efficient systems were available.

The ABM treaty signed on May 26, 1972, established a situation of quantitative and functional symmetry between the two sides, each being permitted to deploy 100 launchers at two sites.[41] It signified that each superpower renounced any hope of defending large numbers of its population from attack by the other side. This renunciation had the more serious consequences for the USSR, since Soviet territory was already within range of Chinese missiles, while the United States was not expected to fall within Chinese reach for several years. The USSR had already deployed 64 launchers around Moscow, while the United States had begun construction at two sites (and contracted some equipment for two others) intended to protect Minuteman survivability. American ABM technology was thought to lead Soviet, but neither side had any real prospect of saving more than a fraction of its population through ballistic missile defense, the gains of which could be readily nullified by increases in offensive power by the other side.

The Interim Agreement on Limitation of Strategic Offensive Arms, also signed on May 26, 1972, had the effect of freezing the levels of ICBMs and SLBMs already deployed or under construction by each country. The agreement is to remain in effect for five years unless replaced earlier by an accord on more complete measures limiting strategic offensive arms. Numerical ceilings for SLBMs are given in a protocol also signed by President Nixon and Secretary Brezhnev (which has, however, not been published in the USSR): The US may have no more than 710 SLBMs and no more than 44 modern ballistic missile submarines (three more than the existing total). The USSR may have no more than 950 SLBMs and no more than 62 modern ballistic missile submarines (up from 56 already deployed or under construction), provided however that the USSR retires 209 older land-based missiles and 30 older SLBM launchers. Though not mentioned in the protocol, ICBM levels were understood to stand at 1,054 for the United States and 1,618 for the Soviet Union in 1972. The total number of ICBMs and SLBMs consistent with the agreement are: for the United States, 1,710; for the USSR, 2,419.

The first ground for concern in the U.S. Senate about the Interim Agreement, then, was that it committed the United States to a lower number of strategic offensive weapons than permitted to the Soviet Union. One White House response to this criticism was that the agreement headed off an even greater asymmetry which would have resulted had the USSR continued her ICBM and SLBM deployment rates of recent years. This argument was a kind of red herring, however, because Soviet deployment rates had already slowed in 1971-72. Indeed, some members of the U.S. negotiating team believed that the Kremlin simply agreed to ceilings which already represented its ultimate targets. The Pentagon, for its part, was not interested in "more of the same" kind of missiles, but was embarked on research and development of qualitatively improved weapons—the Trident submarine and B-1 bomber, which would not be ready for serial production for several years.[42]

The second cause for Senate anxiety was that the Interim Agreement enshrined a "megatonnage gap" in Moscow's favor. This factor was more difficult to analyze than numbers of missiles, but most analyses agreed that Soviet missiles carried a much heavier payload than American: in theory at least, 6.5 million pounds versus 3.8 million pounds in mid-1972. The theoretical payload of American B-52s and FB-111s, however, was estimated at 33.4 million pounds in 1972 as against only 4.8 million pounds for Soviet Mya-4s and Tu-95s.[43] Not only are such yardsticks highly crude and uncertain, they are also quite misleading, because warhead accuracy is much more decisive than yield. If the explosive power of a warhead is doubled, for example, the radius of damage increases by approximately one-third. Perhaps for this reason, many Soviet missiles are thought to carry smaller warheads than their payload capacity would permit.[44]

While Moscow has some lead in numbers of missiles and *missile*-deliverable megatonnage, the United States has a clear advantage in the most critical indices of nuclear power: numbers of warheads, accuracy, reliability, and survivability of delivery systems. In 1972 American strategic missiles and heavy bombers could carry 5,900 nuclear warheads, compared to an estimated 2,200 warheads carried by Soviet missiles and heavy bombers. The Interim Agreement set no restriction on numbers of warheads, and the American total was expected to double between 1972 and 1977. The Soviet Union, according to Defense Department estimates in early 1973, had still not perfected the technology of MIRV (multiple independently targeted reentry vehicles) and it was uncertain whether MRV (multiple reentry vehicles) had been deployed in Soviet missiles.[45]

On August 17, 1973, however, Defense Secretary James R. Schlesinger announced that, since May 1973, the USSR had flight-tested missiles with multiple warheads that could be directed to separate targets. This was part of a new test series involving four new generation missiles, at least two of which (both liquid fueled) carried multiple warheads. Production and deployment of the new missiles could begin in two years, Dr. Schlesinger said, warning that the total number of Soviet warheads could match that of the United States by the end of the decade. Though this development could be used to spur intensified defense efforts in the United States, the fact is that the Soviet MIRV tests had been expected for some time and the 1972 Interim Agreement predicated on the need for revision after five years. Indeed, President Nixon and Secretary Brezhnev pledged at San Clemente on June 21, 1973 to accelerate negotiations to produce a new offensive weapon treaty before the end of 1974. Again they agreed to be "guided by the recognition of each other's equal security interests and by the recognition that efforts to obtain unilateral advantage, directly or indirectly, would be inconsistent with the strengthening of peaceful relations" between the two countries.

From the Soviet standpoint, however, the strategic balance in 1972-73 was hardly tilted in Moscow's favor. In addition to the "warhead gap" resulting from the U.S. lead in MIRV, there was also a significant American lead in numbers (and quality) of long-range bombers: more than 430 B-52s in service and more than 100 in storage, as compared with 140 slower and shorter-range Soviet heavy bombers. The U.S. bombers could deliver some 2,000 weapons on Soviet targets compared to 420 deliverable by Soviet bombers. As the United States equips her bomber force with Short-Range Attack Missiles (SRAM) in the mid-1970s, the number of nuclear weapons on U.S. strategic aircraft could rise to more than 7,500.

While Washington espouses "sufficiency" in weapons deployed, the White House has made clear its intention to retain "superiority" in military technology, i.e., the very research and development potential that accounted for U.S. leadership in MIRV, ABM know-how, nuclear submarines, etc.[46] Soviet leadership in fields such as large missiles was—like steel production—in areas no longer at the forefront of modern technology. Even the initial Soviet tests of multiple warheads in 1973 reportedly involved liquid-fueled rather than solid-fueled missiles such as Minuteman and Polaris.

As Soviet diplomats emphasize, there is also a major asymmetry in that America's dual-purpose aircraft based in Europe and on aircraft carriers could be used not only tactically but for strategic strikes on Soviet territory. Though the USSR continued to target some 700 medium- or intermediate-range missiles on Europe, Moscow had no equivalent to the forward-based systems (FBS) of the United States.

Another important asymmetry is that Soviet submarines must travel much further from their home bases in order to come within firing range of the United States. They can be serviced only from Soviet territory, whereas U.S. submarines can operate out of Spanish and Scottish bases. The movements of these submarines can be monitored as they pass through NATO-controlled waters in the Baltic Sea and the Dardanelles (where there are also the restrictions of the Montreaux Convention to contend with). Finally, the range of Soviet SLBMs was shorter than that of Polaris or Poseidon missiles in 1972. Both superpowers were testing missiles of much longer range, which could reduce considerably the value of overseas bases in the future. As of 1972-73, however, IISS estimates were that only 40 percent of the Soviet submarine fleet could be on station at any one time, compared with 60 percent for the U.S. fleet.

If we look beyond the 1972 agreements to other factors in the balance of power, the perspective from Moscow looks still more dismal. The Kremlin continues to face a significant threat on two fronts. British and French nuclear forces are not limited at all by the 1972 accords, and nuclear weapons continue to be available to West Germany and other NATO members if Washington approves their use in time of war. China's nuclear capability has grown steadily, and Peking has unresolved differences with Moscow. Chinese-American relations, by contrast, improved significantly in the early 1970s. SALT I, in short, limited only the two superpowers. Of the other three nuclear powers (and those with access to nuclear sharing), all seemed to be foes of the USSR.

Like the strategic nuclear balance, the balances of power in Europe, in the Mediterranean, and elsewhere in the world are all complex and difficult to measure. The one dimension in which Moscow seemed to enjoy a clear advantage was in numbers (but perhaps not quality) of tanks and tactical aircraft it has deployed in Eastern Europe. Even these Soviet advantages have to be viewed against the significant improvements being made in anti-tank weapons in Western Europe. The geographical and other factors that enhance Soviet power in Europe are the same ones that make it more difficult for Russia to reach (or control) the seas and to bring North America within range of the bombers and missiles that have long been targeted on Western Europe. Even so, the Mediterranean fleets of *either* France or Italy outnumber that of the USSR, without placing the U.S. Sixth Fleet on the scales.

While Washington was clearly having problems with its allies—from Saigon to Tokyo to Bonn—in the early 1970s, these paled by comparison with those which troubled the Soviet network of friends and allies. Nationalism could again raise its ugly head to disrupt the Warsaw Pact. Détente would make Eastern Europe increasingly vulnerable to the blandishments of the West, turning it into a transmission belt that could poison the USSR as well. Elsewhere, the Kremlin seemed to be riding a series of tigers by the tail. Egypt and other Arab friends were neither grateful for Soviet aid nor amenable to Kremlin guidance. North Vietnam could still disrupt U.S.-Soviet relations. Hanoi like other Soviet friends and allies could also play a Chinese card. As for the Peking leadership, Mao Tse-tung could not live forever, but there was no sign that his successors would return to Moscow's embrace. One of the brightest spots on the Kremlin horizon seemed to be Cuba, which had just joined the Council of Mutual Economic Assistance. Castro was even complementing Soviet practice by conducting businesslike relations with "Revolutionary Peru," with Mexico, and with other Latin countries. If Nixon dropped bait in the Caribbean, however, the halcyon years of the Soviet-Cuban affair could be shaken.

Though both superpowers have serious domestic troubles, the Soviet Union faces a variety of problems quite unlike those confronting the West. First, the Soviet GNP has remained less than half that of the United States. If the GNP of all NATO countries is pitted against those of the Warsaw Pact, the totals (in 1971 dollars) are $1,889,000,000 versus $696,000,000. If Japan's GNP of $225,000,000 is added to those of the Atlantic community, the United States and her most powerful allies have a total GNP of more than $2 trillion.[47] This total could become still more impressive if it included the GNPs of Australia, Taiwan, New Zealand, and other U.S. allies. The contrast would be still greater if Switzerland, Sweden, Austria and other nonaligned nations were considered with the Western totals. While Indochina has drained U.S. resources, Cuba and some other recipients of Soviet aid have also depleted those of the USSR.

While Western nations have acute currency problems, the members of the Soviet-led Council of Mutual Economic Assistance are plagued with persistently sluggish economies lacking in innovation and dynamism.[48] Faced with structural and morale problems, the Communist nations continue to play a version of "musical chairs," hoping that radical reorganization of ministries and planning agencies will supply the missing music. Though all industrialized countries are confronting ecological problems of various kinds, the Western nations confront a more acute danger than the USSR that they may be cut off from oil supplies, at least temporarily. The Communist countries, on the other hand, seem increasingly dependent on the West for food supplies and for the technology necessary to run a modern economy.

Secondly, ethnic and nationality problems within the USSR threaten to be much more disruptive than racial differences in the United States. Russians and other Slavs make up less than 60 percent of the Soviet population. Moscow may hope to submerge the nationalisms of the constituent republics in larger planning units, but this will hardly placate the nationalist feelings which bubble ever closer to the surface.

Third, the Soviet system still has no viable way to cope with dissent except by repression. The prominent physicist Andrei Sakharov, for one, has argued that greater civic freedom is necessary to overcome economic stagnation. The regime also runs the risk that its repressive policies will simply alienate more and more the scientists and young people on whom its future prospects depend.

Fourth, the Soviet system still lacks any mechanism for orderly succession of political rule. General Secretary Brezhnev and his colleagues have proved highly skilled in resolving conflicts among themselves and maintaining at least the facade of collective leadership. Brezhnev, however, might reach for more power just as his mental and physical energies begin to falter. Brezhnev also runs the risk that, like Khrushchev, he may bank on the feasibility of establishing a policy of peace and trade with the United States, only to find that his efforts are sabotaged—if not by the President, then by some other part of the American bureaucracy. If one or two members of the present Moscow triumvirate pass from the scene, the Kremlin's political order could be shattered, especially since KGB and military leaders became full members of the Politburo in 1973.

While the USSR and many other countries had their own domestic scandals and corruption, none gained the publicity attaching to the Watergate and related affairs in the United States. These problems threatened in 1973 to paralyze the domestic if not the foreign operations of the U.S. Government, with unpredictable impact on America's international standing. The early response from Moscow, however, was to stand by the U.S. President, while many European observers considered the exposé of the Nixon White House to show the continued (or renewed) vigor of American self-government—a long-term asset despite its immediate costs.

Thus, though the USSR was "gaining" in some respects on the Western powers in the early 1970s, the overall balance of power—technological, economic, political, as well as military—seemed likely to favor the West for at least the decade, perhaps to a greater extent than in the 1960s if non-military aspects were considered.

Proposition IX:

The 1972 SALT accords appear to serve the best interests of each party. Each superpower is left with more than sufficient power to deter a first-strike attack by the other. Though the 1972 agreements leave each side free to intensify the arms race, they also permit, oblige, and pressure both sides to make further-reaching in accords in SALT II. For the meantime, each can gain from the kind of "stability" and "sufficiency" agreed to in SALT I.

It is premature to say whether one or the other superpower gained the more from the 1972 agreements. Surely, each side made concessions. If the parties put off all agreements until perfect symmetry were attained, either through competition or through negotiation, there would never be an agreed limitation on strategic or other arms. As the International Institute for Strategic Studies has noted, "a large number of quite different 'balances' might be struck between the offensive strategic forces now constrained by SALT agreements. What should also be clear is that the proliferation of such 'balances' demonstrates not only the limited utility of any single criterion but also the frailty of all such crude quantitative comparisons."[49]

The majority of authorities (some 54 percent) represented in the ESP data held that "overkill capacity on both sides makes such distinctions [as superiority] meaningless."

Another 15 percent judged that "parity" existed between the United States and the USSR in 1972. Another 15 percent held that the United States was superior in 1972, only 1 percent believing that the USSR was superior at the time the SALT I accords were signed. Is either superpower moving toward superiority over the next five years? Respondents divided almost equally on this question: 17 percent saying the USSR was moving toward superiority and another 16 percent contending the United States was ahead in 1972 and/or would be superior by 1977. Robert Legvold of Tufts University summarized the strategic balance as one of "effective parity in 1972, asymmetric advantages for both sides, with the United States enjoying a *qualitative* lead in most critical areas." Some respondents objected to the phrasing of the entire question, saying that the alternatives posed did not present sufficiently variegated and sensitive choices. Lawrence Finkelstein of Harvard University noted that the entire question could not be answered apart from the specific situation to which force is relevant. Others complained that the survey left out the option of "parity now and in 1977" (deliberately omitted to make it harder to hedge). A plurality of respondents (60, about 40 percent) stated that the interim agreement on strategic weapons would "stabilize the superpower competition but leave other arms races unaffected." An optimistic minority of 35 respondents thought that the agreement would "contribute to containing the arms race generally." Thirty-eight replied that the accord would "prove meaningless" (as [it is] bypassed through qualitative improvements) and two thought that the agreement would collapse altogether, e.g., by the way it is interpreted.

Some respondents suggested that the interim agreement was an important first step that could lead to stabilization of the strategic balance. Others saw it as freeing resources for a conventional arms race. One thought it improved the relative position of the Soviet Union. Another stated that it afforded some stability but could be bypassed by technological innovations. Several respondents thought the interim agreement useless for containing the arms race, but important for political relations. A highly pessimistic view was that the agreement might result in a stepped-up arms race. At the other pole, one writer suggested that the accord was a first step in the transformation of a system emphasizing military preparedness to one of "global economism." (Cross-tabulations of different answers indicate that those respondents who believe the USSR to be ahead in the arms race had higher hopes for SALT I and II than those who considered the United States to be ahead or those who believed "overkill" to make "superiority" a meaningless concept.)

Most respondents were quite sanguine that the SALT I accords would prove viable, at least for the next four or five years. Eighty-one percent considered it probable that both sides would observe the ABM limitations agreed to in 1972. Sixty-six percent thought it improbable that either superpower would attempt to violate SALT agreements clandestinely so as to gain at least temporarily the upper hand in negotiations from strength. (One foreign expert, however, thought it likely that both superpowers would secretly attempt to evade any future qualitative limitations.) Only 12 percent considered it probable that "a major technological breakthrough . . . will unsettle the rough deterrent parity now existing in superpower relations."

Strategic threats from other centers of nuclear power did not appear excessively ominous, at least for 1973-77. Only 6 percent expected a "major technological breakthrough that will enable one or more of the other nuclear powers . . . to close the gap between their own military potential and that of the U.S. and the USSR." Only 8 percent predicted "the union of two or more European powers to form the embryo of a nuclear superpower." To be sure, 61 percent saw China "moving vigorously to develop nuclear forces more powerful than those of France or Britain at their present levels of development." And 38 percent said that China would soon possess a "nuclear force capable of a significant 'second-strike' against the USSR even if Soviet forces should strike first." Furthermore, only 10 percent considered it likely that a major technological breakthrough "will enable the two superpowers to mount an effective defense against developing nuclear powers such as China." Only 3 percent considered it probable that Chinese leaders would use their "nuclear power less 'rationally' or 'responsibly' than other nuclear powers."

The future prospects of superpower arms control, on the other hand, were viewed rather pessimistically by most respondents. Only 28 percent considered it probable that the U.S. and USSR would reach agreements "in the next round(s) of SALT that are meaningful in restraining their qualitative and quantitative arms competition." Not more than one-fifth of respondents considered it likely that France, Britain, or China would take part in future SALT negotiations.

Only 14 percent expected "the development of more credible guarantees by the nuclear powers against nuclear blackmail of non-nuclear weapons countries." And only 45 percent forecast "additional arms control outside of SALT involving the superpowers and other states (such as nuclear-free zones, CBW, etc.)." Despite this, few respondents considered it probable that Israel, India, or Japan would test and deploy nuclear weapons (26, 14, and 13 percent respectively). (Some argued, however, that Israel may already be in a position to deploy nuclear weapons *without* field testing.) In this same vein, only 4 percent deemed it likely that "a major technological breakthrough . . . will enable lesser powers (Egypt, Pakistan, North Vietnam, etc.) to develop weapons of mass destruction that will give them an effective terror or second-strike weapon analogous to the nuclear weapons possessed by China, Britain, and France."

Will the arms race between the U.S. and the USSR continue at levels as high as in recent years? Forty-nine percent responded "yes" to this question, but 38 percent believed the competition would proceed at reduced levels and only 3 percent assumed it would be at levels higher than in recent years. Several respondents qualified their responses by stating that they expected the *qualitative* arms race (including research and development) to intensify, while *quantitative* aspects (production and actual deployment) would slacken. Joseph I. Coffey of the University of Pittsburgh suggested that the United States arms effort would be higher than in recent years, while the Soviet Union's would be about the same as or lower than in recent years. Answers to this question were generally corroborated by responses to a question about the likely share of the U.S. defense budget in the gross national product in the years 1973-77: 44 percent expected the share would stay about the same; 32 percent believed it would decrease; while 25 percent thought it would increase. (The overall defense budget could readily increase, even while strategic spending was held steady or reduced, due to higher costs for personnel or for non-strategic weapons systems.)

The views represented in the Expert Survey Panel suggest, on balance, that SALT I represented a major step in containing the superpower arms race. Considerable skepticism is indicated, however, on whether future negotiations will succeed in reaching meaningful limitations on arms competition between the superpowers or among other nations.

The *difficulty* of reaching further arms controls, of course, does not preclude the *desirability* of seriously attempting to do so. The Expert Survey Panel may have underestimated both the dynamism of military technology and the determination of the U.S. and Soviet governments to bring it under control. (The survey was completed prior to the Nixon-Brezhnev pledge in June 1973 to reach a new strategic arms accord before the end of 1974 and the announcement that the USSR conducted her first flight tests of multiple, separately targetable warheads had occurred in mid-1973.)

Defense planners both in Washington and Moscow had concern that the other might unsettle the military expectations on which the Interim Agreement rested. The Pentagon, for example, expressed alarm in 1972-73 that the Soviet lead in numbers of ICBMs would be married with qualitative gains posing a theroetical threat to the survivability of the American land-based missile force. Thus, Soviet ICBM accuracy might be dramatically improved through terminal guidance systems, perhaps to the point where any missile that lands could destroy an American missile in its hardened silo. As many as twenty warheads might be deployed on a single Soviet missile—a quantitative change which would pose a threat to American ICBMs, even without improvements in Soviet missile accuracy. Russia's lead in killer satellites provides another asset, for destruction of U.S. reconnaissance satellites could prevent the Pentagon from targeting missiles kept in reserve after an initial wave of Soviet attack missiles. Depressed trajectory missiles, fired from submarines or from land silos, could elude American radars for some time and narrow the warning times for U.S. bombers to take to the skies.

Soviet deployment of mobile missiles (which Moscow denies is banned by SALT I) could further complicate America's defenses. These and other contingencies can be combined into a worst case scenario in which the USSR could destroy the U.S. bomber fleet on the ground and disarm the Minuteman force simultaneously, leaving the Kremlin free to dictate the terms of the peace. The Polaris-Poseidon missile squadrons, the argument runs, would be immobilized by Washington's recognition that their use would bring destruction upon America's cities (as yet spared from Soviet attack) by Soviet forces still held in reserve and hidden from U.S. intelligence by destruction of American satellites.

Soviet planners, of course, could easily generate an even more terrifying worst case study of America's potential—whether for a first- or a second-strike scenario. To begin with, the cautious planners of Soviet strategy could never assume that they could destroy the American retaliatory capacity or neutralize Washington's willingness to slug it out if a nuclear war began. The numbers and accuracy of U.S. warheads, already superior to Moscow's, must be expected to increase. Maneuverable warheads, chaff, decoys and electro-magnetic impulses could readily overwhelm and penetrate Soviet air and missile defenses.[f] Moscow would also have to consider whether China, France and/or Britain might not be dragged into the war, adding to the dangers of escalation no matter which side struck the first blow. U.S. and other NATO forward based systems (including those operated by West Germany) could also be orchestrated in an attack on the Soviet heartland.

Returning to SALT I, we find that two schools of thought have emerged in the West. The first school, which contends the agreements conceded too much to the USSR, is certainly wrong-headed or misinformed. Surely U.S. strategic forces have been and will remain adequate to meet President Nixon's criteria for "sufficiency" (enumerated at the outset of this chapter), at least for the duration of the interim agreement (1972-77). The same may be said for Soviet forces, which are permitted to expand during this period up to specified levels.

The opposing school of thought holds that the 1972 accords did too little and came too late. This school points out that the 1972 accords left each side free to continue with deployment of multiple warheads, the development of more powerful planes and submarines, and explorations in many fields of weaponry which threaten qualitative breakthroughs that could shatter any sense of "equal security." "A little arms control can be a dangerous thing," they point out, arguing that accords like those reached in 1972 (as in 1963) can provoke an intensified arms race.

This line of criticism has more substance than the "sell-out" thesis heard in some quarters of Washington and probably in Moscow as well. But it is too absolutistic. It ignores the historic dimensions of the 1972 agreements: their intrinsic complexity (compared, e.g., with the nuclear test ban); the vital importance of the weapons limited (compared, e.g., with "capital ships" in 1922 or "weapons of mass destruction in outer space" in 1967); and the political and other obstacles—domestic and external—which the parties surmounted in three years of negotiations.

The long-term significance of SALT I may be that it laid a basis for containing the new rounds of intensified weapons competition in the late 1970s. The obstacles and the hopes for rational decision-making in this domain are discussed in the next chapter.

---

[f]Development of the subsonic cruise armed decoy was terminated by the Pentagon on July 6, 1973, in part for economic reasons, but "a vigorous technology program" would continue research on penetration aids.

2

Nicholas II to Salt II: Logic vs. the Organization(s)

In this chapter we shall focus on the elements of continuity and change in Russian policy. Our thesis will be that the role of traditional factors (geography, culture, ideology) has declined, resulting in a tug-of-war between strategic logic and organizational pressures. Looked at in historical perspective, the balance has shifted toward greater acceptance of arms control rationality as a way to enhance the long-term interests of the USSR, even though this entails compromise accommodation with the other superpower. As in the United States, however, Soviet decision-makers continue to hedge their bets by placating hard-line critics who contend, with Laertes, that "best safety lies in fear" (not trust).

Many of the propositions advanced in the preceding chapter are posited on an assumption that the Soviet and U.S. governments have often acted in accordance with the logic of the situation facing them.[1] Taken to an extreme, the propositions assume that a unified Rational Actor sitting in Moscow or Washington employs strategic logic to advance the "interests" of his government. The ninth proposition in particular assumes that—if this Rational Actor were enlightened, with full access to relevant information and with skills for analyzing it in a balanced way—the "Kremlin" and the "White House" would act to maintain and extend the strategic arms limitations agreed to in 1972.

While the first eight propositions have policy implications, they attempt mainly to describe rather than to prescribe Soviet and U.S. behavior patterns. Not all these patterns harmonize fully with a rational model aimed at optimizing the national interest. Thus, some behavior has been clearly influenced by misperception, e.g., regarding the capabilities and intentions of the other side. Some behavior has been anachronistic, suited to meeting a past rather than a current challenge. Further problems arise because Soviet leaders may often have priorities different from American, and different beliefs on how best to achieve their goals. Moscow's logic, in short, need not be Washington's.

Differences in the style and substance of "American" and "Soviet" (Russian) strategic logic derive from substantial differences between the countries themselves:

1. geography (e.g., the advantages of oceanic isolation compared with proximity to Asia and Europe);
2. cultural traditions (e.g., pragmatism and decentralized problem-solving versus absolutism and centralized guidance);

35

3. historical experiences (e.g., little basis for fear of foreign invasion compared with repeated defeats by Asian and European powers);

4. economics (e.g., relative abundance and a position of world leadership compared with relative scarcity and relative backwardness);

5. military experiences (e.g., reliance upon advanced technology versus last-ditch reliance upon time, space, and population mass).

Each government's conception of its "interests" will also be shaped by its own political culture, whether summed up in a formal ideology or in deeply engrained "political beliefs." Each government will perceive and act on problems and opportunities within the framework of its own particular system. Thus, though the two systems may be similar or even "converging" in many respects, there are still myriad ways in which the strategic logic of each superpower may differ, making it difficult for either side to ascertain the degree to which the other is behaving "rationally."[2]

Another way to analyze Soviet and U.S. behavior is to examine the organizational structures which influence and implement each government's foreign policy. We may look at the routines (e.g., standard operating procedures) of each bureaucracy or the bargaining and competition that occurs between and among various components of the decision-making system. Such approaches have been used by Graham Allison, for example, to explain apparently irrational or non-rational components in U.S. and Soviet decision-making at the time of the Cuban missile crisis.[3]

The Organization Model, of course, is only one way to explain behavior that seems out of tune with the logic of the situation. We should also study the cultural influences within a society that may lead to misperception or non-systematic procedures in problem-solving. We might also attempt to penetrate the psyche of individual leaders to ascertain why their decisions seem "hare-brained" even to their colleagues with similar values and access to information. Thus, behavioral patterns of nations, their elites, and those of individual rulers must be considered if we are to anticipate their responses to particular situations.

As Figure 2-1 suggests, the roots of decision-making must be traced to a wide range of influences—cultural, group, and personal. Culture, like ideology, shapes not only the way leaders express themselves but how they think and perceive; it both generates and blocks out trains of thought and feeling. Nationalist and other group sentiments also intrude to shape or be shaped by ideology. Completely contrary to notions about "faceless Communist bureaucrats," there have been wide differences in the personal values and styles of Soviet leaders (e.g., Stalin, Khrushchev, and Kosygin); just as there have been among Western leaders (e.g., Franklin Roosevelt and Harry Truman).

From these sources—cultural, group, and personal—derive the main ingredients *internal* to a decision-maker's actions. But his decisions—even his so-called initiatives—take place in response to an external environment as it intrudes upon

37

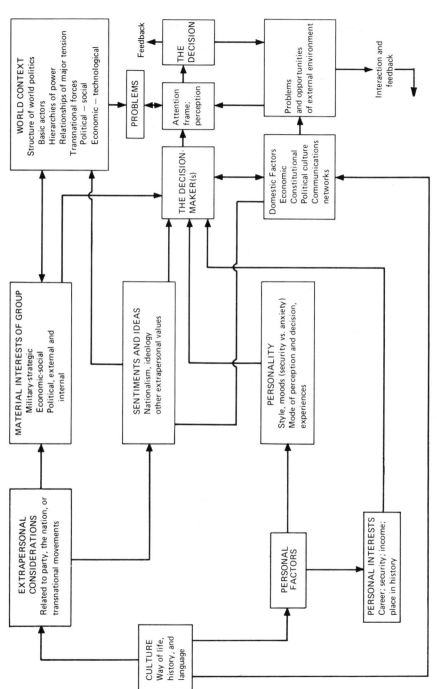

Figure 2-1. Outline of Factors Conditioning Foreign Policy Decisions

his attention frame and as it is perceived by him. This environment, in addition to casting up the problems and opportunities that stimulate decisions, also provides the international and domestic context which further condition the politician's thoughts and deeds. There is both a cause and effect relationship, an interdependence, between the military position and national sentiment of one state and the broader structure of world politics, with its hierarchies of power and transnational forces. The domestic context—economic, constitutional, etc.— will also condition the final decision as well as inputs such as personal interest and national sentiments. There is, of course, a continuous interaction between all the elements outlined and feedback from each decision affecting all factors in the chain. Given the complexity of this system, it is hardly surprising that some decisions will reflect more the logic of the situation while others will suggest more traditional response patterns or even random behavior.[4]

We must underscore that the ideas of the U.S., Soviet and other governments on arms control are not formed in a vacuum. Soviet views on arms competition, for example, naturally reflect a learning experience, the nature of which can be shaped by Washington, Peking, or other centers of power. To the extent that Soviet leaders feel their experiences in arms control matters have been conducive to promotion of their interests, they will be inclined to pursue these negotiations more seriously and vice versa. Thus, one Soviet diplomat told the author of the profound shock and disillusionment experienced by some in the Soviet Foreign Ministry in 1955 when the three Western heads of government ignored, at Geneva, the May 10 disarmament proposals of the USSR, proposals that specifically incorporated much of the Western position up to that time, leading Washington by September of that year to "place a reservation upon all of its pre-Geneva substantive positions . . . [on] levels of armaments. . . ." This incident may or may not be apocryphal, recounted to impress the Western listener, but the principle implicit in the Soviet diplomat's story seems indisputable: Soviet ideas and actions—no less than the West's—will be based upon perceptions and experiences formed in a crucible of interaction.

Explanations of foreign policy decisions must take account of the many and diverse levels at which world politics may be analyzed and the various approaches to this analysis. Linking these two dimensions, the following scheme results:

Levels of Analysis[5]	*Approaches to Explanation*
The Individual	Cultural influences; family backgrounds; personal style and values; career interests and ambitions.
Domestic Politics	Organizational structures and processes; standard operating procedures; vested interests; bargaining between bureaucracies and parties; the warrior

Levels of Analysis	Approaches to Explanation
	class; military-industrial complex; other interest groups—formal and informal managerial, scientific, consumer; informal associations.
Politics Among Nations	Rational Actor: decisions made on the basis of "national interest," operating unilaterally or in response to signals from the other side. Historic behavior patterns. Perception and misperception. Action-reaction patterns.
National and Global Environment	Push and pull of technological dynamism; resource shortages and surpluses; ecological pressures; transnational forces.
International Organization	Mechanisms for coordination and conflict resolution. Weaknesses and strengths of institutions for formulating rules, interpreting and applying these rules, and enforcing them.
Communication Systems	Networks for transmitting, receiving, and filtering messages among individuals, groups, bureaucracies, nation-states, transnational or international organizations.

These frameworks for analyzing decision-making are helpful for understanding the zigs and zags of Soviet and American policies toward arms control over the years. Different levels of analysis and approaches to explanation will be emphasized in different parts of this book. Our particular focus in this chapter, however, is on the growing role of strategic rationality in Soviet policy compared with organizational and domestic inputs.

Organization and Interests, Formal and Informal

The East-West arms race has been marked by both continuity and change.[6] If we look back not only to the first disarmament efforts of the Bolsheviks but also to Tsarist diplomacy, the elements of continuity appear at least as significant as the changes that have affected Soviet policy over the years. Moscow's negotiating behavior even in recent times continues to bear striking resemblances to the approach of Tsarist Russia to the Hague Conference on the Limitation of Armaments in 1899 (and again in 1907).[7] Much of this behavior is explicable in terms of a Rational Actor model: strategic logic has dictated certain policies that tried to compensate for Russia's weaknesses and take advantage of her geopolitical and demographic advantages.

Like Tsar Nicholas II, Soviet leaders from Lenin through Brezhnev have been aware of Russia's technological and material disadvantages vis-à-vis the West. Nicholas, for example, called the Hague Conference in part because he sought to outlaw the rapid-fire cannon available to other powers but not to Russia, unless at great expense. Soviet leaders, in their time, have also sought to negate the West's lead in various fields of military technology: in atomic weaponry (ban the bomb campaigns of 1946-52); the West's plans for tactical nuclear weapon deployment in Europe (atom-free zone proposals of 1956 on); outer space surveillance (denunciations of spy satellites as contrary to international law until Russia also obtained such craft in the early 1960s). Indeed, the Kremlin seems to have finally decided to take part in the strategic arms limitation talks (SALT) with Washington only after the Johnson Administration asked Congress for funds in 1968 to deploy antiballistic missile defenses (ABM), an expensive and complex system in which the United States might produce another "gap" for Russia to contend with. The U.S. lead in the testing of multiple warheads was no doubt another incentive bringing Moscow to the SALT negotiations in 1968-69.[8]

The diplomacy of Nicholas II appealed to pacifist sentiments at home and abroad, much as Soviet propaganda has courted elements of the liberal bourgeoisie, the working class, the oppressed nations of the Third World, as well as the war-weary people of the USSR.[9]

Like Tsarist Russia, the USSR has also been constrained by the views of her allies. Thus, despite its original reasons for calling the Hague Conference and wanting it to succeed, St. Petersburg had to promise Paris that no accords would result before France would consent to attend. Analogous pressures from Pankow and Peking contributed to occasional harsh notes in the Kremlin's negotiations with the West in the 1950s and 1960s.

More ironic even than the cross-pressures from allies were those from within the Tsarist Government. Nicholas was eventually compelled to assure some of his own ministers that Russia would not agree to major arms controls at The Hague because force or threat of arms would be needed to obtain Russia's political and territorial objectives in the Far East (where war with Japan was anticipated) and at the Turkish Straits (near which a number of Balkan wars would ensue prior to Sarajevo).

On this point of comparison we find that Soviet arms control policy has also been the result of conflicting pressures, from Lenin's day to the present (though dissent was surely rather muffled in the years of high Stalinism). These positions have reflected the same kinds of bureaucratic interests and institutional orientations that characterize decision-making processes in the United States and other countries.[10] Thus, a relatively conciliatory position toward negotiations with the West was developed in the Soviet Foreign Ministry (or Commissariat) under Chicherin, Litvinov, and Gromyko—all of them professional diplomats well versed in foreign cultures and languages, but (partly because of their cosmopolitan ways) relatively low in the Party hierarchy (at least until 1973).[11] This professional orientation and its concomitant willingness to explore negotiations was not nearly so pronounced when the Foreign Ministry was headed by Trotsky, Molotov, or Shepilov—in part because these men were ranking Party leaders first (at least two of them ideological hardliners) and only secondarily concerned with diplomacy. Vyshinsky's term as Foreign Minister (1949-1953) coincided with the height of the cold war and internal tensions in the USSR, producing a climate inhospitable to explorations of détente, even if the Foreign Minister had not been notable for his legalistic defense of and other involvements in the purges of the 1930s.[12]

The contrast between the world views associated with the Party hardliner and the professional diplomat was illustrated by the different ways in which Trotsky and Chicherin spoke, in their day, of "peaceful coexistence."[13] This concept can be rendered two ways in Russian: as *mirnoe sozhitel'stvo* or as *mirnoe sosushchestvovanie*. The first of these expressions more nearly approximates "peaceful cohabitation," implying a more active but less enduring relationship than the second term, which literally means "peaceful coexistence," connoting a more stable but also a more formal relationship. Trotsky seems to have been the first Soviet leader to speak of *mirnoe sozhitel'stvo*, a term that he used in a basically revolutionary context from November 1917 until the Brest-Litovsk Treaty concluded in March 1918. He used this term, for example, in the same speech in which he called for "no war, no peace." It was left to Trotsky's successor as Foreign Commissar, Chicherin (once employed in the Tsarist Foreign Ministry), to use *mirnoe sozhit'elstvo* in a more conciliatory sense, as he did in September 1918 when attempting privately to convince the Kaiser's government of Moscow's interest in good-neighborly relations and "peaceful cohabitation." Chicherin later termed Soviet Russia's peace treaty with Estonia in February 1920 "the first experiment in *mirnoe sozhitel'stvo* with bourgeois states" and "a dress rehearsal for understanding with the Entente."

Chicherin also seems to have been the first Soviet spokesman to employ the more formal expression for coexistence when, on June 17, 1920, he called for "*mirnoe sosushchestvovanie* with other governments, no matter what they are." Such niceties, of course, have been blurred in later Soviet treatments of the problem, but Lenin seems never to have used the term *mirnoe sosushchestvovanie*, though in February 1920 he did speak of Soviet policy in Asia as "*mirnoe sozhitel'stvo* with all peoples, the workers and peasants of all nations awakening to a new life, a life without exploitation, without landowners, without capitalists, without merchants." Lenin did, however, speak of *mirnoe sozhitel'stvo* with bourgeois governments in October 1922, when he told the London

Observer that lack of full Soviet participation at the Lausanne Conference would impede trade "so that there would be either no grounds at all left for peaceful coexistence or it would be unusually hampered," and that the League of Nations was without "real equality of nations or real prospects of peaceful coexistence between them."

Stalin, after Lenin's death, used both terms for coexistence, but declared that the period of *mirnoe sozhitel'stvo* was receding into the past, giving way to a period of imperialist attacks. At a moment when Litvinov was presenting Moscow's appeals for total and general disarmament at the League of Nations, Stalin declared that the task was to delay war by buying off capitalists and applying all measures to maintain peaceful relations. "The basis of our relations with capitalist countries," he declared, "consists of admitting the *sosushchestvo-vanie* of the two opposing systems." As Franklyn Griffiths has pointed out in his essay on these changes, Stalin's "acceptance" evolved into Khrushchev's active pursuit of *mirnoe sosushchestvovanie.*[14] If Stalin accepted peaceful coexistence out of weakness, Khrushchev later made it a foundation of Soviet policy at a time of mutual deterrence.

Chicherin and Maxim Litvinov (first his deputy, later his successor as People's Commissar for Foreign Affairs) took the lead in formulating the Soviet position on disarmament at a number of international conferences.[15] It was Chicherin who, in mid-1921, first expressed the Soviet Government's interest in "disarmament of any kind," though he also noted Moscow's skepticism that "guarantees" would be found to assure the implementation of disarmament measures (about to be discussed at the Washington Naval Conference), a point that Comintern statements made in much stronger language. Prior to the Genoa Economic Conference in 1922, Litvinov seems to have drawn up theses on a "pacifist program" to be presented by the Soviet delegation, a procedure approved by the Party's Central Committee. Chicherin was apparently instructed to elaborate the details of the program, which he did in consultation with Lenin, the Soviet Foreign Commissar later presenting this program with great flourish at Genoa. Litvinov, for his part, led the Soviet delegation at the Moscow Conference on the Limitation of Armaments later in 1922, demonstrating much of the style and substance he showed when Moscow joined the League of Nations disarmament talks in 1927. As recent documentation has shown, however, Chicherin in 1922 was rebuked for going too far toward concessions to the West (a fate suffered more visibly by Harold E. Stassen in 1957, alleged by John Foster Dulles to have exceeded his instructions in arms control talks with Moscow). After an exchange of telegrams with Chicherin, however, "the Politburo [to quote a senior Soviet historian] decided that Chicherin was right" and directed him to make "concessions in strict dependence on the amount and terms of the loan granted to Soviet Russia."[16]

Traditions established by Chicherin and Litvinov in the interwar years have been continued in some ways by Andrei Gromyko. All three men seem to have lost no chance to speak for disarmament, when permitted by the political directorate. Some Westerners have seen Gromyko mainly as a professional technician, like the foreign minister of any great state, concerned primarily with diplomacy and *Realpolitik*, leaving ideology to others in the power structure. Gromyko, however, has moved from specialist and adviser in foreign affairs to full membership in the highest policy-making body, the Party Politburo. His career displays a remarkable durability, whether by Soviet or by world diplomatic standards. Taking over the Foreign Ministry in 1957 after Shepilov was brought down with the "anti-Party group" opposing Khrushchev, Gromyko remained in his job for seven years under Khrushchev and—by the time he joined the Politburo in 1973—for nine years under Brezhnev. When Gromyko urged the West to take careful note when arms control proposals were espoused by the Party leadership at the Congress in April 1971, this was on the basis of greater technical sophistication and more political authority than Chicherin or Litvinov enjoyed in the heyday of Lenin or Stalin.

There is, we should note, a worldwide trend for foreign ministers to meet one another frequently; to initiate and respond to proposals from one another as theoretical equals; to develop their expertise on the basis of higher education and professional diplomatic experience—usually without benefit of military training or service, even in developing countries. Within this elite, Andrei Gromyko was already the third best known foreign minister in 1965, ranking only after Couve de Murville and Dean Rusk among those known personally to other foreign ministers.[17] It is not so strange that—fifty years after the revolution—the Soviet Union's Foreign Minister is a part of an international elite of specialists in diplomacy. It is perhaps more surprising that he is part of a tradition that Chicherin and Litvinov established in the interwar years.

To what extent have other segments of the Soviet power structure opposed arms control policies authorized on high and carried out by the commissars and ministers of foreign affairs? By analogy we know that U.S. arms control policies must run a gauntlet which includes a variety of government agencies as well as political and economic pressure groups outside the government. The judgments of the White House, the National Security Council, the Departments of State and Defense, and the Arms Control and Disarmament Agency on arms limitation policies may be challenged not only by one another but also by Congress and numerous business interests which campaign rather openly and certainly more vigorously than would be possible in a less pluralistic community.[a] By the same

[a]By late 1972-73 it appeared that President Nixon aimed to reduce the influence of the Arms Control and Disarmament Agency drastically, cutting its staff and putting an aging career State Department officer at the head of the delegation to SALT II. Though the new head of the ACDA, Dr. Fred C. Iklé, was a respected scholar with university and RAND connections, he was a relative newcomer to the government bureaucracy, though he had long acquaintance with Dr. Kissinger and the new Secretary of Defense, Dr. James Schlesinger. The President, some insiders averred, was making ACDA a sacrificial lamb to placate the hardline Senators and other critics of SALT I. This decision was the more repugnant because ACDA representatives in SALT I had stood firmly by whatever orders

token, of course, public and elite pressures for détente and arms control also receive freer expression in the United States. Indeed, defense decision-making for both superpowers will reflect many of the *sui generis* characteristics of each. The imperatives and inertia of American institutions and bargaining processes will not necessarily be reproduced in the USSR. Comparisons may, however, point to some similarities as well as differences. Both countries, for example, have had their share of ideological hardliners, military and other groups opposed to East-West accommodations on arms control and related matters.

A *Pravda* cartoon of the 1920s showed Chicherin being embarrassed by the revolutionary speeches of Comintern head Zinoviev. Did the Comintern apparatus object to the disarmament proposals of the Commissariat for Foreign Affairs? Were proposals welcomed as part of a coordinated strategy against imperialism, or were they simply accepted as part of a foreign policy on which they—the men most concerned with fomenting revolution—had great doubts? In any event it was not difficult to sabotage the disarmament initiatives of those days by burying them in revolutionary propaganda subversive to the kind of mutual trust conducive for agreement on arms limitation (especially in the interwar era, when France and her allies demanded "moral disarmament" and "security" as the preconditions for "material disarmament"). Later, at the height of the cold war, the Cominform worked in orchestration with various Communist fronts to exploit the bomb banning proposals of Soviet diplomacy in the last years of Stalin's life.

Revolutionary concerns have long been dormant in the USSR, but Khrush-

they had received from Washington (including some which required reneging), while the last minute concessions made late at night in the Kremlin were the work of Mr. Nixon, Dr. Kissinger, and close associates. Though members of the National Security Council had been bugged earlier to plug leaks about SALT and Vietnam, a self-serving interpretation on the work of the President's Special Assistant for National Security was delivered to John Newhouse appeared in Vienna to gather information on SALT I, Kissinger instructed the U.S. delegation not to talk with him. In Senate testimony on September 11, 1973, however, Kissinger admitted that he talked to Newhouse once and authorized his staff to explain positions "that were more or less publicly known and that had already been presented" to the Soviet side. Newhouse could "check his judgments" with the NSC staff, but Kissinger denied authorizing that they check Newhouse's galleys for "accuracy."

Not surprisingly, *Cold Dawn* did not reveal the fact that the rather high ceilings for Soviet SLBMs in the Interim Agreement were originally suggested to Dr. Kissinger by Soviet authorities during his April 1972 trip to Moscow. These levels were among the options which Dr. Kissinger had his staff and other agencies to consider, even though they struck the Joint Chiefs of Staff as well as the U.S. SALT delegation as too high and out of line. Though *Cold Dawn* gives the impression that the President and associates were prepared to depart Moscow without a SALT agreement unless SLBMs were included in the accord, Dr. Kissinger's April talks in Moscow had already shown that SLBMs could be limited so long as Washington accepted the Soviet terms.

While Gromyko and his entourage gained new prestige from SALT I, the resignation of ACDA head Gerard C. Smith was accepted with more relief than regret shortly before SALT II commenced. Only time would tell whether the revelations of *Cold Dawn* (such as Soviet concern over a "provocative" attack by a third party) would inhibit Soviet diplomacy in future negotiations.

chev and his successors have often been criticized by ideological hardliners at home and abroad for their arms control dealings with the West. Assuming that revolutionary concerns have subsided, however, it would seem that their potentially disruptive influence on Soviet arms policy has been more than compensated by the growth of a military-industrial complex within the USSR.

Like military men everywhere, Soviet ministers of defense and their subordinates have generally taken a dim view of letting down moral and material defenses by negotiating with the adversary. There is no evidence that Trotsky (while in power) or his successor as Commissar for Military Affairs, Mikhail Frunze, were opposed to the disarmament line espoused by Chicherin and Litvinov. That line, after all, could be rationalized as part of a one-two punch, in which Comintern propaganda followed through to underscore the futility and hypocrisy of the bourgeois disarmament position. But it is clear that Trotsky and Frunze—despite personal and doctrinal feuding between them—shared a militant, revolutionary outlook concerned with keeping the entire nation and its armed forces in a high degree of readiness.[18] Frunze and other Soviet military men tried to forestall and attenuate the transition of the Red Army toward a small cadre force backed by a large territorial militia.[19] A less independent and revolutionary outlook was shown by Voroshilov, but he too talked of the need for strengthening Soviet defenses in the period of the Five-Year Plans before World War II, on premises that stressed the implacable hostility between the Soviet Union and the capitalist system.[20]

The zero-sum character of the struggle with imperialism and the need for intensified defense efforts have often been emphasized by Soviet military spokesmen, sometimes in harmony with the dominant Party line but sometimes with a discordant note at moments of East-West détente or movement toward cuts in military allocations. There was much evidence at several moments in the 1960s of serious dissatisfaction among the military over (a) reductions of troop strength; (b) allocation of funds to the military budget; and (c) decisions that implicitly favored one branch of the armed services over another.[21] There have also been warnings in the Soviet military press that arms control efforts will be in vain. In his day Frunze had cautioned that chemical weapons would be used in future wars and that no convention or agreement would change the matter.[22] In this same spirit a veritable chorus of Soviet military writers in 1968-1969 offered a series of thinly veiled warnings against joining the United States in SALT. They counseled that security should be sought in enlarging and improving the Soviet missile force rather than in negotiating with perfidious Washington. Once the SALT negotiations got underway, however, objections to the talks receded in Soviet military writing; and shows of force became less frequent and less spectacular on Red Square. Military spokesmen, like Party leaders, came to aver that neither side could benefit from a "new spiral in the arms race," and that the 1972 Moscow Summit agreements were in the interests of both sides.[23]

Defense Minister Grechko was quoted on a 1971 trip to Finland as saying that a decision to use nuclear weapons "could only be made by an idiot or a man who lost his mind," but in 1973 he repeated the familiar warning of earlier defense ministers that the West had not and never would abandon its aggressive aims or resign itself to the existence of Communist nations. Even before Grechko joined the Politburo in 1973, military representation on the Party's Central Committee had gained steadily through the 1960s till it reached 8.3 percent in 1971, contrasted with 2.4 percent in 1952 and 4.5 percent in 1956. If military personnel *candidate* members of the Central Committee and full members of the Central Auditing Commission are also computed, however, there has been a slight decline in the percentage of military representation in the higher organs of the Party through the 1960s till the Party Congress of 1971.[24] While not conclusive, the figures suggested that the highest members of the military hierarchy have been rewarded with full membership in the Central Committee, while otherwise the Party has endeavored to retain its usual position of predominance over the military.

Soviet politicians, especially at moments of crisis when they felt insecure (as in 1954-55 and in 1964-65), have courted the military. It also seems likely that the links between some political leaders and the military have been reinforced further by support from heads of industries engaged in advanced research, development, and manufacture of military and military-related products such as space ships.[25] Thus, what Joseph Schumpeter termed the "warrior class" has found itself in common cause with certain political leaders, with the secret police, and certain industrial interests whose empires may atrophy or be otherwise threatened by a lessening of international tensions, by freer contacts with foreigners, or by decreased investments in certain sectors of the economy.

Compared with the guardians of ideological rectitude, the marshals and the captains of heavy industry, the constituency for arms limitation in the Soviet Union is wide but weak. Writers, scientists, and champions of light industry have not been renowned for their decisive influence at the highest levels of the Kremlin. Though sit-ins, underground chronicles and thoughtful manifestos were given some rein in the late 1960s, the partial liberalization of Soviet foreign policy in the early 1970s was accompanied by a gradual and skillful tightening of domestic repression, accomplished in part by urging the leaders of the "Democratic Movement" to go abroad (and stay). As for the ordinary Soviet consumer, he has been short-changed for well over two generations. "Let them eat promises" has been—at least till the mid-1970s—the Politburo's updating of Marie Antoinette.

The trend toward functional representation at the highest level of foreign policy-making reached its apotheosis in April 1973, not long before Brezhnev was to meet again with President Nixon, when Gromyko, Marshal Grechko, and Yuri Andropov were all named as full members of the Politburo (replacing one member associated with a foot-dragging position on détente and one ally of Kosygin's "consumerism"). This marked the first time since 1957 that a Foreign

Minister or Defense Minister held Politburo rank, and the first time since Beria (1953) that a head of the secret police had climbed so high. Only time would tell whether these three voices would echo the General Secretary or whether they would exercise some independent influence on Soviet foreign policy—representative perhaps of their own institutional perspectives. At least for the short term, however, the Politburo appeared to have been rendered more functional by giving representation to powerful bureaucratic groups concerned with foreign policy. The Politburo would thus be able to deal more effectively with arms and security problems, trade and other issues becoming more salient in an era of more East-West communication. As Brezhnev told some American reporters in June 1973, foreign policy matters came first on the Politburo agenda.

Given another succession crisis, the levers of power controlled by both Grechko and Andropov could shape the outcome far more than the worldwide diplomatic contacts of Gromyko. Allegiance to their patron would no longer be an issue, and each man would presumably try to exercise influence in behalf of himself, his own policy preferences, and possibly his particular bureaucracy. The political culture of the Soviet Union militates for the subjection of all particular interests (including the military) to the will of the Party. In a free-for-all among technocrats representing a variety of special interests, however, the voices of military and the KGB might prove to be weightier than in the immediate past.

Returning to our main theme, we see that organizational interests as well as cultural influences have left their mark on Soviet arms and arms control policies over the years, just as they did in Tsarist times. While analogies with the American scene are imperfect, they are at least suggestive. Policies which leaders in both countries might prefer on "rational" or "objective" grounds can be altered—either in conception or in implementation—by reason of particular interests militating against arms control and for expansion of military power.

Logical Imperatives

While each bureaucracy may have its own axes to grind in matters of arms and arms control, the top party leadership has generally tried to take account of the arguments pro and con, balancing them according to the needs and opportunities of the moment. What we find, on balance, amounts to a secular trend toward greater acceptance of strategic logic, one that recognizes the positive role for arms control in Soviet defense policy, even though this entails compromise accords with the ideological foe. The weight of competing organizational interests, clustered within institutions or around particular issues, has probably increased with the advancing complexity of the Soviet society, compelling the Party leadership to balance claims of competing interests.

Virtually the entire evolution of Communist thinking on arms limitation from before the Bolshevik Revolution to the 1970s was anticipated by shifts in

Lenin's views on this subject. Lenin's attitude toward disarmament passed through two fairly well defined stages, but contained the seeds of a third stage that seems to have become increasingly influential in Soviet thinking in recent years. First, from before the 1905 Revolution until after the October 1917 Revolution, Lenin opposed disarmament negotiations because they engendered pacifist illusions harmful to a revolutionary mentality. The task of the proletariat, he urged, was rather to "disarm" the bourgeoisie and to end war by terminating the class struggle. While maintaining his theoretical opposition to such schemes as the "plague of nations," however, Lenin in 1919-1920 presided over the conclusion of many arms control arrangements embodied in peace treaties with Russia's western neighbors. By 1921-1922 a second stage emerged as Lenin endorsed disarmament negotiations as a way to buy time and exploit contradictions in the enemy camp. This second stage in Lenin's thought, however, contained elements of another, less revolutionary orientation, one that treated disarmament not only as a tactic but as a possible long-range objective of Soviet policy. Lenin in 1922 urged Soviet diplomatic support of the pacifist wing of the bourgeois camp "as one of the few chances for the peaceful evolution of capitalism to a new structure. . . . "[26] The first positive Soviet policy toward arms control came in treaties terminating hostilities along Russia's western front in 1918-22 (demilitarized zones, etc.); next, in 1921, as a means of seeking Soviet participation in the Washington Naval Conference, where Moscow wanted particularly to take part in negotiations about the Far East; in 1922, as a means of dividing the bourgeois governments facing Soviet Russia at Genoa and generating support from the working classes and pacifist bourgeoisie of Europe; later in 1922, as a means of pressuring Russia's East European neighbors to make the same kinds of manpower reductions already planned for the Red Army.

Lenin, though disposed to rule out disarmament talks on *a priori* ideological grounds, recognized the pragmatic utility of such talks as a means of strengthening peace sentiment as well as revolutionary movements in the West. He also anticipated the day when military technology would make war counterproductive as an instrument of policy. In these waverings he adumbrated considerations and policies that would later emerge under Stalin and the several regimes that have succeeded him.

Stalin's regime used disarmament diplomacy basically as a way of neutralizing alleged or actual threats to Soviet security from Europe in the interwar years and from the United States and her allies after Hiroshima.[27] The approach taken was basically that of "Stage II" Leninism, i.e., advocacy of far reaching measures unlikely to be accepted by Moscow's negotiating partners, but which might contribute to a climate that would forestall attack and/or buy time for the USSR to build up her own forces. There was a revolutionary motif to Litvinov's presentations at the League of Nations from 1927 to 1934, for the Comintern could point to the rejections of Soviet initiatives as "proof" of the hypocrisy inherent in bourgeois diplomacy.[28] Soviet efforts in the years 1946-1953 sought a wider base among the partisans for peace to hamstring America's nuclear weapon leadership and to undermine the West's moral position in the Korean war (by charges of bacteriological warfare).[29]

Russia emerged from the world war favored by a new girdle of compliant, "friendly," Stalinist-type regimes along her western frontiers. This gain for Soviet security was undermined, however, by changes in military technology that left the USSR vulnerable to airborne attack with nuclear weapons even though Soviet troops stood athwart the historic invasion routes of the East European plains and mountains. Though Soviet scientists tested their first atomic bomb in 1949, it was not until 1954-55 that numbers of Soviet long-range bombers were amassed capable of striking the territory of the United States. Thus, though the USSR did not possess numerical equality with U.S. strategic forces, the Soviet Union by the mid-and-later-1950s acquired—for the first time in Russian history—a minimum deterrent capable of dissuading any rational opponent from an attack. This important fact enabled Soviet negotiators for the first time to negotiate with the West on the basis of relative equality, both sides considering measures that could be to their mutual benefit.

Other changes accumulated in rapid succession.[30] The first summit conference since Potsdam and the opening rounds of the cold war brought the British, French, Soviet, and U.S. heads of government together in 1955. Despite some negative results of these meetings, Western and Soviet leaders left Geneva persuaded that both sides acknowledged the futility of nuclear war as an instrument of policy. By 1958 the first conference of "experts" was held, thereby acknowledging the role of technological expertise in resolving problems of arms control, e.g., in the matter of nuclear test detection and identification. The years 1958-61 witnessed a three-power moratorium on nuclear tests, though France entered the atomic club in 1960, and held her first nuclear tests. The first arms control treaty involving the superpowers (on Antarctica in 1959) was followed by others in 1963, and then by a succession of accords leading toward the SALT agreements of 1972.

The limited accords of the early 1960s demonstrated that arms controls were possible between Communist and non-Communist powers. They also showed—for all to see—that world communism was not monolithic, nor was the Western alliance. The nuclear test ban treaty of 1963 helped to expose and to seal the rift between Moscow and Peking; it increased tension between Adenauer's Germany and the leaders of Britain and the United States; France, like China, also refused to sign the treaty and separated herself still further from her alliance partners.

Despite Khrushchev's penchant for "subjectivism" and occasional gambles, the rational actor model of strategic calculus came to the fore in his regime. First generation rockets would not be mass produced if skillful bluffing might gain political advantage and facilitate economic savings. Ground forces would be downgraded when strategic rocket forces appeared to be the decisive factor in modern war. If arms control agreements with the West were criticized within the country or by Moscow's allies, a Party declaration would respond most pragmatically: the "atomic bomb does not adhere to the class principle."[31] Defying opposition elements within, and without, Khrushchev would seek to establish his historical contribution on the success of "peaceful coexistence." One man's form of "rationality," however, looked like "hare-brained schemes" to others. Even while Khrushchev remained in power, the drastic cuts in manpower were curtailed in 1961 (partly in response to U.S. actions during the Berlin crisis that year), and steps taken to establish greater balance between modern and traditional components in the Soviet armed forces. Such moves, of course, could be due to organizational pressures as well as to some form of strategic logic. Indeed, looking at the buildup of Soviet conventional forces in Europe in recent years, one must wonder to what extent this has been the result of rational calculations or a way of satisfying interest groups militating for a share of the defense budget.

After some initial delays and despite some anomalies, both Kosygin and Brezhnev seem on balance to have followed Khrushchev in endorsing a rationalistic belief that arms control accords with the West can serve the interests of both sides. Though some Western negotiators regarded him as highly "ideological" in the late 1960s, Brezhnev clearly acquired by the early 1970s an ability to discuss not only generalities but to negotiate specifics on a wide range of foreign policy matters, including strategic arms and the problems of East Central Europe. Whether Brezhnev or Kosygin could ever be usefully depicted through such terms as "hawk" or "dove" is doubtful, though Kosygin's commitment to greater consumer goods production was more marked in the 1960s and his travels abroad were much more extensive than Brezhnev's. By 1972-73, however, Brezhnev had established not only his own competence in foreign affairs but also his claim to power and to historical eminence through the success of his "peace program." He had conducted top level negotiations with Westerners such as Willy Brandt and Richard Nixon in the USSR and on their home turf. His signature—that of the CPSU General Secretary—was affixed to the main accords reached in Moscow, Bonn, and San Clemente in 1972-73. Among Brezhnev's many medals was added that of the Lenin International Peace Prize. His glories and the accomplishments of the Soviet Peace Program were amplified by a series of peace congresses and meetings of "broad strata" of leading and popular representatives of culture and science from many countries converging on Moscow throughout 1973.[b]

---

[b]The White House, for its part, did nothing to quash the campaign launched by Senator Hugh Scott and *Finance Magazine* to nominate President Nixon for the Nobel Peace Prize in 1973. The USSR, in turn, nominated Marshal Tito as Nobel Laureate. Brezhnev himself received the International Lenin Prize "For Strengthening Peace Among the Peoples." *Pravda* (May 2, 1973, p. 4) praised Brezhnev for proclaiming "the majestic peace program" at the 24th CPSU Congress. Congratulations came in, e.g., from Communist Parties of Spain, Syria, England, Peru, Rumania, and Canada. Telegrams came also from Outer Mongolia, Bangladesh, President Tito, and Asian-African People's Solidarity Organization. *Izvestiia* (May 5, 1973, p. 3) declared the USSR had "launched an unparalleled 'peace offensive',"

Lenin to Brezhnev

If we survey Soviet strategic and arms control policies from 1917 to the 1970s, we find a series of modifications both in ideology and in *praxis* designed to cope with changing situations at home and abroad:

Table 2-1
Environmental Change and Soviet Response

1917-1921:

Initial weaknesses of Soviet regime.	Two alternating strategies: trust in and support a German Revolution, create Communist International.
Failures of German Revolution.	Self reliance. Come to terms with non-Communist government of Germany and other Western countries. Form Red Army.

1921-1927:

Domestic weakness and collapse of revolution throughout Europe.	NEP; Stage II Leninism in negotiations; clandestine arms cooperation with Germany; shift to cadre-militia forces.

1927-1928:

Economic reconstruction of USSR coupled with "scissors crisis" and other problems. Imperatives of modernization.	Five-year Plans. Litvinov to Geneva. Continue cadre-militia forces.

Mid-1930s:

Threats from Germany and Japan.	Rebuild regular forces. Collective security at League.

1939-1941:

Failure of League system.	Nonaggression pacts with Berlin and Tokyo. Divide East Europe with Hitler.

1941-1945:

German *Blitzkreig*.	Doctrine of "permanently operating factors." Ally with the West. Crash program to develop modern rocketry, planes, and nuclear weapons.[32]

1945-1953:

American nuclear monopoly. Cold War. "Containment." Koren War.	Stage II Leninism in negotiations. Accelerate technology development. *Zhdanovchina* at home and in Eastern Europe. Maintain large theater forces. Disparge value of surprise attack and nuclear weapons.

the fruit of which was already seen in the end to the "political blockade of the GDR. *Pravda* on April 30, 1973 stated that world conditions now favored anti-imperialist advances, as seen from election results in France and Chile. Looking eastward, General Petrushevskyi urged China's People's Liberation Army not to be influenced by Mao's attempts to make the PLA "hostile" to the USSR and Soviet people. He instead urged the unity of "socialist countries' armed forces" for counterblows against imperialism. He noted that he had served four years as "chief ministry adviser in the PRC" and had taken part in May Day parades in Peking (Moscow in Mandarin to China 1230 GMT 2 May 1973).

Table 2-1 (cont.)

1954-1957:	
Soviet nuclear weapons and some long-range bombers vs. U.S. superiority in numbers and proximity of strategic forces.	Upgrade role of surprise attack and destructiveness of atomic war. Move toward Stage III Leninism in negotiations. Stress difficulty in containing nuclear war. Reduce Soviet theater forces.
1955:	
Germany's entry into NATO.	Form Warsaw Pact.
Mid-to late-1950s:	
Deployment of tactical nuclear weapons in NATO countries.	Stress impossibility of localizing nuclear war. Work on developing Soviet tactical nuclears. Propose atom-free East Central Europe.
1954 to mid-1960s:	
Western superiority in air- and sea-lift capabilities for interventions.	Argue difficulty of localizing any wars. Develop Soviet air- and sea-lift capabilities. Establish bases in Middle East.
1957-1961:	
Apparent Soviet lead in ICBMs.	Maximize image of this lead. Exploit it in bargaining with West and China.
1961 to mid-1960s:	
U.S. ICBM-bomber superiority. Counterforce and flexible response doctrine.	Emphasize adequacy of minimum deterrent. Argue impossibility of "limited" nuclear war. Resume nuclear tests 1961 and attempt to deploy missiles in Cuba 1962.
1962-1963:	
Failure of Cuban missile gambit. Economic burden of arms race.	Cultivate Spirit of Moscow and some arms controls. Claim ABM and orbital weapon capabilities.
Mid-1960s:	
Threatened spread of nuclear weapons to Germany (MLF) and elsewhere.	Threaten West Germany. Negotiate NPT and pressure others to adhere. Discuss possibility of "local" and "limited nuclear" wars.
Late 1960s:	
Strategic parity with the United States, coupled with threat of U.S. advances in MIRV and ABM.	SALT and continued deployment of missiles on land and sea to redress balance. Intense R & D in modern technology.

The three stages implicit in Lenin's attitudes toward disarmament have been manifested in the outlook and policies of the Soviet, Chinese, and other governments claiming to follow the precepts of Marxism-Leninism. Stage I of Lenin's thinking on disarmament has provided the model for Mao Tse-tung and other revolutionaries skeptical about the prospects of peace so long as capitalism remains a world force; the instrumental view of disarmament implicit in Stage II Leninism provided the basic model for Soviet policy at the League of Nations and the United Nations until Stalin's death in 1953; the inchoate aspects of Stage III were developed under Khrushchev, who tried to make disarmament and arms limitation a strategic goal of Soviet policy. Even when model III came to the fore under Khrushchev, however, the influence of model II continued to be marked: profound doubts about the willingness or ability of bourgeois governments to enter into balanced, long-term accords with Communist regimes; a kind of Bolshevik (or Russian) proclivity for all-out solutions such as GCD (general and complete disarmament) instead of "mere" arms control; corollary to these points, a rejection of the view that "security" assurances and on-site inspection procedures need to precede disarmament.[33] Nonetheless, Malenkov and then Khrushchev turned Soviet policy away from exposure tactics and toward a line that would strengthen "sober forces" in the West and make it feasible for both sides to agree to "partial measures of disarmament" (which the West termed "arms control").

Under Brezhnev and Kosygin Soviet policy has wavered between the second and third stages of Lenin's thought. The first years of their regime, coinciding with tensions over Vietnam and Czechoslovakia, saw a certain reluctance to give the same weight that Khrushchev assigned to peaceful coexistence and arms limitation as goals of Soviet foreign policy. Maintaining a certain centrist position, Brezhnev joined Gromyko at the Twenty-fourth Congress of the CPSU in April 1971 in making sober proposals for arms limitation addressed to attentive western audiences and endorsing statements designed to maintain Moscow's chosen posture in propaganda bouts with Peking.

The policies of Brezhnev and his associates in 1972-73 suggested that they had moved rather squarely into a third stage of arms control thinking. Both sides gained, the Soviet press declared, from the ABM and interim agreement of 1972. Both accords were justified on pragmatic as well as ideological grounds. Though contradictory signals emitted from both Moscow and Washington, many signs indicated that the Brezhnev regime wanted in the mid-1970s to go beyond SALT I. Soviet strategists suggested to American colleagues the need to create a "no-war system" that would stabilize and contain the competitive aspects of "peaceful coexistence." They urged the establishment of a legal regime that would permit change while outlawing the use of force. Portions of this idea, picked up by Litvinov from Messrs. Kellogg and Briand, had been revived under Khrushchev. In the late 1960s they had been translated into bilateral treaties in Central Europe and a diplomatic campaign at the United Nations. Soviet specialists also indicated a willingness to reexamine the Military Staff Committee and the problems of using Third World forces as agents of U.N. peacekeeping machinery. In harmony with Marxist premises, Soviet specialists argued also that an economic base of East-West trade would enhance the long-term prospects for peace.

Will the third stage of Soviet thinking on arms control persist in the years ahead? To make the most of the new realism and objective potentialities for improving U.S.-Soviet relations, statecraft must rise like a Phoenix from the destructive ways of cold war struggle. As in 1889, so also in the 1970s, diplomacy can be spiked by powerful factions within the country or by external allies opposed to a broad agreement. Technology proceeds with its own mad momentum. Having examined the challenges, we can now study the record of recent years so as to focus the necessary conditions for arms limitation.

3

The Conditions for Arms Control: Cuba to Salt II

The history of arms control negotiations between the United States and the Soviet Union—from the first efforts to control the atom after World War II to the first and second phases of SALT—suggest that there are a series of underlying conditions that must be met before East-West agreements are possible to control the arms race. These conditions emerge from the record of U.S.-Soviet negotiations, particularly from the understandings and agreements that followed the Cuban missile crisis, and hence apply specifically to the two countries which, at least in this period, have been "superpowers." If these conditions were adapted *mutatis mutandis*, however, they would probably be applicable to arms control efforts among medium and lesser powers as well.

We do not seek to establish here whether arms control can be a useful instrument for the promotion of world peace or the interests of particular countries. A broad analysis of these questions would be highly complex, requiring analysis of situations in which negotiations were not even attempted; cases of unilateral restraint (with or without any effort at bargaining); and still other cases where negotiations were attempted but stalled short of agreement. We also omit any discussion of the aftermath of particular agreements, including such possible by-products as cheating, mutual recriminations, intensified competition in other spheres, etc.[1] Our focus is much more narrow: an attempt to discover the domestic and external conditions in which adversaries believe it in their interest to enter into tacit or explicit agreements with each other to regulate the development, production, deployment, or use of armaments.

Despite the narrow focus of this chapter, the results may challenge earlier views on the general requirements for arms control. Most American writers have examined arms control from a technical military viewpoint, a perspective that has led them to neglect or minimize political considerations which may be promoted in negotiations and in agreements. This attitude has led to a quest for mechanical solutions, e.g., verification procedures, appropriate ratios for force regulations, etc.[2]

The opposite approach emphasizes the "moral" prerequisites for arms control. Influenced by France, the League of Nations Assembly in 1922 affirmed that "moral disarmament is an essential preliminary condition of material disarmament, and this moral disarmament can only be achieved in an atmosphere of mutual confidence and security."[3] This same dichotomizing terminology was used at the Moscow Disarmament Conference in 1922 when Poland and the Baltic States pressed for a non-aggression treaty while Soviet diplomats urged actual force cuts.[4]

All through the League of Nations period Soviet spokesmen made clear what disarmament is and is *not*. It is not, they argued, an increase, a preservation, or an imperceptible reduction of armaments. It is not a mock or "show" reduction touching only obsolete or secondarily useful forms of armaments. It is not a formula which puts off actual disarmament for a distant or undefined future moment, or until an impossible-to-achieve mathematical formula is arrived at, or which strives to maintain or improve a state's power position by relating disarmament to "security," "defense," "sacred," or "international obligations." Disarmament meant rather "the complete elimination or a perceptible reduction of armaments."[5] And if bourgeois governments were not ready for total disarmament, the USSR backed partial reductions across the board.

Moscow, in those years, was relatively weak. The Kremlin's interest was to reduce more powerful states to the same low level of armaments as that possessed by the USSR, thereby enhancing the non-military factors of power available to Russia. Following World War II, however, the Soviet Union (like Germany between the wars) has sought equality. Specifically, Moscow has sought the symbols and the substance of parity with the United States. The 1972 summit talks in Moscow, for example, are said to have been "productive precisely because they were conducted under strict observance of the principle of equality and equal security of the parties, the rejection of the use of force or of threats, reciprocal respect of interests, and in the spirit of the implementation in international relations of the principle of peaceful coexistence of states with different social systems." All this gave a "realistic approach" to the Moscow summit.[6] Looking ahead, another Soviet analyst in 1972 discounted Western arguments about the need for asymmetrical reductions in Europe, saying that "objective analysis shows that all argumentation about 'military inequality' between NATO and the Warsaw Treaty Organization in the area of conventional forces and the necessity for asymmetrical reduction does not withstand criticism." The only principle possible was therefore said to be "reduction on the basis of parity [*paritetnogo sokrashcheniia*] which would retain the general balance already existing to a lower level." "Such a reduction on the basis of parity would answer the main requirement: it would not inflict a sacrifice on the parties taking part in the reduction."[7]

Quite a different set of conditions has been spelled out by Chinese spokesmen in response to such U.S.-Soviet steps as the nuclear test ban and the most recent SALT accords. Like Soviet spokesmen in the 1920s and 1930s, Peking has denounced these as partial measures that create a smokescreen facilitating an intensification of the arms race in other domains. China's representative to the United Nations was no less eloquent in 1972 than Maxim Litvinov had been when he proposed total disarmament at the League of Nations more than forty years before. Indeed, Chen Chu's position was even closer aligned with that of Lenin before the Bolsheviks came to power, when Lenin denounced disarmament as a utopian myth designed to draw attention from the need for "disarming the bourgeoisie." "Imperialism is the root cause of war," China's representative argued. Assertions that the arms race is the root cause of war cover up a basic demand that the people of various countries abandon their struggle and "disarm themselves before the intimidation and aggression of imperialism, colonialism, and neo-colonialism." The "disarmament experience" which Soviet diplomats say has been accumulated since 1963 is a hoax, for the superpowers have gone on to expand not only their nuclear but their conventional arsenals, and to use them for threats and intervention all over the world. Although China favors the "complete prohibition and thorough destruction of all nuclear weapons," Peking would not attend a general disarmament conference until the necessary conditions were created: there had to be no possibility of nuclear blackmail against the participants. This meant that the Soviet Union and the United States (1) had to promise not to be the first to use nuclear weapons at any time, particularly not to use nuclear weapons against non-nuclear weapons countries "at any time and under any circumstances"; and (2) they had to "withdraw from abroad all armed forces and dismantle all military bases including nuclear bases set up on foreign soil."[8]

The reality, we believe, is at once more complex and yet more hopeful than these extreme views—uttered by haves and have-nots in different times and places—would suggest. Arms control possibilities between the United States and the USSR are not mechanically governed by the correlations of military forces between them. Political and other interests have often served as a useful incentive or *quid pro quo*. Indeed, agreements have often been possible despite the absence of symmetry or even of rough parity, agreements which hard-headed analysts nonetheless judged to enhance their country's interests. Cognizant of the many factors affecting the feasibility of accords, we may begin to understand also the preconditions for their continued viability.

The conditions affecting arms control are multifold and relate to many dimensions of conflict and cooperation: the balance of security and other interests; research, development, and deployment; the style and substance of negotiations; the character of available arms control proposals; the quality of adversary relations; alliance factors; Third World international crises; domestic, political, economic, and sociological factors; and international trade.

Certain conditions appear to be indispensable for the success of arms control negotiations, while others are merely helpful but not absolutely necessary. Still other conditions are harmful to the cause of arms control and may prevent an agreement even if most conditions favor one. Though all the essential conditions presented here appear *necessary*, they are by no means *sufficient* to induce an accord or to keep it viable. For this, political will and leadership, not to speak of luck, is also required.

We begin by listing the critical conditions and discussing the way that they have affected East-West negotiations. The arguments presented, of course, are hypotheses or partial models about the conditions for arms control. Later in this chapter we shall attempt to validate the hypotheses by reference to periods that appeared favorable for arms control and others that were inauspicious.

One caveat throughout: The conditions presented here seem consonant with the historical record; this does not mean that the conduct of U.S. and Soviet decision-makers was either logical or ethical or that their behavior will necessarily be repeated by future policy-makers. For example, the interests of all parties might have been enhanced if Moscow had accepted various measures to freeze the arms race before Soviet acquisition of a minimum deterrent or, later, rough parity with the United States. The Soviet leadership sought to advance its interests by acquiring equal rank with the United States, rejecting any kind of Avis posture for the long haul. Some may believe that the United States should not have attempted for so many years to maintain nuclear superiority; that Washington could have short-circuited the arms race long ago by agreeing to reduce its capacity to the Soviet level or by standing still while Soviet forces increased, instead of letting this option be imposed by the weight of history and inertia. Other decisions might have been wiser or more moral; but the critical conditions presented here are the ones that emerge from the actual course of action adhered to by each superpower in a particular environment.

The Balance of Interests
(Security and Others)

Essential: (1) *Mutual satisfaction that the proposed arms control will enhance the basic interests of each side as perceived and defined by its own government, based on security and other considerations.* (2) *Sufficiency (as conceived by each party) in the forces regulated—despite or because of the proposed controls.* (3) *If the agreements cover forces central to the strategic balance, there must be parity if not symmetry.* (4) *Credible second-strike forces must remain after the agreement, and not just a delicate balance of terror that could be upset by marginal accretions by either side.* (5) *Accords on peripheral areas of military competition, however, are attainable without parity or symmetry, and many have been concluded.* (6) *If there is neither parity nor symmetry, agreements are still possible if each side—for its own reasons—believes that they enhance particular objectives.*[9]

Helpful: (1) *Parity or symmetry in the forces to be regulated facilitates agreement but is not essential, since trade-offs are possible in other domains.* (2) *Recognition and action by both sides at roughly the same time ("in-phase") to promote parallel interests.*[10]

Harmful: (1) *A sharp imbalance in the forces to be controlled which the weaker party is determined to redress—either through mutual agreement or through unilateral actions—and which the other party is determined to preserve.* (2) *Insistence by either party on absolute "equality" in some domain, regardless* *of asymmetries or trade-offs that may make the proposed agreement advantageous to both sides. Such equality could theoretically be achieved by agreements reducing the forces of the stronger party or by permitting the weaker side to build to that same level; or by unilateral policies without any agreements.*

Comment: All the U.S.-Soviet accords since 1958 (the moratorium on nuclear testing) have been concluded against a backdrop of mutual deterrence, even though Soviet strategic forces have generally been weaker than American. The first promising moves toward arms control took place in 1955, i.e., at the very moment the USSR first acquired numbers of long-range bombers capable of delivering nuclear weapons to the United States, thereby giving the USSR for the first time a terror weapon to deter external attack.

"Sufficiency" may be a highly elastic concept covering postures so diverse as the minimal deterrent of the Khrushchev period to the pre-emptive posture to which some Soviet and American strategists seem to have aspired. Whatever the actual balance of power, each side must consider that the proposed arms control will leave it with forces "sufficient" for their task before it will enter in and abide by this measure. SALT I, for example, left Washington with fewer ICBMs than those permitted to the Soviet Union, but the White House clearly assumed its missiles would be "sufficient"—at least for the five-year period in which further negotiations would take place. While neither superpower could hope that the ABM defenses permitted under SALT I would permit it forces "sufficient" to defend significant numbers of the population, both sides seemed to recognize that—given the state of the art—no conceivable ABM defense could achieve that objective. Some Washington planners, however, may have rationalized that the North Dakota ABM sites permitted by the 1972 treaty would "suffice" to ensure the survivability of some U.S. ICBMs in case of a Soviet attack.

As indicated below, many U.S.-Soviet accords have been concluded despite the absence of parity or symmetry in the forces to be controlled. Wherever these forces were considered vital to the East-West balance, however, parity or sufficiency have been present, as in the 1963 limited test ban or in the 1972 SALT accords. Even these measures, however, did not require perfect symmetry in the forces to be controlled.

Where existing or proposed asymmetries are not acceptable to one of the parties, of course, no voluntary agreement will be possible. This situation ruled out Soviet acceptance of the Baruch Plan before the USSR acquired nuclear weapons as well as Chinese or French acceptance of the limited test ban treaty. It made it infeasible for Moscow to accept a freeze on strategic delivery systems when President Johnson proposed negotiations[a] on both strategic offensive and

---

[a]Though some writers have traced the origin of the SALT negotiations to 1967 or late 1964, the first U.S. proposal for such negotiations came in President Johnson's message to the Eighteen-Nation Disarmament Committee on January 21, 1964: "The United States, the Soviet Union and their respective Allies should agree to explore a verified freeze on the number and characteristics of strategic nuclear offensive and defensive vehicles." Follow-up statements by Secretary Rusk stressed that "the development of this concept would be a

defensive weapons systems in 1964.[11] Indeed, the USSR turned down several American proposals early in the first round of SALT that could have produced much more radical agreements than those signed in 1972. One proposal offered to reduce ICBMs (but not SLBMs) by one hundred per year, with the option that, if the USSR would begin by reducing her large SS-9 missiles, the United States would begin by cutting long-range bombers from her arsenal on a one-for-one basis. Soviet negotiators, apparently ordered to legitimize a formal parity, insisted rather that both sides first agree to an upper limit (one presumably high enough to permit Soviet forces to grow in the interim).[12] They also rejected a ban on flight tests of MIRV systems, without exploring whether some *quid pro quo* could be established that would negate or adequately compensate for the U.S. lead in multiple warheads.

Absolute equality in the quantity and characteristics of U.S. and Soviet forces is probably unattainable and perhaps undesirable, because each country is faced with unique geographical and political situations. Formal symmetry in their forces' structures, for these same reasons, would be unlikely to produce actual parity between the superpowers. Parity, then, is not only possible without formal symmetry; it is likely to result from particular combinations of asymmetries. These asymmetries need not trouble either side (or prevent arms control accords) if the forces of each are "sufficient" for their particular functions.[12]

Asymmetries may be expected not only because of *sui generis* geopolitical conditions facing each superpower, but also because of historical accidents and traditions. Thus, Russian forces have long had a "police function" in Europe even before the October Revolution, a mission they continue to fulfill in ways not expected of the U.S. military in Europe.

Historical experiences as well as the proximity of nuclear China also make it more likely that Russia would put a greater premium on defensive measures than the United States. As indicated earlier, differential progress in technology helps account for the Soviet reliance upon medium- and intermediate-range missiles targeted on Europe and on giant warheads for ICBMs, weapons which the United States has bypassed in favor of more sophisticated systems.

The problem of aerial reconnaissance as a way to verify arms dispositions

---

matter for consultation with our Allies before negotiations with the Soviets." (He stressed that the idea for a multilateral missile fleet within NATO "could and would be protected.") But ACDA Director William C. Foster told the ENDC that the United States would also have kept the door open for suggestions on the weapons freeze from not only the USSR but from other members of the ENDC. (*Documents on Disarmament, 1964* [Washington, D.C.: U.S. Arms Control and Disarmament Agency, 1965], pp. 7-21.)

The 1964 initiative differed from the SALT I accords in several respects. First, it hoped to restrict weapons characteristics as well as numbers. The 1973 treaty does set severe limits on characteristics of ABM systems that may be deployed under the treaty, but the interim agreement leaves the door open for improvements in offensive weapon characteristics. Second, Washington's 1964 initiative endorsed limited on-site inspection to verify the accord, whereas the 1973 accords are clear that "national means of verification" will be used. Third, the 1964 proposal placed a much greater emphasis on consultation with allies than was the case in SALT I, especially in 1973.

illustrates how asymmetries can prevent or facilitate agreements on arms limitation. Moscow was cool to an agreement on "open skies" in the 1950s because the USSR was a closed society and the United States relatively open for intelligence gathering purposes; because the USSR lagged the United States in aerial reconnaissance technology; and also because Khrushchev sought to exaggerate the size of Soviet strategic forces. This situation changed through the 1960s as the USSR acquired her own reconnaissance satellites and as Soviet ICBM deployment overtook and then surpassed the United States in missiles deployed. Comparatively speaking, however, the Soviet Union remained a highly closed and secretive society. Despite this major asymmetry and a variety of cultural differences between the USSR and the United States, their ABM and offensive weapons accords in 1972 provided that neither side would "interfere with the national technical means of verification of the other Party" or "use deliberate concealment measures to impede verification by national technical means of compliance. . . ."

Some means had to be found to verify the agreements to the satisfaction of the U.S. Government; both sides had grown accustomed to the idea of satellite overflights; the USSR gave no one-sided concessions since she enjoyed a kind of parity both in satellite technology and missile deployment; Moscow could still maintain its own closed society and benefit from American openness.[13]

The 1972 ABM treaty was concluded despite the absence of symmetry or parity in defensive systems. The U.S. Government apparently concluded that the Soviet monopoly in ABM defenses around the capital city did not significantly affect the strategic balance, presumably because U.S. forces were sufficient to overwhelm such defenses. U.S. negotiators, to be sure, ultimately sought equality of rights and obligations in the ABM treaty, so that both sides were entitled to construct a site with one hundred interceptor missiles to defend the capital city and a missile site 1300 kilometers distant. In agreeing to this treaty, however, official Washington probably reckoned that it would never cash in this ticket.

Asymmetries may also be tolerated where there is little likelihood of confrontation. Estimates on threat perception, of course, are highly subjective. But revised Western estimates on the danger of war in Europe may make it more feasible for NATO to accept European arms controls in the 1970s than was the case in the 1950s and 1960s. Subjective judgment also comes into play when weighing possible military losses against political gains that could result from great power disengagement in Central Europe, but such trade-offs are inherent in any accords between NATO and the Warsaw Pact countries.

Research, Development and Deployment

Essential: *Little or no prospect of radical shift in the balance of power to the advantage of one side only through a technical breakthrough; a political* *development (e.g., a reversal of alliances); or a redeployment (e.g., missiles to Cuba) altering the strategic and other interests affected by the proposed arms controls.*

Helpful: (1) *A sense that the weapons to be curbed have reached a techno-logical plateau or are peripheral to the arms race, so that both sides have a kind of sufficiency in these weapons. This perception may be linked, however, with some fear of accretions by the other side which could drive the arms race to more expensive levels without improving the security position of either side. (2) Confidence that the proposed accords will not be jeopardized by arms developments in other countries not affected by the agreements (e.g., China).*

Harmful: *Possibility that military developments or deployments by one side may offer significant political-military advantages of great importance in the short-run, even though they may be negated in the middle or long term.*

Comment: The resumption of nuclear testing by the USSR in 1961 and the attempt to install strategic delivery systems in Cuba in 1962 were both Kremlin attempts to compensate for sharp asymmetries in the strategic balance, even though Soviet forces probably provided a minimum deterrent without these developments.

Conclusion of a nonproliferation treaty (signed 1968) was impossible so long as Washington sought and Moscow feared a loophole that might permit a West German finger on the nuclear trigger through multilateral forces, which could have effected an important shift in the balance of power.

The 1967 outer space treaty was possible despite the Soviet testing of FOBS (fractional orbital bombardment systems), because Washington assumed that this asymmetry would not give the USSR any significant bargaining power and that it could be matched or countered by American technology if needed.

While Moscow and Washington were able to conclude agreements in areas where they had a sufficiency (atmospheric nuclear testing, fissionable materials, etc.), or where deployment of mass destruction weapons would not favor either party (outer space), the USSR signed no agreements that would foreclose the possibility of approaching parity with the United States in intercontinental delivery systems. When parity in this central domain became attainable in the late 1960s, serious SALT negotiations could begin.

The 1972 ABM treaty recognized that city defense is not likely to be attainable and that second-strike forces can be protected or assured through other measures than missile defense.

The interim agreement on strategic missiles recognized that neither super-power is likely to achieve such strategic breakthroughs that they may upset the rough parity attained by 1972, at least in the next five years.

The Negotiations

Essential: *A style and content that indicate seriousness of purpose and feasibility of agreements: Ideally, (1) each side must be well prepared and staffed; it* *must be willing and able to discuss specifics. (2) If the talks are to be private, they should generally remain private. (3) If a proposal is made, it must be adhered to for a reasonable period. (4) Available proposals must exist that enhance the security and other interests of each side without (a) insurmountable "jokers" or (b) verification requirements for intensive physical intrusion by foreign inspectors. This kind of negotiating style and content may be violated at times by bargaining tactics designed to put pressure on the adversary or to mollify hard-line elements at home. But the net effect of these tactics must not be such as to undermine fatally the credibility of either side.*[14]

Helpful: (1) *The existence of regular, private negotiating channels or fora.* (2) *An ability of the negotiating countries to fractionalize the points at issue, reducing them to parts that can be negotiated one by one.* (3) *Ability to put proposals in the form of "yes-able" propositions conducive to affirmative replies by concerned parties (as distinct from ambiguous statements of principle).*[15] (4) *The presence of deadlines (such as a forthcoming American election) to introduce a sense of urgency.* (5) *The willingness of top policy-makers on each side to intervene personally to break negotiating deadlocks and reach compromise accords.*

Harmful: (1) *Proposals that are clearly one-sided or that do not fairly or effectively cope with anticipated technological or political change.* (2) *Proposals that threaten the internal security—political, economic, or technological—of either party.* (3) *Proposals so manifestly unnegotiable that they are counterproductive even for setting ultimate goals.* (4) *Exploitation and subordination of arms control to an instrumental role in pursuit of other zero-sum objectives.* (5) *Reneging on proposals after they have been accepted by the other side.*

Comment: Lack of thorough preparation and staffing has hampered negotiations. Some Soviet as well as Western observers have belittled the character of the USSR delegation in the first one or two sessions of SALT, stating that its lack of expertise and authority betrayed a desire to stall for time while Soviet missile construction could proceed apace.

Both Soviet and U.S. negotiators could ask whether the other side was not merely providing a diplomatic front to deflect attention from significant missile developments: in Russia, the rapid deployment of SS-9s and the preparation of sites for additional large missiles; in the United States and in U.S. submarine bases, the deployment of multiple warheads.

Well before SALT, the United States' image as a reliable negotiating partner was undermined when Washington seemed to renege on its own arms control proposals after they were endorsed by the USSR (e.g., in 1955, 1959, 1962). Given Soviet sensitivities on this score, a steadfast position might have been expected of the United States during the SALT negotiations. Nonetheless, this dismal pattern occurred again in 1970 after Washington proposed two ABM options to the USSR: either a zero ABM posture or a capital city defense for both countries. When Soviet negotiators brought back a favorable response to the first of these choices, Washington shifted ground and upped the ante. This shift was rationalized in part in terms of a common understanding that nothing in the SALT negotiations was definitively agreed to unless everything—a total package—was nailed down. The SALT delegation was instructed now to insist upon an asymmetrical arrangement that would give the United States a 4:1 lead, assuming Minuteman defense in North America and capital defense in the USSR. Unbeknownst to any members of the U.S. delegation, Dr. Kissinger had already proposed a 3:1 variant of this scheme to Ambassador Dobrynin. The final accord embodied in the 1972 treaty seemed to constitute virtually a mechanical compromise of these earlier positions, one that could be diagrammed as an arrangement 2:2 (*de facto* 1:0::0:1 or *de jure* as 1:1::1:1[16]). This accord, however, was ultimately achieved *despite* the sharp switch in Washington's posture in 1970. Had the White House stood by its original options, we might have had an ABM treaty that required dismantling of existing ABMs or one that put much more severe limits on future deployment than the May 1972 treaty.

It may be impossible to generalize about the optimum mixture of negotiations conducted at the front door (by the official delegations); those at the rear (*ad hoc*, like those between Kissinger and Dobrynin); and those in the side yard (unilateral statements to the media). Since action in all these domains is probably inevitable, it should be guided so as to avoid eroding the credibility of either side's negotiating effort. In the mid-1950s, for example, news leaks by both sides poisoned the climate of the negotiations and helped point them to a dead end. Strict secrecy was maintained by both Moscow and Washington in most of 1969-1970. Though news leaks into the U.S. press in 1971 led to Soviet protests, the train of negotiations leading to the 1972 accords was not derailed. While the leaks upset the Soviet delegation, it is conceivable that they helped prepare the American public for the agreements to come. As arms control talks become increasingly technical and as asymmetries become the object of bargaining, however, there seems little use in preliminary news stories which fuel speculation about which side is "winning" until both parties concur on measures they consider mutually acceptable.

The Kremlin's intentions have also been called into question by a series of Soviet actions and inactions. Thus Soviet delegations have often preferred to talk in generalities and abstractions, refusing even in SALT to be specific about their own weapons using any more precise nomenclature, for example, than "heavy missiles," the character of which the United States had to spell out in a unilateral statement. While Moscow has downplayed the emphasis once assigned to General and Complete Disarmament, it has continued to address the galleries in such proposals as a World Disarmament Conference (presumably to upstage Peking). More troublesome, Moscow has at times orchestrated apparent concessions in arms control as part of a broad diplomatic offensive. Both Nixon and Brezhnev endorsed General and Complete Disarmament in 1973, thereby adding to suspicions about the substance of their San Clemente summit.

The fact that top leaders of both superpowers have engaged their personal prestige and political influence in the successful outcome of arms control negotiations has been important in bringing about many of the accords reached by Moscow and Washington. Chairman Khrushchev was the first such leader since 1945 to gamble on the possibility of East-West accords to halt the arms race. His gamble undermined his position at home when he was confronted with the U-2 flight and with shifting U.S. positions on acceptable numbers of on-site inspections for a nuclear test ban. In 1963, however, President Kennedy, along with Khrushchev, staked his political fortunes on the feasibility of arms limitation and personally supervised the small number of trusted aids who laid plans for the test ban signed in Moscow that summer. The personal intervention of President Nixon and Dr. Kissinger was also instrumental in breaking the several impasses which obstructed the road to the May 1972 accords; e.g., in spring 1971 and, most notably, in talks with Brezhnev in Moscow in April and May 1972. Kissinger and Soviet Ambassador Dobrynin also discussed SALT directly on many occasions. On the debit side, these high-level interventions eroded the authority of the SALT teams negotiating in Helsinki and Vienna; on the credit side, they permitted compromise accords which could be made most readily only at the highest levels.

Linkages

Essential: *Linkage between specific arms control measures and other issues in East-West relations should not be essential if the arms accord is sought with roughly the same intensity by each side.*

Helpful: *Proffering a reward in some other domain for acceptance of an arms control accord may help induce agreement by the less interested party. Creation of a broad package of agreements, in arms control and other areas, helps assure each side that possible losses in one domain will likely be compensated by gains in another. Such linkages will be especially important when political or economic considerations appear more weighty than the limited arms measures under consideration.*

Harmful: *Excessive complexity can prevent agreement, even where the arms control proposals under discussion are of interest to both sides. Such complexity can arise from (1) linking arms control with other proposals (jokers) unacceptable to the other side; (2) insisting on adding more negotiating partners; (3) widening the number of targets (e.g., China or India) to be influenced or controlled through the accord.*

Comment: The root problem here is how to distinguish "separable topics" for fruitful negotiations, given that all "armament problems, be they strategic, tactical or logistic, are interrelated at some level. Moreover military and political considerations can never be entirely separated: the success of arms control negotiations and the subsequent implementation of the resulting agreements depend greatly on the political context and vice versa. The level of armament of any one nation affects all other nations to some degree; thus the justified concerns in a world pressing for arms control are becoming increasingly multilateral."[17]

The USSR sought with scant success in 1963 to link the test ban with a NATO-Warsaw Pact nonaggression pact. In the mid-1960s Moscow cited the bombing of North Vietnam as a reason for not discussing arms control with the United States. Linkage between NATO's forward-based systems in Europe and strategic offensive and defensive weapons has been argued by Soviet diplomats in SALT I and II, and rejected by Washington. The nuclear have-nots managed with more success to extract concessions from the superpowers as conditions for adhering to the nonproliferation treaty. The Western powers also achieved some results in making movement toward a Conference on European Security and Cooperation contingent upon the outcome of other negotiations over divided Germany and signs of Soviet interest in MBFR. Coerced into the CESC somewhat against the preferences of most NATO governments, the Western governments raised the ante further by insisting in 1972-73 that the conference give major attention to a notion traditionally anathema in Moscow: freer exchanges of persons and ideas. The SALT I accords, however, were inter-mingled with a large package of linked concessions by each side: Moscow would encourage Hanoi at the Paris peace talks and the White House would pressure Congress to grant Most Favored Nation status to the USSR, *et cetera.*[b]

The involvement of top leaders from both sides is the more important when compromise accords are based not only on arms control but on other issues such as trade. While Moscow resisted American attempts to create such linkages in President Nixon's first term, it seems clear that the more matters of common concern are involved, the easier it becomes to accept a "loss" in one domain if there are "gains" in other areas. Simplicity has its virtue, making a partial ban on nuclear tests easier to conclude than one that also prohibits underground testing. Where the arms control issues at stake are close to the vital interests of each side, and are quite complex or difficult to measure in terms of gains and losses to each side, it is probably advantageous to move toward a total *Gestalt* of East-West accords which—taken together—demonstrates a commitment to strategic and economic interdependence, if not "ideological coexistence."

"Bargaining Chips"

Essential: *Neither rewards (through linkage) nor threats (cashing in bargaining chips) should be necessary if arms control measures are sought with roughly*

---

[b]Insight into the pros and cons of linkage may be gained from analysis of European resistance in 1973 to U.S. attempts to create a wide front of negotiations on military, economic and other issues. Since most European governments considered themselves dependent on the U.S. militarily, it would be to their advantage to prevent coupling their strategic interests with America's economic problems.

equal intensity by both sides. What is essential is that each party be motivated—for whatever domestic or external reasons—to pursue the negotiations to a successful conclusion.

Helpful: *Threats may be helpful in cases where the other side is complacent with the status quo or the drift of events. The bargaining chip tactic holds out options to an opponent, making it clear that in the absence of specific agreements our side will be obliged to undertake programs not otherwise needed. From the standpoint of arms control, however, the threatened deployment can be justified only if it can reasonably be defended as necessary, and if it can be halted if negotiations prove successful.*[18]

Harmful: *Such threats may well spark another round of military competition rather than serious negotiation. Even if relatively serious negotiations are commenced, they may prove incapable of terminating the deployment of a new weapons system once its development and procurement have begun.*

Comment: The two major cases in which Washington has explicitly utilized bargaining chips concern ABM and the Trident submarine. Moscow seemed unwilling to negotiate on ABM and offensive limitations until 1967-68, when Congress started to fund an American ABM system. When cost-efficiency arguments failed, supporters of ABM could still claim that an American deployment was necessary to coerce the Soviets to negotiate.

Was the American tactic successful? If the Russians preferred to waste their resources on an ABM that could easily be overcome by small increments to the U.S. strike force, why should Washington have sought to match such folly? Was not the more salient consideration for Moscow the fact that, by the late 1960s, the Soviet ICBM force had drawn alongside the American so that both sides could negotiate from a basis of roughly equal security? From this foundation they could talk about how to forestall future rounds of arms competition, apart from any Damoclean sword which one party might hold over the other. Indeed, as argued in Chapter 1, the Kremlin's most destabilizing moves in East-West relations seem to have been inspired by a sense of inferiority. The Russians, like others, pride themselves in resisting intimidation.

By 1972 the ABM segment of SALT produced an agreement that left each superpower free to build to much higher levels than it then planned—what W.K.H. Panofsky has called "arms control by supplemental purchase"—with both sides agreeing to "permit each other to *add* to their respective ABM inventories the particular kind of force which the other side already possessed or had in advanced stages of construction."[19] This treaty, however, facilitated a sharp decline in funding for deployment of the ABM Safeguard system: from $996 million in 1972 to $600 million planned for 1973 to $402 million requested for FY 1974. Development of a site defense, however, leapt to $170 million proposed for FY 1974 from $60 million funded in 1972. Funds for identification and development of advanced ABM technology increased from $96 million in 1972 to $100 million proposed for FY 1974.[20]

Partly as a result of accepting inferiority in numbers of ICBMs in SALT I, and partly to prepare for SALT II, the White House opted in 1972-73 to push for deployment of an advanced submarine (Trident) and long-range bomber (B-1) by 1978. The very threat of the new submarine, it was argued, made the Russians more willing to include SLBMs in the 1972 interim agreement. But the West's lead in submarine missilery over the USSR was already gigantic, as discussed in Proposition VIII in Chapter 1. And the cost to the American taxpayer of this new program would also be stupendous: Funding for Trident would jump from $105 million funded in 1972 to $795 million planned for 1973 to a proposed $1,712 million for FY 1974. Continued development of the B-1, meanwhile, would produce an increase of $104 million for FY 1974 over the $370 million spent in 1972.

The FY 1974 budget requests also included a variety of other "hedges" against future threats or requirements, or against breakdowns in SALT negotiations. These included $15 million for submarine-launched cruise missiles, $95 million for advanced ballistic missile reentry systems, $6 million for mobile ICBMs, $35 million for early warning radars for a possible submarine threat, and $17 million for a low-frequency radio communication system.

Would such vast sums be spent and the results renounced if Moscow agreed to the right terms? The case of MIRV and other previous experiences pointed in the other direction. As Shulman has put it: the use of the bargaining chip tactic has probably "stimulated armament programmes more than it has negotiations, and . . . left us saddled with programmes which would not have been supported on their merits."[21]

The philosophy of bargaining chips runs contrary to that of tension reduction. To be sure, the stick is often more appealing as an instrument for influencing others than the carrot. Some mixture of the two is probably essential in human relations. But the stick has played by far the predominant role in East-West relations since 1945. More effort at de-escalation and less bluster and escalation would probably serve both sides well in the 1970s.

Another relevant guideline had been proposed by Dr. Schlesinger himself some six years before he became Defense Secretary in 1973. This was known as "Schlesinger's Uncertainty Principle," summarized by Robert E. Kuenne in *The New York Times* (July 30, 1973) as an informal procedure of "informed procrastination." Given the difficulty in applying formal systems techniques to handle the problems of an unknowable future, the decisionmaker should not lock himself into a technological commitment until events present him with the need to act. As Kuenne points out, the rationale for Trident in 1973 was based on future contingencies for which there was no immediate need to act except to carry out a program of continuing research (e.g., on anti-submarine warfare). The Uncertainty Principle, Kuenne concluded, "cries for application."

Adversary Relations

Essential: *Perception and recognition by each government that there are responsible forces in the other country that favor arms control agreements of value to both sides.*

Helpful: *Serious efforts by each side to strengthen these forces in the other government or in its society generally. This will not be done by subversion, which could easily backfire. Rather, this aim will be pursued both in word—recognizing the commitment of the other side to peace and affirming the principles of non-zero sum competition; and in deed—refraining from provocative actions and cultivating a spirit of "graduated reciprocation in tension reduction," or what Khrushchev called "disarmament by mutual example."*[2 2]

Harmful: *Actions that undermine moderate influences and strengthen hawkish forces on the other side.*

Comment: Since the mid-1950s Soviet media have commented on the existence of "sober" forces and "madmen" in Western ruling circles. They have used this distinction to justify arms limitations domestically and ideologically, but Soviet diplomacy has also sought to strengthen sober forces in the West, citing Lenin's advice to the Soviet delegation to the 1922 Genoa Conference as a model. The blurring of such distinctions in Soviet media or diplomatic practice, on the other hand, has been an indicator that the moment is not ripe for arms negotiations.

Understandably, the Western governments have been less certain which Soviet leaders have been *pro* or *contra* arms control. Both Moscow and Washington have come far toward recognizing that both sides can profit from pursuit of parallel or common interests. Soviet ideology has phrased the positive sum concept in practical terms: "Life itself dictates peaceful coexistence."

Alliance Factors

Essential: *Support for proposed arms controls by allies or, failing this, a willingness by each party to overlook its allies' objections.*

Helpful: *Sense of common cause vis-à-vis respective allies. Self-restraint toward possibilities of exploiting contradictions in the other camp.*

Harmful: *Virtual veto power by one or more allies.*

Comment: The superpowers' respective allies have both spurred and restrained progress in the negotiations. Britain has generally supported the U.S. position and worked to bridge the gap between Washington and Moscow, as did France before de Gaulle. Poland, Czechoslovakia, and Rumania have generally taken a more progressive stance in arms control than their Soviet ally. Both

Bonn and Peking exerted a checking influence at key moments in the middle and late 1950s, and the nuclear test ban was signed over their objections. Under de Gaulle and his successors France has taken a position analogous to China's, which Washington—like Moscow—has been compelled to overlook if agreements were to be reached. From the late 1960s through 1972 Bonn has welcomed most arms control measures while Pankow has often tried to constrain Moscow.

The Third World

Essential: *A multilateral treaty directly affecting the Third World will bind only those states that sign and ratify it, but Third World attitudes and actions can have only marginal impact on arms control decisions of the superpowers.*

Helpful: (1) *Support for proposed measures by Third World states which one or both superpowers hope to influence, e.g., toward affirmation of certain security policies including arms control.* (2) *Sense of common cause vis-à-vis the nonaligned states of the Third World: not merely to gain their moral approval but to motivate certain countries not to invest in nuclear or other armaments.*

Harmful: (1) *Opposition to proposed measures by Third World states which one or both superpowers hope to influence.* (2) *Attempt by negotiating parties to compete in winning favor of Third World nations, leading to propaganda appeals in the negotiations and in other fora.*

Comment: The lack of decisive influence of Third World opinion was illustrated in 1961, when the Soviet Union resumed nuclear testing and conducted the largest atmospheric tests in history almost concurrently with the Belgrade Conference of Nonaligned Nations. On the other hand, Soviet concern to include an escape clause for wars of national liberation prevented a U.S.-Soviet accord in 1964 on outlawing the use of force to alter frontiers. A variety of treaties since 1967—outer space, nonproliferation, seabed, biological warfare—have been negotiated bilaterally and amended only marginally to take account of Third World preferences. If a Third World country does not like the accord, of course, it can hardly be compelled to comply (*cf.* India or Israel and the NPT).

The other side of the coin is that the fewer parties directly affected by an arms control measure, the easier it will be for the superpowers to agree to it (assuming the two governments wish to, for whatever reasons). *A fortiori*, the fewer countries expected to sign or otherwise approve the measure, the easier it will be to negotiate. It is possible for the great powers and others to create a bandwagon effect, pressuring all and sundry to sign a treaty such as the limited test ban or the nonproliferation treaty. The countries deeply opposed will not sign, however, or, if they do, they will keep their options open. Thus, India signed the test ban, but has refused to adhere to the NPT and retains a capability to go nuclear in a short time if she chooses. This is not to say that the effect of an arms limitation sponsored by the superpowers and others has no inhibitory effect upon the others. If India, Japan, Israel, or other countries believed that their basic interests required flouting the nuclear test ban, however, they would be less restrained by considerations of treaty law than by possible sanctions.

International Crisis

Essential: *An international atmosphere that permits conclusion of East-West arms controls, even if it does not directly encourage them.*

Helpful: *International crisis that stimulates the superpowers to seek agreements that will prevent the outbreak of war or agreements that, even if they do not bear on the immediate crisis, will help generate an atmosphere of restraint and some relaxation of tensions.*

Harmful: *A crisis so intense that serious negotiations bearing on East-West security become infeasible.*

Comment: Crisis has become endemic in parts of and epidemic in the whole of the international system. In a world of rapid communications and manifold interdependencies, trouble even in areas remote from the superpower confrontation may have an important impact on U.S.-Soviet relations. This presents us with an epistemological problem: How can we know whether particular arms control agreements have been facilitated, hindered, or not at all affected by crises in various parts of the world?

The fact that the Cuban missile crisis was followed by a series of arms control measures suggests the hypothesis that "things must get worse before they can get better," perhaps because governments need a traumatic stimulus to remind them of the dangers in unbridled military competition. The Vietnam war may have had a similar effect. The Soviet media, at least, argued in 1966-67 that the Indochina war made it all the more imperative to ease international tensions by such measures as the treaty on outer space.

A different kind of hypothesis could result from the study of various other crises. The Hungarian-Suez incidents of 1956 gave the *coup de grace* to the 1955 "Spirit of Geneva," a blow administered to the "Spirit of Camp David" by the Soviet and American handling of the 1960 U-2 incident. In this same vein, Moscow's initial response to the U.S. bombing of North Vietnam in 1965-1966 was to act as though arms negotiations were impossible while a "sister socialist state" was being attacked. Soviet diplomats argued at that time that the Moscow ABM had to be expanded in case the Indochina conflict escalated. More dramatically, both President Johnson's scheduled trip to the Soviet Union and the beginning of SALT were cancelled in 1968 by the Warsaw Pact intervention in Czechoslovakia. The interplay between the Czechoslovakian events and SALT illustrates how crisis—even if it is not perceived as threatening to either superpower—may so affect the climate of world (and domestic) politics that sensitive negotiations become infeasible.

Finally, there are cases where arms control negotiations seem to have been immune to fluctuations on the international fever chart. The Six-Day War of 1967 did not unsettle the movement toward a Nonproliferation Treaty, though it did give Soviet and U.S. leaders some experience in crisis communication over the hot line. Subsequent events in the Middle East and in Vietnam were kept out of the SALT deliberations, both the U.S. and Soviet delegations reassuring each other that their negotiations would not be affected by events in other parts of the world.

Strategic logic and intuition suggest that, on balance, crises in the Third World have pushed the U.S. and Soviet governments toward arms control—or arms control negotiations—as a vehicle for conflict control. If these crises had escalated to superpower confrontations, of course, negotiations on arms control would have been impossible. As we have seen, the détentes of 1955-56 and 1959-60 were terminated by crises, and that of 1972 was threatened before it was born.

Soviet acquiescence in the American mining and bombing of North Vietnamese ports and rail lines on the eve of the May 1972 summit conference demonstrated that the Kremlin put a larger premium on the other issues at stake. Moscow would not permit an embarrassment in a remote area of competition to prevent agreements on arms control, trade, and other matters of vital interest to the USSR. The Nixon Administration, however, could hardly have been certain that escalation of the fighting in Indochina would not scuttle the forthcoming summit, just as the U-2 incident had done in 1960. Indeed, the President has been reported to have judged this to have been a 50/50 possibility. Due to skillful U.S. diplomacy, however, not only Moscow but also Peking now saw reason in 1972 to tolerate the blockade and to encourage Hanoi to serious negotiations later in the year. Both Soviet and Chinese readers, of course, could note in their press that "patriotic forces" were besieging the "puppet" elements in South Vietnam and Laos, a point that would help explain the American bombings to these audiences.

A multiplier effect can develop between arms control and international crisis. To the extent that the superpowers make progress in controlling their own arms race, they may feel more confident that they can cooperate to tranquilize conflict in other parts of the world—and vice versa. Peace may not be "indivisible," for a war in Abyssinia need not produce conflict in Europe. Successful negotiations in one area, however, can have a positive impact in other domains, unless they merely permit the shifting of fighting power from one region to another. The SALT records of 1972, at any rate, seemed to be followed by superpower moves to restrain or reduce fighting and tensions in the Middle East and Indochina.

Domestic Politics

Essential: (1) *Domestic political strength sufficient to permit each government to commit itself to international agreements with far-reaching consequences;*

alternatively, a sense on the part of the ruling group that its domestic position can be strengthened through successful conclusion of certain arms controls. (2) A certain period of adjustment in which a new administration can determine its general attitude and specific policies toward arms and arms control.

Helpful: *Domestic support, both from elites and the broad public, for the proposed arms controls. The more responsive the government and the more complex the issues, the more understanding will be required to obtain this support. A president (or a Soviet Party leader) with an established reputation for taking a tough or a firm position toward the other superpower may be in a better position to make arms control compromises than one thought to be "weak" in standing up to the other side. A political culture and legal system conducive to respect for and observance of arms accords.*

Harmful: *Hawkish influences exerting a veto power or undermining treaties signed. Making arms accords contingent on domestic changes in the other side.*

Comment: President Kennedy restricted the planning and negotiating of the 1963 test ban to a small group within the government. When the treaty appeared within grasp, he moved to prepare public opinion (e.g., his "Strategy of Peace" address) while attempting to retain the favor of allies (*"Ich bin ein Berliner"*). To win Senate approval he undermined the spirit of the treaty by commitments to intensified underground testing. Khrushchev also had to cope with strong domestic opposition to détente, which seemed to falter when Kozlov became ill in April 1963.

President Nixon was cool to SALT when he was elected in November 1968, and he pressured the lameduck Johnson administration not to enter into any new commitment to Moscow to open negotiations. The momentum of bureaucratic politics inherited from the Johnson years, in turn, put pressure on the new president to take a more positive position on strategic arms control. The White House ordered the National Security Council to review all aspects of SALT, especially verification capabilities, before the United States could be committed to the negotiation table again. Such a procedure seems logical and natural for a new president, though review could as well have turned up pretexts for postponing further negotiations. By late 1969, however, SALT had formally begun and the United States was unilaterally taking measures to curtail biological weaponry. By 1971, if not before, the President saw arms control as a way to vaporize liberal opposition within the country, while appeasing hard-line elements by continued commitments to high defense spending and "bargaining chips." Even after his prestige was attached to the SALT I agreements, Nixon stood by while Henry Jackson and other senators backed a Congressional Resolution that ran contrary to the basic principles of the understandings reached at the Moscow summit.

Bureaucratic expertise on arms control has been facilitated in the USSR by a greater continuity in top posts in the Foreign Ministry and Defense Ministry than obtains in the United States between administrations. Soviet scholars report that Brezhnev and Kosygin also ordered a review of arms and arms control policies inherited from Khrushchev when they took power in October 1964.

They had to contend not only with the legacy of the 1962 Cuban debacle but with the new challenge of mounting U.S. involvement in Indochina, including the bombing of North Vietnam. They deliberated also the new threat of a widening gap in deliverable warheads resulting from the U.S. lead in MIRV technology. By 1968-69 Soviet specialists were still puzzled (according to conversations held in 1972-73) about American intentions in SALT, a situation that may help explain the Soviet tendency in those negotiations to await specific initiatives from the U.S. team.

Brezhnev's commanding position within the Kremlin was affirmed shortly before the May 1972 summit with Nixon when Politburo member Shelest was removed from his position at the helm of the Ukrainian Party organization. Whereas Frol Kozlov's illness in April 1963 created a free hand for Khrushchev prior to the Moscow test ban negotiations, Shelest's downgrading (and that of the Georgian Party Secretary just after the summit) seemed to reveal a firm hand which Brezhnev already enjoyed. This posture was further demonstrated in the fact that he personally signed many of the summit agreements as "General Secretary of the CPSU" without any formal position in the governmental hierarchy. In April 1973, however, prior to Brezhnev's travels to Bonn and Washington (when mischief could take place at home), Shelest was removed from the Politburo along with Gennadi Voronov, reputed to have been aligned with Kosygin's economic orientation. Three executors of the Brezhnev line then joined the Politburo—Gromyko, Andropov, and Grechko—signalling (at least for the time being) a harmonious coordination of external and internal security policy at the highest level.

Economic Factors

Essential: *No vested interests so powerful that they can prevent accords to damp the arms race.*

Helpful: (1) *Perceived utility in reducing resources devoted to the military establishment and its technological base and transferring them to other sectors of the economy.* (2) *Support—from the general public and elites—for such transfers.* (3) *Feasibility studies on how to make such transfers.*

Harmful: (1) *Belief that one's own economic wellbeing requires a high level of military-oriented spending or that* (2) *it is possible and desirable to drive the adversary into economic bankruptcy by maintaining high levels of military competition; alternatively, that he will make significant concessions to obtain arms control agreements.*

Comments: Many economists including Soviet and East European specialists concluded in the late 1950s-early 1960s that the arms race is a burden not only for developing nations but also for industrial countries such as the United States, and that it would be both desirable and feasible gradually to shift resources from the defense to civilian sectors. The obstacles to such a shift, they concluded, are more political than economic.[23]

In support of this outlook (and contrary to the assertions of some New Leftists), the Pentagon Papers suggest that America's participation in Indochina seems to have been motivated more by ideological, strategic, or sheer bureaucratic concerns than economic considerations.[c] Though some private interests have gained from the war, the economy as a whole has suffered, a point recognized by the stock market as it has reacted positively to each serious report of impending peace. These facts notwithstanding, one may also note the rise and fall of particular stocks correlating with the apparent prospects for an American ABM system. Particular companies surely have a vested interest in continuation of the arms and space races, even if the economic wellbeing of the country generally suffers.

The burden of defense has been much higher on the USSR than on the United States. Though Soviet decisions on arms control have been influenced marginally by economic concerns, there is no evidence that they could not be justified primarily in terms of international security requirements. Some Soviets continue to fear that Washington, as in the time of John Foster Dulles, may be attempting to spend the USSR into financial and political ruin.[24]

China, like the USSR, seems to be willing to pull in her collective belt (or keep it pulled in) in order to spend the necessary manpower and other resources the Peking leadership believes necessary for defense.

Arms decisions in communist countries are also affected by preferences of economic and technological elites with vested interests in high levels of spending for defense and defense technology. As in capitalist countries, these elites ally with hard-line political and military leaders opposed to a relaxation of tensions and improved relations with the ideological foe.

Sociological Factors

Essential: *No vested interests so powerful that they can prevent accords to damp the arms race.*

Helpful: *Support for arms control from concerned elites and the public. Positive and friendly attitudes toward foreigners including the ideological adversary. Government confidence that its position will not suffer and may gain from cultivating East-West détente and promoting arms control.*

---

[c]This assessment is indirectly substantiated by the ESP data, which showed an overwhelming majority (76 respondents) holding that "power politics" was the most important force shaping U.S. policy-making in the .1969-72 period. Next in order came "ideology" (26), "misunderstanding of other peoples" (23), "nationalism" and "economics" (14 each), "human nature" (10), and finally "ecological factors" (1). Other factors not included in the original list were emphasized by Richard Merritt and J. David Singer. These included "domestic politics," "bureaucratic pressures and inertia," and "presidential politics." One State Department official said that correct "understanding of other peoples" had also been an important influence.

Harmful: *Belief that one's basic political security requires a society that is economically deprived, cut off from the outside world, and hostile to the ideological foe. Belief that negotiated arms controls can be made domestically palatable only by significant measures to placate hawks opposed to détente and arms control.*

Comment: Fortunately for world security, neither the U.S. nor the Soviet governments seem to have believed in recent years that scares of a "red tide" or "capitalist encirclement" are needed to promote the interests of the ruling regime. There is little mass support for brinkmanship vis-à-vis the ideological foe. Rather, most observers find a weariness with war and a widespread yearning for what Herman Kahn has called "hedonism." In both countries, to be sure, agencies of internal security and watchdogs of political purity continue their opposition to détente and freer communications by citizens of East and West, and "ideological coexistence" continues to be officially taboo in the USSR. Aggravation of domestic ills in each superpower, such as race or nationality grievances, could alter this pattern, leading the government to seek refuge in building the image of an external bogey (a role which can be and has been assigned at time's to China). There remains also the possibility that the military would not only influence but dominate the government from behind the scenes, especially in Moscow where succession procedures are ill-defined. In the USSR as in the United States, however, there is a long tradition of military subordination to civilian rule which has rarely been directly challenged.

International Trade

Essential: *No fear that access to necessary resources will be impaired as a result, direct or indirect, of arms control and associated agreements.*

Helpful: *Concern to expand East-West trade for its own sake or as a means of providing a material stake in conflict control.* [d]

---

[d]The ESP respondents' belief in the non-aggressive intentions of the Soviet leadership was expressed indirectly in their response to a question about the role of trade in U.S.-Soviet relations in recent years. Forty-six respondents stated that "trade has been of much greater interest to the USSR than to the U.S."; 44 held that "trade and political settlements have been of roughly equal importance in bringing both governments to the negotiating table"; 31 stated that "both governments have sought to use the promise of increased trade primarily as an instrument to achieve political settlements"; and 22 asserted that "both governments have been vitally concerned to achieve political settlements that would permit a great increase in trade." Only three suggested that "trade has been of much greater interest to the U.S. than to the USSR."

Most ESP respondents seemed to believe that the great powers are increasingly interdependent economically and technologically, and that their awareness of this condition has affected their basic policies. Still, politics sets limits to economics. Despite the perceived interest of both superpowers in achieving an expansion of trade and in political settlements, there is little expectation that either side will make "significant political concessions to

Harmful: *Assumption that other side's need for trade or foreign markets will lead it to make far-reaching concessions in arms control and other security matters.*

Comment: From the mid-1950s through the early 1970s the USSR has been concerned to expand East-West trade, while Washington has been more interested in an exchange of culture and ideas (what Moscow calls ideological subversion). Soviet policy may have been genuinely influenced by a Marxian belief that a sound material base in international trade would help assure a superstructure of peace (just as a material base of heavy armaments is likely to influence the political superstructure, most logically toward violence). Washington's general aloofness to Soviet trade overtures changed only in the early 1970s as (a) the imbalance in U.S. imports and exports grew more critical; (b) Moscow raised U.S. hopes that it would influence Hanoi toward an acceptable negotiated settlement in Vietnam; and (c) specific deals (wheat, gas, machinery, etc.) became not only politically feasible but economically thinkable. Over the years, however, Washington has probably overrated the degree to which it could command arms control or political concessions in return for economic favors.[25]

The Record, 1962-73

The argument is that the presence or absence of the "essential" factors enumerated above has been critical to the success or failure of attempts to curb the U.S.-Soviet arms race in the last two decades. This argument may be tested by looking at three major periods conducive to arms control (November 1962-October 1964; January 1966-July 1968; November 1969 through 1972) and three "times of troubles" with little or no progress toward arms control (May 1960-October 1962; November 1964-December 1965; August 1968-October 1969).[26]

Let us recall here the positive achievements of the three periods conducive to arms control. To the right of each accomplishment we will also note whether the forces affected by the agreement were (a) symmetrical; (b) in a state of parity; (c) otherwise "sufficient" for each side; (d) regulated as part of a trade off in which arms control concerns were weighed against and bargained with other kinds of interests.[27]

obtain improved trade relations" with the other. Only 20 percent thought it likely that Moscow would make such concessions to Washington; 12 percent that Peking would make them to the United States; and 15 to 18 percent that Washington would make them to Moscow or Peking. As for "trade and political relations between Washington and Tokyo, only 20 percent of respondents expected significant improvement in 1973-77. But 45 percent forecast significant improvement in Japan's relations with the USSR, while 74 percent looked for major improvement in Tokyo's trade and political relations with Peking. (As noted earlier, most respondents thought Japan unlikely to go nuclear in the next four years, and less likely than Israel or India.)

Table 3-1
Arms Control Accords, 1962-73

October 1962-October 1964	Symmetry	Parity	Sufficiency	Other Trade-Offs
	(In the forces controlled after the agreement)			
—Apparent U.S.-Soviet understanding on Cuba in late October 1962; no Soviet missiles deployed: no U.S. invasion; subsequent withdrawal of U.S. missiles from Turkey;	No	No	?	Yes
—Washington-Moscow hot line, agreed to June 20, 1963;	Yes	Yes	N.A.	Yes
—Limited nuclear test ban; signed August 5, 1963;	No	?	?	Yes
—Understanding on outer space endorsed by U.N. General Assembly, October 17, 1963;	Yes	Yes	Yes	Yes
—Announcement of reductions in Soviet defense budget and possible troop reductions by Khrushchev, December 13, 1963;	No	No	Yes	Yes
—Simultaneous declarations by Soviet, U.K., and U.S. governments of an intention to cut back production of fissionable materials (April 20, 1964)	No	?	Probably	Yes
January 1966-July 1968				
—Outer space treaty (negotiated bilaterally and multilaterally), signed January 27, 1967;	No	Yes	Yes	Yes
—Nonproliferation treaty (negotiated bilaterally and multilaterally), commended by U.N. General Assembly, June 12, 1968 and opened for signature July 1, 1968; entered into force March 5, 1970;	No	Yes	Yes	Yes
—Security Council adoption of tripartite resolution regarding assurances to non-nuclear weapons states in case of aggression, June 19, 1968;	Yes	Yes	?	Yes
—Plans for SALT laid in 1968 (aborted by Czechoslovak events, August 1968).	No	?	?	Yes
November 1969-1973				

—SALT commences November 17, 1969, and continues into other rounds. Deadlock on relative priorities of defensive and offensive weapon limitations apparently broken by agreement in principle announced by President Nixon and Radio Moscow on May 20, 1971: to break the stalemate in the SALT negotiations by concentrating in 1971 on curbing

November 1969-1973	Symmetry	Parity	Sufficiency	Other Trade-Offs
ABM but "together with concluding an agreement to limit ABMs," to agree also "on certain measures with respect to the limitation of offensive strategic weapons."	No	Yes	Yes	Probably
—Some reaffirmation by Moscow as well as Washington of an understanding reached in 1962 on missiles in Cuba (late 1970);	No	No	?	Probably
—On November 25, 1969, President Nixon renounces use of lethal or incapacitating biological agents and weapons and all other methods of biological warfare; repeats that United States will not be first to use lethal chemical weapons; and extends this no-first-use pledge to incapacitating chemicals. President specifies that toxins would be included in the U.S. renunciation of biological agents, February 14, 1970. On August 19, 1970, Nixon resubmits the 1925 Geneva Protocol to the U.S. Senate for advice and consent to ratification. United States supports British proposal (August 1969) for a prohibition of production or stockpiling of biological weapons (amended at the United States suggestion in 1970 to include toxins). Soviet government announces in March 1971 that it will also support such a prohibition, dropping previous insistence on linking it with a similar ban on chemical weapons; convention on Prohibition and Destruction of Biological Weapons signed April 10, 1972;	Yes (in biological, but perhaps not in chemical weapons)	?	Yes	Probably
—Progress toward an all-European security conference in 1969-1973; Soviet acceptance of North American participation in January 1970; agreements reached in Four-power Berlin negotiations, 1970-1972, and in GDR-FRG negotiations;	No	?	?	Probably
—Nonproliferation treaty enters into force, March 5, 1970; later progress in formulating an agreed system of safeguards under auspices of the International Atomic Energy Agency;	No	?	Yes	Probably
—Renunciation of force treaties signed between Bonn and Warsaw, December 7, 1971; ratified in 1972; and between Bonn and Prague in 1973;	No	No	Yes	Yes
—Seabed treaty (drafted bilaterally and multilaterally), approved by United Nations First Committee,				

November 1969-1973	Symmetry	Parity	Sufficiency	Other Trade-Offs
November 17, 1970, signed on February 11, 1971; entered into force May 18, 1972;	?	Yes	Yes	Yes
—Force reductions in Europe endorsed by NATO Council (1968-1972), and by Warsaw Pact ministers (Budapest, June 1970), and by Secretary Brezhnev, (March-May 1971), NATO specifying the reductions should be "mutual and balanced." Movement toward multilateral negotiations throughout 1972-73;	No	No	?	Yes
—Nuclear accidents agreement, signed and entered into force on September 30, 1971;	?	Yes	Yes	Yes
—Agreement to modernize hot line, signed and entered into force on September 30, 1971;	Yes	Yes	N.A.	Yes
—ABM treaty, signed May 26, 1972;	No	Yes	Yes	Yes
—Interim Agreement on strategic offensive arms, signed May 26, 1972;	No	Yes	Yes	Yes
—Nixon-Brezhnev pledges on war prevention and SALT II objectives, June 1973.	No	Yes	Yes	Yes

Progress toward arms control in each of these three periods appeared to correlate strongly with the essential conditions listed above, while periods of little or no forward movement coincided with the absence or weak presence of essential and helpful conditions, times which were rather dominated by conditions harmful to arms control. Though some underlying conditions remained relatively constant, changes in any critical factors could and did have decisive effects.

The absence of many essential conditions seemed to account for the time of troubles from May 1960 through October 1962. The U-2 flight raised doubts for Moscow whether "sober forces" wishing to negotiate could regain the upper hand in the United States ruling circles; the expansion of the Minuteman program under President Kennedy widened the asymmetries in the balance of power, reducing the confidence of many Kremlin leaders in the deterrent and political capabilities of the Soviet strategic forces; Khrushchev's personal style and policies were under fire from domestic critics, many of them hard-line in foreign affairs; Soviet troubles with Peking were growing, exacerbated by any sign of Soviet interest in accommodations with the West. All these pressures (and others, e.g., related to Berlin) helped to impede negotiations in 1960-62. Moscow's decision to resume nuclear testing in 1961, exploding the largest warheads ever tested, and to emplace missiles in Cuba in 1962 showed that the Kremlin was deeply concerned to redress the balance of power primarily by unilateral action. If negotiations took place, they would be from a position of strength.

The role of altered perceptions became evident after the Cuban missile crisis, because the strategic balance underlying the arms controls of late 1962-1964 was not objectively much different from that of 1961-62. But the Cuban confrontation showed not only the resolve of the American President (perhaps doubted in Moscow), but also his unwillingness to exploit aggressively the United States lead in strategic weapons—all of which served to revive confidence that a credible deterrent existed on both sides, one that was not destabilized by the agreements of 1962-64.[28] After Cuba there was no longer any immediate prospect of a technological or political quick-fix that could radically alter the balance of power. Any Soviet interests in that direction would require rather a long-term building program. Lacking true parity with the United States and confronted with many asymmetries in force structure, the USSR could agree to a variety of arms control measures that helped bring the arms race under control (e.g., preventive measures for outer space) and that had political benefits at home and abroad (strengthening Khrushchev's interpretation of peaceful coexistence). They also had the effect of tranquilizing East-West relations in a way that would permit the USSR gradually to build up her ICBM and sea-based forces toward a level of parity with the United States.

The movement away from the 1963 "Spirit of Moscow" became marked only in late 1964 following Khrushchev's ouster and the heightened involvement of the United States (also the USSR) in the Indochina war. For one or two years the USSR acted as though the bombing of a "sister socialist state" was the main impediment to U.S.-Soviet arms control talks. While the political embarrassment of Vietnam weighed heavy, other factors were probably more important in keeping Soviet diplomats from the negotiating table: first, the new Brezhnev-Kosygin regime wanted to placate the marshals who had been compelled to endure Khrushchev's subjectivisms so long; second, a political-military assessment had to be made of the "lessons of Cuba"; third, proceeding from these two considerations, the Soviet Government committed itself to the missile building program that would bring it to rough parity with the United States toward the end of the decade. Until that level was reached, serious negotiations on levels of strategic and defensive arms (pressed by Washington as early as January 1964) were almost unthinkable.

As the Vietnam war became more violent, however, Moscow came to argue that it made arms control talks more urgent: Both Moscow and Washington moved in 1966-67 to formalize by international treaty the 1963 gentlemen's agreement outlawing the deployment of mass destruction weapons in outer space. Far from curbing Soviet plans for expansion of strategic forces, this treaty permitted continued testing of fractional orbital bombardment systems, one of the tracks the Kremlin was still pursuing in its manifest efforts to reach parity with Washington. Once the multilateral nuclear force (MLF) proposal was given a decent burial in 1966, Moscow also moved seriously to close the gap between the United States and Soviet draft treaties on nonproliferation of nuclear weapons. This yielded a treaty which would confine Washington and its allies (Western Europe, Japan, Israel) more than it would the USSR (much less disposed to trust putative allies with advanced weapons). The NPT, like the outer space treaty, would not restrict the expansion plans of Washington of Moscow, though each pledged to set a good example for the nuclear have-nots.

By the end of the 1960s strategic equivalence was in sight for the USSR. Moreover, if strategic arms talks did not get underway, the United States threatened to destroy the strategic balance by deploying a wide network of ABM defenses more advanced than Soviet technology and resources could provide for some time. Mutual agreement to commence SALT was itself disrupted by political events of greater immediate significance: Moscow's decision to regain control of Czechoslovakia by imposition of Soviet occupation forces. This development, like the bombing of Vietnam in 1965, made East-West negotia-tions politically infeasible for the rest of 1968, by which time President Nixon had been elected to replace Lyndon Johnson. A resumption of momentum toward arms control had to await a reassessment by the new American administration of the strategic and arms control programs inherited from the Johnson Administration.

The Nixon Administration signaled a serious approach to arms control by several important changes in the United States strategic doctrine: sufficiency instead of superiority of strategic forces; forces adequate for one and a half instead of two and a half wars; ABM defenses to defend missiles rather than cities; in the third world, a low profile. At the same time, Washington kept up the pressure on Moscow by continuing work on the first ABM sites in North Dakota and Montana and by proceeding with the testing and deployment of multiple warheads. The USSR, for her part, was drawing ahead of the United States in numbers of land-based missiles. Expansion of Russia's "heavy missile" and submarine programs also promised to redress the balance of power. By 1970-72 the two governments had reached or soon would reach a kind of strategic parity. Strong asymmetries persisted, probably giving the United States an overall superiority. If so, this superiority was hardly meaningful in political terms, and the variety of deterrence systems on both sides ensured that they could not be removed by a knock-out first strike. (See the ESP data cited in Chapter 1.) Confronted with a mass of asymmetries, the two governments made the necessary compromises to achieve an ABM treaty and an interim agreement on strategic offensive arms.

The May 1972 summit and November 1972 American elections provided salient deadlines for the United States negotiators. Moscow was brought to respect this deadline also by virtue of global American stratetgy: in Vietnam, in

Peking, and in trade negotiations. The USSR, hungry for an expansion of United States-Soviet trade, saw cause to seek a basic accommodation with Washington.

Some of the essential factors remained relatively constant through good and bad periods for arms control. Shifts in one or more of the critical underlying conditions, however, could have decisive effects, ruling out or facilitating an agreement. Such changes derived from a variety of complex sources, for example:

1. *Altered Perceptions:*

We noted earlier the role of altered perceptions in facilitating the transition from the Cuban confrontation to the "spirit of Moscow" in 1962-63. Various images also had to change to make possible the arms controls of 1971-72. Richard Nixon had been a *bête noire* of world communism before taking office in 1969. As President, however, his views on the utility of communicating and negotiating with Communist regimes seemed to differ greatly from those he held in earlier years. His actions persuaded Soviet, Chinese, and other Communist leaders that their assessment of him should also change. By 1972 both Peking and Moscow seemed to believe that Mr. Nixon's re-election offered the best hope for continued negotiations with the United States, and Moscow explicitly "cleared" him in summer 1973 statements on Watergate.

2. *Altered Rates of Growth:*

The rapid increase in the United States strategic forces early in the 1960s and of Soviet strategic forces in the late 1960s raised major questions about the intentions of each party, especially since these increases were accompanied by occasional suggestions in strategic doctrine about the feasibility of a pre-emptive strike or of victory in nuclear war. The rapid buildup of United States forces in the early 1960s was itself *partly* due to a misperception about the growth rates of Soviet forces at the time. Soviet anxieties about the significance of the United States buildup were partially allayed by Washington's restraint after the Cuban confrontation. If the rapid buildup of Soviet forces tapered off at levels of rough parity with the United States in the 1970s, this would tend to allay Washington's anxieties.

3. *Multiplier Effects:*

The Kremlin's willingness to break with Peking on arms control and on other issues in the early 1960s had wide ramifications affecting other conditions as well. Once this Rubicon had been crossed, it contributed to an outlook in which the Soviet leadership seemed to think of China as a greater threat than the United States, and to the growth of a mentality in Washington as well as in Moscow that viewed the superpowers as joined in a common cause against China. The break with Peking also encouraged Khrushchev to claim that disarmament accords demonstrated the validity of his interpretation of Marxism-Leninism, a point stressed in Soviet domestic propaganda, in the Communist movement, and in media addressed to the Third World.

4. *Threshold Effects:*

The economic burden of the arms race crossed a perceptible threshold for the USSR in 1962, serving to reinforce the Kremlin's reasons for seeking arms control accords in late 1962-63. Economic problems became severe again for the USSR in 1971-72. Similarly, the burden of the entire defense effort became perceptibly onerous for the United States economy in the late 1960s, though this was due more to the Indochina war than to present or anticipated expenditures on strategic weapons that might be curtailed in SALT. Apart from economic factors, it seems likely that a certain degree of conflict in the Third World, e.g., Indochina or the Middle East, might not interfere with SALT and might even spur arms control negotiations. If this conflict intensifies beyond a certain threshold, however, it could so dominate East-West relations that arms agreements with the adversary would be politically infeasible.

5. *Gating Factors:*

A change in the domestic or international political scene may open or close the gate to arms control accords otherwise possible. This occurred in April 1963 when Frol Kozlov, a leading opponent of Khrushchev's conservative opposition, became physically incapacitated, and in June 1963—in alliance relations—when Moscow and Peking broke publicly. The replacement of Khrushchev by Brezhnev-Kosygin *et al.* in October 1964 tended to close the gate for a while if only because the new leaders felt compelled to placate the Soviet military for a time and to test out the chances for rapprochement with Peking. The removal of Petr Shelest from leadership of the Ukrainian Community Party (but not from the Politburo of the CPSU) on the eve of the May 1972 Moscow summit was a sign that "conservative opposition" to the upcoming negotiations would not be tolerated. The fact that General Secretary Brezhnev himself signed most of the summit accords showed not only that he was more than equal with his colleagues, but that—like Khrushchev—he was seeking to establish his reputation and record in part on East-West arms limitations.

To sum up, a comparison of the 1963 test ban treaty and the 1972 SALT accords reveals a remarkable uniformity of many crucial conditions within the Soviet Union.

Both sets of agreements (like the Yalta accords) were signed in the USSR. Both were preceded or accompanied by conditioning factors in 1963 and 1972 which included:

1. A shared belief in mutual deterrence, despite asymmetries in the military components to be controlled;
2. Growing economic pressures (on both sides in 1973);
3. Demonstrations that each superpower wished to pull back from dangerous involvements in the Third World (Cuba and Vietnam);
4. The recent failure of still another Soviet attempt (apparently rather half-hearted) to mend fences with Peking;
5. The illness or downgrading of a leader of the Soviet conservative opposition to détente;
6. A more positive attitude in Moscow toward Yugoslavia, often the bellwether of East-West détente;
7. Favorable notice in Soviet media of "sober forces" in the West;
8. The public commitment of the top Soviet leaders to the feasibility and desirability of arms control agreements;
9. Assertions that Lenin favored arms limitations;
10. Soviet efforts to commit the West for further security agreements in Europe (a NATO-Warsaw Pact Nonaggression Treaty in 1963; a European Security Conference in 1973) and to movement to liberalize and energize U.S.-Soviet trade;
11. A cordial but businesslike demeanor in the negotiations (perhaps firmer in 1972 than in 1963).

After the accords were signed in Moscow, the Soviet media:

1. Argued that the agreements benefited both sides; were realistic and in tune with the facts: i.e., the end of Western hegemony and the bankruptcy of America's attempt to proceed from "positions of strength";
2. Portrayed the accords as a victory for the enlightened leadership of the CPSU and as a demonstration of the decisive importance of the Soviet Union in world affairs;
3. Asserted that the accords would strengthen the "progressive, peace-loving forces" struggling against imperialism and for peace; denied that the accords would in any way retard the forces of revolution;
4. Failed to publicize Western actions that might countervene the apparent spirit of the accords (plans to test underground; pledges to maintain technological superiority of the U.S.);

5. Treated Western opponents of the accords as a somewhat demented minority out of touch with the masses and enlightened leadership;
6. Reported support from Communist and revolutionary sources throughout the world and wrote off Chinese carping as out of touch with the true principles of Leninism;
7. Issued more assertions that Lenin favored arms limitation.[29]

Before and after the accords went into effect, the Soviet leadership sought to:

1. Maintain the momentum of détente and arms control by further agreements and some unilateral acts;
2. Use the improved political atmosphére to accelerate trade relations with the United States;
3. Tighten ideological-political controls at home.[30]

What of the future? Most of the conditions that appear essential for accords appear to be fairly positive for the mid-1970s. Many of them, however, can shift from positive to negative quite rapidly, if only in the way they are perceived. The potentials for danger may be seen, for example, in:

1. The Strategic Balance. If the United States insists upon equality (symmetry) in all aspects of the strategic balance, agreements based on parity (permutations of asymmetries) will be impossible.
2. Research and Development. If both superpowers intensify the quest for technological supremacy, one or both may feel that the promise of technological innovation should rule out future agreements and perhaps cancel existing ones.
3. Objections of allies. These may be overwhelming as negotiations try to include forward-based systems in Europe or Soviet missiles targeted on Europe; negotiations on MBFR also promise to cause splits among allies.
4. Non-intrusive inspection. This may be inadequate for verifying limitations on qualitative characteristics of missiles envisaged in SALT II, or on general purpose forces discussed under MBFR.
5. Domestic support for arms control and political stability. These may fluctuate with the health and fortunes of Soviet and United States leaders.
6. International crises. Conflicts in the Middle East or Indochina or along the Sino-Soviet frontier could escalate, casting a pall over the negotiations.

If these negative conditions do not arise and if positive ones hold, will SALT II and other U.S.-Soviet arms control efforts move toward fruition? There is no such assurance. *First*, the list of "essential conditions" hypothesized here may be incomplete or inaccurate. It may have missed a key factor by taking it for granted, the significance of which will be seen only when it changes. Further, the testing methods used here have depended heavily on verbal definitions and subjective interpretations that may not be scientifically adequate for coping with the problems assayed. *Second*, if the list if valid for the decade or so studied, it may be time-bound in ways that render it insufficient for application to subsequent (or previous) periods when the basic structure of international politics may be quite different (e.g., tri- or multipolar instead of bipolar).

A *third* and more important liability is that the essential conditions posited are thought to be necessary but not sufficient to ensure arms control success. How the world is perceived by leaders on both sides is at least as important as its objective content. How they act and react to this world is still more important. If they act as though parity exists, this is more important than the statistics in world almanacs. Whether there are asymmetries or symmetries in the balance of power, leaders can pursue or reject proffered arms controls, depending on their values and their assessment of other trade-offs. Indeed, one lesson of the 1960s is that arms control agreements have often been concluded because of hoped-for gains in the political or economic spheres rather than in the military confrontation directly affected by the accords. Even if both sides want agreement, the style with which they approach each other and conduct the negotiations is crucial. Sloppy planning, arrogance, or sabotage from within the regime (or by third parties) can undermine an agreement which both sides were inclined to want.

To overcome these obstacles and to convert necessary conditions to sufficient ones, a "modernist approach" to arms control is needed. Its requirements are discussed below in Chapter 5.

4

The Arms Control Road to Peace: Pros and Cons

Beyond Moralpolitik and Realpolitik[1]

Arms control offers an approach to peace that is at once less hopeful but more attainable than disarmament.[a] If all swords could be hammered into plowshares, this might provide a respite to armed conflict—at least until the plowshares were refashioned into instruments for war. Even without sophisticated weapons, however, men can fight with their fists, with knives, and with clubs. Unless we are sure that we have eliminated the reasons for aggression—whether they are

---

[a]The distinction between "disarmament" and "arms control" varies with time, place and author. "Disarmament" usually implies a reduction or abolition of armaments, although it has been used, especially between the World Wars, to denote mere limitation of arms. "Arms control" is a more inclusive concept having to do with any regulation or limitation on the construction, maintenance, or use of arms. It could therefore provide for a severe reduction, but possibly for an increase in arms. The term "disarmament" is favored in Moscow and the phrase "arms control" in Washington. Steps such as the nuclear test ban are euphemistically labeled "partial disarmament measures" by Soviet spokesmen.

From the time of the Baruch Plan to the mid-1950s or early 1960s, however, the term "arms control" occasioned many East-West debates, partially rooted in semantic differences. In Russian as in French, "control" signifies "inspection" or "checking," without the broader meanings included in English or German. The use of "arms control" by Western diplomats therefore tended to reinforce Soviet suspicion that the West wished only " *control* over armaments" (legalized espionage) instead of arms reductions. The term "arms control" was often translated in just this way (*kontrol' nad vooruzheniiami*). See, e.g., V.A. Zorin, ed., *Bor"ba Sovetskogo Soiuza za razoruzhenie, 1946-1960 gody* (Moscow: Institut Mezhdunarodynkh Otnoshenii, 1961), p. 73. For a critique of armaments control (*kontrol' za vooruzheniem*) in the German Federal Republic resulting from the terms of the Western European Union, see N. Nikolaev, *Atomnaia stavka Bonna* (Moscow: Mezhdunarodnye otnosheniia, 1969), pp. 126-133. For an exegesis of the terms "disarmament" and "regulation of armaments" in the United Nations Charter, see O.V. Bogdanov, *Razoruzhenie—garantiia mira* (Moscow: Mezhdunarodnye otnosheniia, 1972), pp. 38-60.

The lexicon of arms control took on a more definitive form with the signing in Moscow of the U.S.-Soviet treaty on the limitation of ABM systems (*ogranichenii sistem protivoraketnoi oborony*) and the interim agreement on certain measures with respect to the limitation of strategic offensive arms (*o nekotorykh merakh v oblasti ogranicheniia strategicheskikh nastupatel'nykh vooruzhenii*). These documents spoke of curbing (*sderzhivanie*) the race in strategic offensive armaments and taking effective measures toward reductions in strategic arms, nuclear disarmament, and general and complete disarmament (*effektivnye mery v napravlenii sokrashcheniia strategicheskikh vooruzhenii, iadernogo razoruzheniia i vseobshchego i polnogo razoruzheniia*). Many military terms are also provided, such as additional fixed land-based ICBM launchers (*dopolnitel'nye statsionarnye puskovye ustanovki MBR*). See texts in *Izvestiia*, May 30, 1972, pp. 1-2. As of late 1972 the Soviet press had not published the protocol to the interim agreement specifying in detail the limits that each side may reach under Article III. English texts and official commentaries are in *Weekly Compilation of Presidential Documents,* VIII, no. 23 (June 5, 1972) (U.S. Government Printing Office).

imbedded in human nature, in particular cultures, or in our material environment—the pursuit of total disarmament is likely to divert us from efforts to make peace more likely, given the disposition of men toward egotistical, aggressive behavior.[2] If total disarmament could be achieved, men would still be likely to fight one another; in time they would rearm (unless prevented by some central authority). But this is not the overriding consideration, for surely we would welcome a decrease in the destructiveness of organized warfare. The more compelling point is that—based on the historical record—large-scale disarmament cannot be "negotiated." It can only be imposed on defeated nations, as after World War I and II. If social conditions throughout the world led men and nations to want a world government, perhaps they would voluntarily surrender their individual weapons to a central authority. By definition, the problem of maintaining the peace would have withered away.[3] But this is not the world we know or the one that is foreseeable in the decades ahead. Instead of a peaceable kingdom we are confronted with profound conflicts arising from ethnic self-consciousness; from the perceived contrasts between "haves" and "have-nots"; and from a planet whose capacity for sustaining life is shrinking in the face of population increase and heightened demands for scarce resources. It is also a world in which many of the most destructive forms of military technology are becoming cheaper and more accessible to individual men and nations. To pursue disarmament under such conditions is to forgo possible improvements in the human condition in quest of utopia.

Arms control differs also from the cynicism of pure *Realpolitik*. The extreme schools of political realism would counsel that all negotiations with the enemy are likely to be fatuous and—even if they produce accords—short-lived. These schools look on such negotiations as a trap or as a game. Such games can be dangerous, especially for Western democracies whose publics generate unrealistic pressures for concrete results. Negotiations on arms limitation should be avoided or, if one is quite confident, manipulated for one-sided advantages. Even if they produce no accords, they may win propaganda points if conducted skillfully.[4] They may also foster a climate in which the other side is inhibited from using or even from producing certain kinds of armaments.[5] Alternatively, from a revolutionary standpoint, they may help to "demonstrate" the hypocrisy of the other side and the infeasibility of real peace without a social revolution.[6]

Arms control attempts to avoid the utopianism of *Moralpolitik* and the utter pessimism of *Realpolitik*.[7] It seeks rather to incorporate the long-term, goal orientation of political idealism and the pragmatism of the realist outlook. Taking human nature and society as they are, arms control pursues three major objectives: It seeks first to limit the cost of arms competition; second, to make war less likely; and third, to make war less destructive if it should occur. It also seeks what Panofsky has termed "arms race stability," i.e., "removal of the incentive for both parties to increase the number and complexity of their strategic forces."[8] If realized, these goals would not ensure heaven on earth or even peace to men of good will. They could, however, be vital to the survival of the human race and to the improvement of the quality of human life. Unlike disarmament, which calls for the reduction or elimination of armaments, arms control objectives could be pursued through a decrease, a stabilization, or—in some cases—an increase in the quantity or quality of armed forces.[b]

Direct Benefits: Economy and Survival

Whereas examples of voluntary disarmament are difficult to find, there are numerous instances of arms control measures—some formalized in treaties, some the result of tacit bargaining, some the product of unilateral restraint. Not all have been long-lived. Some may have been counterproductive in the long run.[9] Some of the parties to the accords may have felt coerced; some may have nursed a variety of ulterior motives; but virtually all these measures were ostensibly aimed at one or more of the three objectives listed above.

Limiting the costs of the arms race has been an objective of arms control negotiations from the Washington Naval Conference in 1921-22, which set ratio limits on capital ships, to SALT. Ecological as well as economic costs have helped to inspire accords such as the nuclear test ban treaty of 1963 and the outer space treaty of 1967. Accords such as the nonproliferation treaty signed in 1968 have been concerned with the costs of the arms race for developing nations as well as for highly industrialized countries.

Other accords have aimed more directly at limiting the likelihood of war, especially through improved communication systems. This objective has been served by summit conferences, from that held in Geneva in 1955 to those in Peking and Moscow in 1972. Following the Cuban trauma of 1962, both superpowers moved to establish a direct communications link—the so-called hot line—between Moscow and Washington, an institution later adopted by other

---

[b]Assuming that we are limited to the world of power politics, a plurality of 65 respondents from the Expert Survey Panel ranked "efforts to achieve a balance (equilibrium) among the five major powers" as the most hopeful road to peace. "Arms control" came next, with 33 votes. "Disarmament" received only nine votes, though it did better than "the quest for national superiority—military and otherwise" (two respondents). Ranked below "arms control" but higher than "disarmament" were "bipolar condominium and spheres of influence." (21 votes) and "collective security through alliance" (13 votes). A variety of other approaches were singled out by 16 other respondents.

Apart from assessing the questions of power politics, the ESP respondents were asked to evaluate the relative importance of other factors for peace on a scale ranging from "highly important" (one) to "not important" (five). At the top of this list came "economic development; trade; technical cooperation; foreign aid" (median score 2.2). This was followed by "education and culture (emphasizing empathy, interdependence, tolerance, cosmopolitan outlook, etc.)" (2.5); "revolutionary change in the domestic political and economic institutions of one or more countries" (2.7); "strengthening international institutions: the United Nations, international law, the International Court of Justice" (3.0); in last place, "an ecological perspective, including for example, zero growth policies for populations" (3.2).

nations as well. This link was modernized in 1971, taking advantage of satellite technology. The same year saw further U.S.-Soviet accords to reduce the chances of accidental or unauthorized war and efforts to decrease the danger of collisions at sea between the ships and planes of the two countries. Even without treaties, unilateral steps have been taken to reduce the chances of inadvertent war, e.g., by instituting improved command and control procedures over nuclear weapons systems.

Efforts to make war less destructive have also been made, though with less visible success. Thus, U.S. strategists have argued that nuclear war need not escalate to Armageddon, suggesting instead that it might be limited to the use of tactical nuclear weapons on battlefields; to attacks on the missile forces of the other side; or to blows against some but not all cities. These suggestions, on the whole, have struck Soviet commentators as infeasible. Their virtuosity has itself reflected the strengths in the U.S. posture compared with the Soviet, at least in the early and mid-1960s. Nonetheless, the fact that both superpowers are able to agree on limiting their anti-ballistic defenses (ABM) is itself mute testimony to their joint belief that civilian defense on a large scale is impossible, and that relative security may be found in stabilized deterrence. From this view it is not a giant step to the conclusion that, if missiles are fired, it could be on a selective basis, directed perhaps toward "disarming" the foe rather than crippling his cities.

It must be seen as some gain that the many wars fought since 1945 have not escalated to direct engagements between the superpowers. Major conflicts involving any great power have usually been characterized by qualitative restraints in terms of the types of weapons used and the targets attacked. The most bloody confrontation between great powers took place between Chinese and U.S. armies fighting in Korea. In both Korea and Indochina however, the United States has fought in a way that remained far below any nuclear threshold. Having been burned in Korea, America's conduct of the Indochina war sought to assure Peking that Chinese territory would not be threatened by U.S. attack. American bombing of North Vietnam, though it has killed many civilians, generally focused on military concentrations. If Soviet antiaircraft crews were killed by U.S. bombs in Vietnam, neither side advertised this fact. The Sino-Soviet frontier is another major danger zone, though the Ussuri River battles in 1969 were clearly limited to conventional weapons. Rising Soviet involvement in Middle Eastern affairs, if it extends to major actions against Israel, could however put the superpowers on a collision course, as almost happened in 1967.[c]

---

[c]Even in the area judged most explosive by the Expert Survey Panel, the Middle East, most respondents (78) expected the Soviet military presence to remain about the same; 36 said it would be basically dependent upon the character of the U.S. presence. Those expecting the Soviet presence to be significantly increased (14) was exceeded by those who said it would be significantly reduced (15). One respondent foresaw a gradual increase in Soviet naval facilities. Others indicated that the Soviets would inch forward, their progress depending upon such factors as domestic conditions within Middle eastern countries and the incidence of major wars.

The most immediate contribution of arms control, then, is to facilitate survival—not just of one nation, but of the world, given the destructiveness of modern war. Arms control can purchase time, time in which to build the social foundations that could undermine the sources of human aggression. This would be no mean accomplishment, since sheer survival is the *sine qua non* for any other form of human progress.

What goals were most important for the U.S. and Soviet Governments in SALT I? Almost half the ESP respondents agreed that the most important goals of each superpower was to relax tensions with its rival (77, US; 62, USSR). Next, 48 respondents held that the U.S. wanted to freeze and possibly reverse the arms race, a goal which 30 respondents also assigned to the USSR. (More salient for Moscow was the goal of freeing resources for non-military sectors of the economy [41 respondents], an objective which only 10 respondents marked as important for Washington.) Third, 19 respondents stated that Washington's objective was to gain domestic political benefits, a goal which only nine assigned to Moscow. Another 10 respondents said Washington wanted to assure compliance by non-nuclear nations with the nonproliferation treaty (only four attributed this interest to Moscow). Machiavellian interests in lulling the other side or gaining a free hand in the qualitative arms race were ascribed to Washington by nine respondents and by only three to the USSR. Eighteen, however, said that Moscow wanted SALT I "to cope better with China."[d]

Collateral Benefits

The medium-term contribution of arms control is that it can be an instrument not merely of war prevention but of détente. The very act of entering arms control negotiations can symbolize a larger desire to contain conflict and move toward cooperative relations with the other side. This has been a major by-product of U.S.-Soviet negotiations since the mid-1950s. Arms control and relaxation of tensions can feed upon each other; one without the other is unlikely. The outstanding example of this phenomenon occured in 1962-64, following the Cuban missile confrontation. It extended from the agreement under which Soviet missiles were removed from Cuba, to the hot line, to the nuclear test ban treaty, to a gentleman's agreement not to orbit weapons of mass destruction, to an accord on slowing down production of fissionable materials. Other arms control measures were discussed, such as reductions in defense spending; momentum was maintained in such steps as the U.S.-Soviet wheat deal. Even greater momentum of this kind developed in 1971-73.

[d]Robert Legvold and Harry Gelber cited Moscow's desire to halt or avoid an ABM race, while another respondent pointed out that the Russians were able to "freeze in a position quite favorable in comparison with the past." Others stressed Washington's interest in checking Moscow's expanding deployment of SS-9 missiles and SLBMs. At another level, one scholar complained that questions like this presupposed that governments "act and think with one voice"—patently a "false assumption."

While a middle-range contribution of arms control is to build the bridges and contacts that lead from conflict to cooperation, the long-term consequences of this approach have a still broader scope. Four of these contributions will be singled out. First, arms control efforts contribute to an ecological perspective on world affairs. Figure 4-1 illustrates the interface between major concerns of ecology and those of international relations. Environmental conditions like overcrowding tend to parallel or to reinforce political behavior injurious to peace and prosperity. The link between environmental disruption and political action is the image that policy-makers and their publics have of 'what is' compared to 'what ought to be.' Governments and publics that feel secure and satisfied will tend to endorse the status quo, whereas those that feel deprived will want radical change and be willing to engage in high-risk policies to achieve it. International cooperation might offer the most rational way to optimize the objectives of each group, but haves will tend to proceed slowly while have-nots will want results in a hurry. Environmental factors such as food shortages may be perceived as injustices which call for political action to bring about a redistribution of wealth. Depletion of natural resources may be seen as a threat which militates for a more belligerent foreign policy.[10]

Although environmental conditions may themselves change quite rapidly, man's beliefs about how to cope with his opportunities and challenges are quite resistant to innovation. Yet, if left unchecked, each of the problems outlined in Figure 4-1 tends to exert a multiplier effect, making the others more acute—both in the ecological and in the political spheres. We see how arms races and war both result from and contribute to ecological malaise. Nuclear testing is but one example of the ways in which arms competition poisons the global environment. As our world becomes more crowded and as its resources are depleted, however, we may witness more frantic and frenetic political behavior as nations fight for resources and for space, and as their domestic life becomes more anxious and conflict-ridden. It turns out that arms races are special examples of the ways in which modern technology is exploited (in part for political reasons) in ways that damage the environment. We can probably derive useful lessons for the control of technology in general from the history of arms control and from such efforts as the campaign to ban supersonic transport (SST) development.[11]

Second, study of arms control helps to generate a preventive approach to the problems of world affairs. This approach is elaborated in Chapter 5 and in

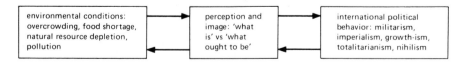

Figure 4-1. Feedback Model

Appendix C. Suffice it here to assert that an accord that forestalls deployment of some weapon is more feasible than disarmament after the fact. Similarly, the United Nations and other agencies have a much greater capacity for preventive diplomacy—damping crises before they explode—than they do for international peacekeeping or peace-making action.[12] Extrapolating from these lessons, it seems clear that preventive ecological measures—limiting population growth, limiting pollution, limiting the unbridled use of natural resources—should be more feasible than "therapy" to cope with overcrowding, smog, and economic scarcity.[13]

Third, arms control (like ecology) provides an excellent focus for interdisciplinary study. The ways of containing arms competition must be at least as diverse as the sources for human aggression. There is real potential for relevant insights from practically every scientific discipline from anthropology to zoology. To be effective, however, they must concert their efforts, sharing the results of individual or team research with others in non-specialized terms. The Joint M.I.T.-Harvard Arms Control Seminar has been a leader in this field, with economists such as Thomas Schelling, engineers such as Jerome Wiesner, biologists such as Matthew Meselson, and mathematicians such as Jeremy Stone talking with political scientists such as Lincoln Bloomfield. The structure of the U.S. Arms Control and Disarmament Agency in the 1960s also recognized the diversity of relevant approaches, its four main bureaus dealing with: International Relations; Science and Technology; Weapons Evaluation and Control; and Economics. Multidisciplinary and interdisciplinary studies have also dominated the *Journal of Conflict Resolution*; the *Journal of Peace Research*; and the *Papers, Peace Research Society (International)*.

Spinning off from the general recognition of the multifaceted character of war/peace studies, there has also been a more explicit understanding of the various levels at which these problems need to be examined: within the individual; within the nation-state; and within the international system.[14] We have come to understand also that it is not sufficient to look at conflict-prone factors within particular states, such as economic structure or ideology, but that we must examine action-reaction patterns between any sets of conflicting parties (be they man and wife or two superpowers). We have come to appreciate more deeply that any understanding of conflict will require us to see ourselves as others see us. Whereas Hans Morgenthau could deride "misunderstanding" as a source of conflict in the 1940s and 1950s, historians of the cold war as well as behavioral scientists have increasingly noted the place of "misperception," "self-fulfilling prophecies," and other psychological factors in generating conflict spirals and arms races.[15]

Fourth, the ascendance of the arms control approach has paralleled and contributed to a much increased sophistication in strategic thinking generally. As the superpowers no longer hope to defend their populations from all-out enemy attack, so they no longer hope for general and complete disarmament. Defense has given way to deterrence, and disarmament has surrendered to arms control.

This approach is consonant with the realities of the nuclear age, when the supreme, overarching interest is survival. If preventive war or pre-emptive attack is not likely to destroy the other's side's retaliatory capability, mutual interest requires that all parties work for a condition of stabilized deterrence in which none of them has reason to fear a first strike from the other.

This line of thinking leads to the conclusion that openness and effective communication are essential to security. The other side should know that we are strong enough to mount a second strike, but that we do not intend to initiate a war. Ideally, it should be manifest that we are not capable of striking a blow that might disarm his retaliatory forces. This reasoning applies to the superpowers, but it might be adapted also for their relations with lesser nuclear powers. China's assurance against nuclear attack could consist in a relatively small number of missiles, but only if the superpowers do not attempt to achieve invulnerability through large-scale ABM defenses.

Prisms of Decision-Making Analysis

These contributions of arms control—some of them more potential than actual—can be looked at in terms of different models put forward for the analysis of decision-making.[16] Looking through these different lenses, we may evaluate more deeply the negative as well as the positive aspects of the arms control approach to world peace.

(1) The Rational Actor Model. As already suggested in Chapter 2, the arms control approach (like that of deterrence) places a premium on the rationality of decision-makers on all sides. It assumes that they will act on the basis of enlightened self-interest. It assumes that the effort to communicate is worthwhile. On these assumptions, American arms controllers attempted to engage their opposite numbers in the USSR to dissuade them of the value of ABM defenses for the Soviet Union. Contrary to these assumptions, the extent to which U.S. strategists called for a "thin" ABM defense of North America against an "accidental Soviet attack" or a "low-level Chinese attack" indicated their fear that the deterrence system would not function, either because of accident or irrationality. If André Malraux may be believed, however, Mao Tse-tung understood the logic of a minimum deterrent at least by 1965, in harmony with the rationalist premises of strategic thinking.[17]

Assuming that all parties are rational, all can be engaged in a non-zero sum game, i.e., relationships in which mutual interests are recognized as well as conflicting ones. This leaves the door open to argument about the ways in which the former might be gradually expanded to overshadow the latter.

What we have perceived as "irreconcilable conflicts of interest" may turn out to be reconcilable if we manipulate the total system in certain ways. What appeared to be bedrock premises of a particular ideology or a particular nation's geopolitical situation may be altered or subsumed in some new framework. Peaceful change, ideally, will take the place of attempts to maintain or to change the status quo by violent means.

(2) The Bureaucratic Model. Having eschewed the all-or-nothing style of disarmament thinking, the arms control approach should be more inclined to examine closely the entire system of inputs that leads to "decisions" on matters of arms procurement and arms control. Only by understanding this system—within as well as between governments—can the arms spiral be brought under control. If we apply this approach to decision-making within particular countries, it readily leads to the insight that apparent "decisions" are the result of many conflicting pressures and interest groups, formal and informal, within and without government, some harmonious and some in conflict. One subset of these forces are the government bureaucracies dedicated to performance of certain tasks, often operating according to standard operating procedures (SOPs) and established routines.

The momentum or the inertia of particular bureaucracies as they cope with old or new problems will determine to a large extent the "policy" a government pursues on issues of arms or arms control. Vested interests will work for or against a solution that enhances their own position. At the time of the Cuban missile crisis, some officials of the Naval Department in the Pentagon saw it as their duty to enforce the quarantine of Cuba in a rigorous fashion. They wanted to "follow the book," and might have if not restrained by Secretary McNamara who, with others close to the President, had a more global view of how the confrontation might be peacefully resolved. Even after Moscow announced its willingness to withdraw the missiles from Cuba, some on the Joint Chiefs of Staff still wanted to remove them with U.S. bombs.[18]

While we know less about Soviet policy at this time, it seems likely that the many puzzles and internal contradictions in Soviet actions may have resulted from (a) Khrushchev's desire to mollify a number of competing interests in Moscow with one grand plan; and (b) the pursuit of their "job" by diverse agencies of the Ministry of Defense and Foreign Ministry without close coordination (such as construction of medium-range ballistic missile sites before setting up appropriate camouflage or anti-aircraft missiles).

If we apply these insights to the SALT negotiations, it would hardly be surprising if the military representatives on the two delegations raise sharp objections to schemes that could thwart their bureaucratic interests, while the delegates from the Soviet Foreign Ministry or the U.S. Arms Control and Disarmament Agency attempt to achieve a place of honor for their constituency. Alternatively, if the U.S. Defense Department is headed or staffed by arms control-minded civilians, while the State Department is dominated by cold warriors, these roles may be reversed. This was the case during most of the tenure of Secretaries McNamara and Rusk. While the bureaucratic model will not predict which of these inflections may predominate in particular departments, it will at least alert us to the probability that the SOPs, habits and styles of diverse bureaucracies (and bureaucrats) will be reflected in apparent "decisions" on arms control.

These insights, like some of those generated by the Rational Actor model, help to downplay the role of ideology and zero-sum thinking in arms control matters. If the United States tests multiple warheads at the same time that Washington negotiates with Moscow on strategic arms limitations, this situation is due in part to the momentum of competing bureaucratic interests, imperfectly harmonized at the top. To be sure, many U.S. Presidents have wanted to "negotiate from strength," and President Nixon has generally continued this policy. The same may be said of Soviet leaders, who have overseen the massive increase in Soviet offensive forces including some 300 SS-9 missiles as SALT got under way. The Bureaucratic Model suggests, however, that neither Washington nor Moscow is necessarily using the negotiations merely to lull the enemy while military buildups continue.

(3) The Bargaining Model. Not only do bureaucracies pursue their routine functions in a routine way, they also struggle actively for power. Beyond the government bureaucracies, there are a host of other competing domestic forces that affect decisions at the top. On the issue of multiple warheads, for example, there are also the corporate concerns that will profit from development and procurement of advanced missilery. There may be some spinoffs for NASA and the space industry generally. Against this there have been revolts within the Republican Party, led by Senator Edward Brooke, as well as organized criticism from leading Democrats and various academics. Depending on the state of the national economy, labor leaders are also likely to come down for or against certain decisions on weapons procurement. All these forces act with a view toward maximizing some particular interest rather than the general interest, though they often legitimize the former as being good for the latter. For the President and for many of his opponents, every decision taken will be viewed in terms of its impact on election day. For a Soviet leader, the day of reckoning could come at any time.

Analogous pressures exist in most countries. Aware of these pressures, the arms control approach will be not only more tolerant of egotistical or contradictory behavior by the other side; it will also counsel ways of intervening in the domestic affairs of the other party so as to affect the balance of power in ways conducive to arms control.

Mindful of the contending factions within other governments, strategists have emphasized the need for communicating not only with words but also with deeds to reassure moderate forces on the other side. Tacit signals may be given much more attention than verbal ones. The most important of these signals from the United States may be the size and character of the annual defense budget. While official Soviet defense statistics are not taken at face value in the West, the Kremlin has adjusted them up (as in 1961) and down (as in 1964) to convey its reaction to the world's tension level.[19] Weapons actually deployed are a more radical indicator, but their significance can also be misread, since we may not fully understand the reasons (bureaucratic, technological, etc.) for their procurement. Thus, America's encirclement of Russia and China with forward bases in the 1950s may well have looked as though the United States was bent on a preventive war strategy, whereas Washington conceived these bases as vital links in a global deterrent posture necessitated by Communist expansionism.

Cognizant of the conflicts within other countries and how we may misperceive the actual reasons for their apparent actions on arms control matters, we may be better able to avoid the psychological distortions noted before, e.g., self-fulfilling prophecies. On the positive side, we may be more likely to develop and carry through strategies for the gradual reduction of conflict. As President Nixon summed up his administration's thinking in 1969 about how to improve relations with China: "We faced two major questions. First, how to convey our views privately to the authorities in Peking? Second, what public steps would demonstrate our willingness to set a new direction in our relations?"[20] The mere posing of these questions suggests a great leap beyond the self-righteousness that characterized much earlier official thinking in Washington on America's relations with China. Putting the questions this way could serve as virtually a direct application of the strategy suggested years earlier by Charles Osgood under the rubric of "GRIT"—graduated reciprocation in tension reduction.[21]

The combined insights of the Bureaucratic and the Bargaining Models help to counter nine of the major sources of misperception which fuel the arms race. To paraphrase Robert Jervis:[22]

1. There is an overall tendency for decision-makers to see other states as more hostile than they are;
2. Decision-makers tend to see the behavior of others as more centralized, disciplined, and coordinated than it is;
3. If the *effect* of another's action is to injure or threaten the first side, the first side is apt to believe that such was the other's purpose;
4. When decision-makers have intentions that they do not try to conceal from others, they tend to assume that others accurately perceive those intentions; only rarely do they believe that others may be reacting to a much less favorable image of themselves than they think they are projecting;
5. It is hard for a decision-maker to believe that the other can see him as a menace; it is often even harder for him to see that issues important to him are not important to others;

6. When messages are sent from a different background of concerns and information than is possessed by the receiver, misunderstanding is likely;

7. When people spend a great deal of time drawing up a plan or making a decision, they tend to think that the message about it they wish to convey will be clear to the receiver;

8. Decision-makers often do not realize that actions intended to project a given image may not have the desired effect because the actions themselves do not turn out as planned;

9. Decision-makers tend to overlook the fact that evidence consistent with their theories may also be consistent with other views.

To the degree that we are able to recognize and countervail these sources of bias, arms control should be more feasible. It may be argued that the statesman is wiser to err on the side of caution (suspecting the other side of the worst intentions) than to risk gambling for peace. Such is the lesson which Soviet and Western leaders alike draw from the appeasement of Hitler before and after Munich. Since World War II, however, the pendulum has swung in the opposite direction, the superpowers piling up what appears to be a superfluous capacity for "overkill."[23]

A Balance Sheet

Each of these models embodies its own nemesis, a danger inherent in the very strengths of the particular approach. The Rational Actor model, implicit in deterrence theory and much arms control thinking, exaggerates the degree to which human affairs are (or can be) regulated by reasoned discourse. Each statesman may have his own form of logic (or psycho-logic), but it may not be fully understood by his associates and allies much less by his adversaries. The nine sources of misperception listed above may be moderated but not entirely eliminated. If so, bluffs and bargaining counters may be misunderstood; deterrence itself may fail. The balance of terror may turn out to be more fragile than strategists presume. The proponents of disarmament—if any of us are still alive—may say: "We warned you this would happen. Given the atomic bomb, our fate really did hang upon an all-or-nothing solution."

The game theorists may readily err in imputing probabilities and values to various courses of action which are weighted and assessed quite differently by other nations. The worth of invading Czechoslovakia and the costs of doing so were viewed quite differently in Moscow in 1968 than they were in Prague or by many Western observers. Wishful thinking is but one source for expectations that do not accord with reality. Where intangible values are at stake—such as the vitality of Soviet leadership in the communist movement—one is hard put to calculate the "rationality" of a particular policy.

Systems analysts may reach a degree of apparent sophistication unmatched by earlier students of domestic or foreign policy. They may understand in some depth the inputs and interaction patterns that underlie national and global politics. Computer programs may be designed that show the "propensity" of each country to settle disputes by resort to force. Nonetheless, this approach is almost certainly bound to falter upon the *hubris* of its designers. Even if they should understand many components of the system, they are not likely to master all or even the most important variables affecting particular crises. The output of their computer programs will not excel the quality of the inputs. Where traditional historians working with case studies cannot agree on the degree to which certain nations are addicted to force, it is still less likely that a systems analyst will be able to computerize such variables to accord with the real world. Still less will he be able to forecast the effects of synergism and serendipity upon national power. Least of all will he be able to forecast what individual(s) will occupy the seats of power and how they will cope with the problems and opportunities confronting them in years to come.[24]

Those who argue that nations will respond to enlightened self-interest and seek non-zero sum solutions may also be destined for profound disappointment. The USSR for several years deployed ABM systems and refused to negotiate on this subject despite the arguments of American arms controllers. China built her own nuclear force although Moscow said this was not necessary and might encourage the West Germans. France has also gone her own way despite similar admonitions from the United States. Assuming that France and Britain want to remain members of the nuclear club, bureaucratic and other factors make it unlikely that they will collaborate on a joint force despite the "rational" reasons for doing so.[25] Various threshold powers such as India may decide to exercise their nuclear option, like China, despite reasoned appeals from internal and external observers.

Gibbon has cautioned that "history is indeed the record of the crimes, follies and misfortunes of mankind." If so, the Rational Model may founder, sooner or later, perhaps in a catastrophic way.

The Bureaucratic and Bargaining models point up some of the shortcomings of the Rational Actor assumptions. Both approaches point to the irrational element in decision-making, the fact that a "decision" will likely reflect the forces of bureaucratic inertia and in-fighting rather than a game theory solution on how to optimize values vis-à-vis some foreign adversary. Indeed, many aspects of arms procurement probably defy analysis in terms of the action-reaction models of strategists concerned with world affairs. Decisions on arms buildups may reflect basically internal considerations—helping industry or alleviating unemployment—or a belief that an "absolute need exists for such an increase regardless of the actions of other states."[26] This seems to have been the case in the 1880s and 1890s, when the United States Navy was expanded apparently without regard to the actions of posture of any foreign power. More recently, one or both superpowers may have been running a race with itself as much as with the adversary, responding more to domestic pressures and the expanding capacity of its technology rather than to threats or restraint from the other side. Seen in this light, Moscow's ABM deployment or its emphasis on SS-9 rockets could not really have been averted by improved channels of communication, nor could Washington's decision to procure multiple warheads or to move toward development of a new generation of Trident submarines. Alternatively, the Kremlin and the White House may take their decisions on the basis of a general presumption of intense competition from the other side rather than on the adversary's specific actions (or inaction). In this case, as in that of domestic factors, the decision process has progressed to a large degree beyond the point where it can be modified by arguments based on symmetries or asymmetries of the international situation. In a related vein, India might choose to go nuclear—not for lack of security guarantees against China—but because she wanted a "spiritual bomb."

If the Bureaucratic and Bargaining models alert us to the various factors— domestic, ideological, technological—that shape arms decisions independently of world politics, they may also imply a counsel of despair. They may make us more tolerant of what appears to be aggressive behavior by the other side, but they also suggest the degree to which the adversary's decisions are beyond our capacity to influence. If Country X is imperialistic because it wants markets or resources, we may be able to persuade it that its economic ambitions can be optimized better through cooperation than through force of arms. But if it is imperialistic because of its domestic political and social institutions, the members of which feel they must expand or atrophy, there is little we can do to change the ways of its warrior class. Similarly, if Soviet or American arms buildups are a response mainly to actions by the other side—real or exaggerated— unilateral acts by the opposite number could turn down the arms spiral. If either superpower's arms buildup is determined by its economy or power structure, however, external intervention may be largely in vain—short of successful revolution engineered or abetted from without. This, as we have seen, was Lenin's Stage I view of all proposals for peace and disarmament, which he took to be counterrevolutionary unless they demonstrated the ultimate necessity for overthrowing the capitalist system.[27]

The ultimate criterion for the efficacy of the arms control approach is its pragmatic success or failure. Since 1945 we have not had a world war or even a small nuclear war. There have, however, been over fifty non-nuclear wars and several approaches to the brink of a nuclear conflict, as in 1962. Still, most of the wars fought since 1945 have involved tacit acceptance of certain arms control provisions, such as a taboo on the use of nuclear weapons or direct attacks on population centers. Even in the tensest confrontations, the great powers have operated so as to avoid putting one another in a *cul de sac* from which retreat or negotiation was impossible. "Communication" has become a shibboleth—not only in sensitivity training groups but in inter-state relations.

We can also point to an unprecedented number and range of formal arms control agreements, from Bonn's entry into the Western European Union in 1954-55 to the 1959 Antarctica Treaty to the latest SALT accords. These treaties have bound not only the large, relatively "have" nations of the globe but also some of the smaller have-nots. The major powers defeated in World War II—Germany and Japan—have accepted severe restrictions on their right to rearm and have gone on to achieve a sense of national fulfillment in non-military domains, a situation quite different from that which followed World War I. Though Moscow and Peking have warned about the danger of revived German or Japanese militarism, these warnings seem directed against somewhat remote contingencies and have been overshadowed, at least in recent years, by appeals to commercial interests and investors in the erstwhile enemy states. Unless Moscow should panic as France did when faced by the Austro-German Customs Union in 1931[28]—the prospects for the continued peaceful evolution of economic integration in Europe appear hopeful.[e]

We could evaluate the relative success of arms control in various ways. We could count the number of treaties signed; the number of nations participating in these accords; the number of hours spent in negotiation; the number and quality of research efforts being conducted within and without governments and the United Nations; the relative sophistication of citizens at large on such matter.[29] By all these standards, considerable progress has been made relative to the interwar period.[30]

Alternatively, we could plot the upward thrust of the arms race; the spread of sophisticated weapons to additional countries; the number of human and material resources being devoted to military purposes; the buildup in nuclear megatonnage and poison that could engulf the planet if a major war did occur. We could count the conventional bombs dropped in Indochina by the United States (more than the tonnage dropped by all parties in World War II). We could

---

[e]Of all parts of the world, ESP respondents foresaw the most quiet on the West European front in 1973-77. Peace and growing prosperity seemed to be the dominant forecast for Europe. Ninety-two percent of all respondents expected the continued viability of the European Common Market (EEC) as an economic institution. They were almost evenly divided, however, on the prospects for a "significant increase in movement toward political unity of Western Europe." But 49 percent expected a significant *increase* in economic and political conflict between EEC countries and the United States, while 38 percent ranked this as 50-50. The outlook for Pan-European cooperation was somewhat brighter: only five percent thought it probable that COMECON would develop along lines that would integrate East European economies and isolate them from the West, while 76 percent expected a "significant increase in trade and other non-political transactions between EEC countries and COMECON." Only 24 percent thought it likely, however, that there would be a "significant decline in technological lag and disparity of living standards between EEC and COMECON countries."

Only 5 percent expected an "attempted social-political revolution in a West European country" and 10 percent in an East European country (though written comments suggested this percentage might have been higher had Yugoslavia been explicitly included). Only 8 percent expected "non-cooperation with the WTO by some member country besides Rumania," though 41 percent judged this to be 50-50. Nine percent thought it probable that Soviet military intervention will take place "against some East European country," and 44 percent deemed this to be 50-50.

count the number of nuclear tests since the 1963 treaty on nuclear testing (more tests underground by the signatories since 1963 than they had conducted above or below ground prior to the treaty—not to speak of the French and Chinese atmospheric programs). We could count the number of persons killed or wounded in inter-state violence from 1950 to 1970 and compare it with the comparable figures for 1919-1939. Indeed, we would have to consider also, the casualties inflicted in internal wars (e.g., East Pakistan in 1971), at least to the extent that such domestic conflicts are due in part to international politics. We would also have to throw upon the scales the ecological damage resulting from the conduct of these limited wars (such as deforestation in Vietnam) or from arms buildups and testing programs, both of which deplete resources as well as pollute the environment.

If we compare the explicit achievements of arms control with the ongoing costs of arms competition and the destruction that a major war would bring, were it to erupt tomorrow, the proponents of peace seem to be engaged in a losing battle. They are running a kind of treadmill, falling further behind. This may be a specific case of the gap between social science and control, on the one hand, and technological change, on the other.

Without the insights and accomplishments of arms control, however, the world would probably be in a worse state. Spaceship earth continues to exist and most of it remains habitable. The very crises through which we have been passing could be the prelude to a more general awakening to the imperatives of non-zero sum politics in the nuclear age. As in 1962-63, looking at the brink of destruction may impel us to policies aimed at cooperation more than conflict. If the statesmen and people of the world have the will, the advances in arms control and related fields of scholarship could provide some of the answers on how to proceed.

While we do not try to tally the overall balance sheet, and while we recognize the negative consequences that certain arms controls may engender, we presume that—given the disposition to make the worst possible case and to err on the side of caution—any agreement which Soviet and U.S. leaders consider to be in their country's interest will probably be useful in countervailing the general thrust toward unrestrained arms race. Unless the superpowers seek jointly to impose their arms control conceptions on lesser states, it is hard to see how U.S.-Soviet constraints can damage the security interests of third parties. Not unless strategic arms levels were drastically reduced would the protective shield offered to Moscow's and Washington's allies be affected by self-imposed limitations like those adopted in SALT I.

Arms control is necessary for peace, but is it sufficient? Wedded to old concepts of *Realpolitik*, arms control will at best succeed in outfoxing the adversary for the time being. If it grows rather from the political idealism incipient in the consciousness of an interdependent world, it could be an important instrument in the struggle to make that world safer and more harmonious.

5 A Modernist Approach to Arms Control: Toward Interdependence

The possibilities and requirements of arms control in the 1970s will be determined *au fond* by the nature of world politics. Two polarized models are possible—the Hobbesian and the Chardinist. The first presumes that international relations, like the relations of men in a primeval state of nature, are anarchical—a perpetual struggle by atomized units against one another, using all means available, and without any ordering principle except the drive to conquer and survive. Juxtaposed to this notion of ceaseless conflict, Teilhard de Chardin proposes that man moves in stages toward hominisation, toward the expansion of reason, the realization of personal fulfillment in a pluralistic community. The distinction parallels that between the extreme conceptions of *Realpolitik* and *Moralpolitik*. These two notions, as E.H. Carr has pointed out, arise from a series of dichotomous views about the nature of man and world politics: the possible vs. the desirable; short- vs. long-range; means vs. ends; pragmatic vs. speculative; *a posteriori* vs. *a priori*; man as self-seeking and unchangeable vs. man as altruistic and malleable.

If one wishes to predict or prescribe, which of these two models should he assume? Neither image is a sufficiently complex representation of reality, for human life—including politics—contains a constantly changing mix from both sets of polarities. If we assume that men are basically good, we will be unprepared for their acts of self-seeking. But if we assume they are exclusively egotistical, we will ignore possibilities for persuasion and inspiration. Similarly, if a government thinks only in terms of utopian blueprints, it will find itself lacking in the means to achieve them. But if it focuses only on the apparently feasible, it will build up the means—primarily the instruments of power—with little idea of their place in an overall strategy.

If hominisation were a *fait accompli* instead of an ideal or a process, by definition there would be no arms control problem, for the global feeling of good will and security would undercut the arms race and any desire to wield arms against others. But while the world contains elements of the Chardinist model and may be moving toward its fuller realization, international politics at critical moments still resembles more Hobbes' war of each against his neighbor. Statesmen, at least, must assume that their governments must protect against a breakdown of the more humanized order so as to be ready for the lupine assaults of external foes. Since we are unlikely in the foreseeable future to eliminate the possibility of a reversion to pure power politics, the arms control problem remains. Indeed, it grows in importance as the engines of destruction become

105

more powerful, cheaper and easier to acquire, spreading to larger numbers of independent actors.

A kind of dialectical approach may be useful, if only to avoid the kind of utopianism-cynicism cycles that accompanied the founding of the League of Nations and United Nations, followed by a failure to achieve their highest expectations. Thus, E.H. Carr has suggested that we should first define our ideals, then seek to implement them, and thirdly—learning from experience—reformulate our ideals and the means for pursuing them.

Assuming that policies on arms and arms control will have to be geared to the survival problems of a Hobbesian world, can these issues be dealt with in a manner that facilitates movement toward a Chardinist world? Can we devise tactical solutions adequate for national competition that are also consonant with progress toward a more humanist and universal order? Such conflicts between means and ends, of course, are not new. Nor are they easy to resolve, as witnessed by the dilemmas of the revolutionary who kills to achieve social justice, the statesman who hides the truth from his people in the name of democracy, or the parent who degrades himself to earn, so that his child may have a better life. Indeed, such choices virtually seem endemic in the human situation.

Design Theory and Policy Science

How can knowledge be utilized to build a more peaceful and prosperous world? Addressing the problem of "Knowledge for Purpose," Alexander George has suggested that students of international relations turn to design theory for procedures that would assist them in translating their scientific insights into action programs.[1] The burgeoning field of policy science is also concerned with problems of application. Some scholars resent suggestions that—like engineering—international studies might be more concerned with application than with pure discovery. But surely there is room for both pure and applied studies in international relations. While there are dangers in developing these ties (*cf.* the geopolitics and anthropology of Hitler's Germany), there may also be mutually beneficial feedback between search and *praxis*. Given the stakes at issue—the survival and quality of human civilization—it would be fatuous to relegate international studies to the ivory tower.

Design theory, Professor George contends, provides analytical frameworks which help policy-makers to understand their options and to formulate procedures, rules, and policies likely to optimize their goals. The establishment of rules to harmonize with subjective values is common currency in most cultures. The American legal system, for example, is structured on the premise that the accused is innocent unless proven guilty. Where there is doubt, jury procedures and other rules tend to favor release of the accused. In medicine, on the other hand, where symptoms or pain exist, doctors are trained to remain suspicious and continue their probes until all doubts have been removed.

Design exercises aim at developing forecasting and other techniques for policy purposes. How do existing situations relate to our basic values? What options are available that would better enhance our basic goals? What are the necessary and sufficient conditions for realizing a preferred alternative future situation? How do we set about moving from "here" to "there"? We may not be able immediately to embark on a rapid journey to a better world, but can we develop a monitoring system that will warn us both of dangers and opportune moments for action?

This chapter attempts to follow these steps in ways that point toward policy principles which, if applied, would enhance such values as war prevention, economic welfare, ecological balance, and social justice.[2]

Current Trends

If we conduct a situational analysis, scanning social and economic indicators, we find that current trends in world arms competition conflict rather seriously with positive human values. We find, for example:

1. A high incidence of wars, large and small, though apparently well below a nuclear threshold;
2. A number of disputes and conflicts which could readily escalate into full-scale violence, with weak machinery for channeling them into peaceful settlement;
3. Heavy investment in most countries in "defense" projects with only limited spillover benefits for urgent domestic problems;
4. Ecological damage resulting from resource depletion and pollution aggravated by arms competition and war;
5. Weapons that could produce unprecedented damage if a major war were to erupt;
6. Military force levels which, though generally growing, produce little or no absolute increase in "national security";
7. Anxieties about shifting balances of power;
8. Weapons of mass destruction not immune to unauthorized or accidental use;
9. Concentrations of influence in persons with special interests in the development and even in the use of modern weapons;
10. Relative neglect of the cultural, social, and economic values which modern governments are expected to promote. Corresponding psychological malaise.

What are the underlying reasons for these trends? This question illuminates the many levels on which the arms race must be studied and the various forces which promote military competition at the expense of arms control.[3] Even where strategic logic might dictate policies conducive to arms limitation, these conclusions may be thwarted by individuals and groups within the power structure with vested interests in the arms race. The *individuals* who make up governments, interest groups, and citizenries have a psyche which, as Thomas Hobbes noted, is diffident and fearful. It may even be aggressive, whether from nature of from nurture. *Domestic pressures* also weigh heavily on decision-makers. Frequently, it appears, the "power elite" will be much more responsive to political hawks, the military-industrial complex, and aggressive forms of "patriotism" than to the constituency favoring arms control, consumerism, brotherhood, and reverence for life.

Conventional forms of *politics among nations* also drive the arms race. Our ESP data showed that "power politics" and "nationalism" are thought to be the most dangerous threats to world peace, followed closely by "misperception and misunderstanding"; "ideology or clash of values"; and "economics (drive for profits or resources, technological dynamism)." "Human nature" and "ecological malaise" were deemed least dangerous among the factors listed.

Do nations seek more "power" because they fear one another or because of internal compulsions (nationalism, the warrior class, military-industrial complex, etc.)? The admixture of external push and internal drive (*Eigendynamik*) probably depends on the time and place. Both have fostered many decisions of the cold war era. Thus, many instruments in the U.S. and Soviet armories have been rationalized if not motivated by the alleged necessity to match or exceed the opponent in every domain of cold war competition, including the arms race. The interaction model is simple but lethal: Nation A perceives a challenge from Nation B (a bomber or missile or ABM or MIRV gap). Frequently, A over-responds, both because he exaggerates the threat and because he prefers to err on the side of caution. If Nation B behaves along similar lines, the resulting spiral is extremely difficult to suppress. The model is not perfect, for Washington and Moscow have sometimes ignored the compulsion to maintain "multiple symmetry" and have often built weapons regardless of the other's specific strengths. But the model explains at least part of the cold war arms race and suggests a mechanism by which the competition could be perpetuated.

The limits which *international organization* places on cold (and hot) war competition are minimal, as illustrated in 1973 by France's refusal to observe an injunction by the International Court of Justice to postpone nuclear testing in the Pacific. Existing international mechanisms for rule formulation and enforcement are quite primitive; the bases for a wide consensus are superficial (compared with residual nationalism and habits of self-sufficiency); the incentives to entrust security and other goals to cooperative programs are weak and inchoate.

The world *environment* adds further complications, for the great (and small) powers respond with alacrity to the whip of technology, even if population and resource pressures are as yet only weakly expressed in most foreign policy decisions. Whatever weapons systems *can* be developed tend to be developed if not deployed. MIRV, for example, was originally rationalized as a means for penetrating the Soviet ABM defenses. Even after those defenses turned out to be rudimentary and even after they were curbed in SALT I, America's MIRV deployment continued. (Russia too presumably continued to work on MIRV development, though she outnumbered Washington in ICBMs and the U.S. ABM was also limited by treaty.) What Robert S. McNamara has termed the "mad momentum" of technology thus adds a synergistic fillip to the insecurities of individuals, the vested interests of certain pressure groups, and the tendency in military decisions to behave "prudently," i.e., on the basis of worst case expectations. The result is a hydra-headed challenge to dispassionate strategic rationality. Even if the logic of the situation calls for arms controls to contain a common threat, nations in conflict may be unable to identify cooperative solutions that would enhance their joint interests. If some leaders perceive these solutions, they may be unable to act on them—due to domestic resistance or non-reciprocation by the adversary. Confronted with such pressures, "rationality" of governments may resemble the traditional wisdom of prisoner's dilemma, as presented by Anatol Rapoport and other specialists in game theory. Given the structure of this predicament, each prisoner tends to choose options that hurt the other prisoner and protect himself if the other prisoner also defects from the common cause. Each prisoner, according to this logic, receives a moderate sentence but avoids execution. Had both thought in terms of a meta-logic emphasizing their interdependence (*prisoners'* dilemma), they could have both gone free (though neither would have received a reward as well as freedom).

Alternative Futures

What are the alternatives to the current trends in military competition? The logical spectrum runs from (1) all-out war to establish some new equilibrium; (2) a more intensive arms race in search for hegemony by one side or another; (3) stabilizing or freezing present military forces, for the superpowers if not for all nations; (4) decreased allocations of men and materials for defense; to (5) broad measures of disarmament (or de-armament).

Since the first two alternatives conflict with war prevention and other humane values, they should be rejected and policies pursued that make them less likely. The last alternative, disarmament, has been the dream of many philosophers and statesmen, but it has only been reached when one side has been defeated in a major war (as in the treaties curtailing Germany's military forces after World Wars I and II). Given the human psyche and the habits of millennia, it may also be that broad-scale disarmament would be dangerous for international peace. Alternatives (3) and (4), while not the best of conceivable worlds, would promise an improvement over the present situation. Policies should therefore be geared toward action programs that would lead to future conditions in which military programs are stabilized or reduced—consonant with the criteria that they make (a) war less likely; (b) the potential damage of war less destructive; and (c) the costs of defense less onerous economically, socially, and politically.

How can the present situation be converted to correspond more with preferred futures? Part of the answer may be derived from the findings of Chapter 3, which concluded that a wide range of underlying conditions were essential to the arms control measures reached by Moscow and Washington in the years from Cuba to SALT I. These conditions ranged across a wide gamut—technological, strategic, political, and economic. Some affected the superpowers from within and some from without; some, directly, others indirectly, e.g., through problems focused in the Third World. Certain conditions appeared as *sine qua non* or at least helpful for arms control, while others seemed harmful. Whether a particular factor exerted a positive or a negative influence depended sometimes on its intensity, for its impact could be reversed if a critical threshold were crossed. Interestingly, symmetry in the forces to be controlled was not always essential for agreements, because acceptable trade-offs could sometimes be found in other domains.

This picture of the conditions favoring arms control in the 1960s and early 1970s may be incomplete, but even if it were perfect, there is no assurance that the requirements of the past would automatically fit the problems to come. Leaderships change; expectations shift; new configurations of forces and inter-relationships emerge. Granted that the structure and character of world politics continue to evolve, we have little choice but to consider the lessons of the recent past as a rough guide to the prerequisites for future arms controls. These lessons must be applied, *mutatis mutandis*, to the different and more complex problems appearing on the horizon: reducing as well as limiting the arsenals of both superpowers; applying qualitative as well as quantitative controls; linking SALT and European arms control; bringing China and other nuclear powers into SALT; strengthening and expanding the nonproliferation treaty and other accords affecting nonnuclear nations.

Design theory urges scientists and governments to "keep score" on the economic and social indicators germane to the values which policies seek to enhance. We should also monitor the movement of underlying conditions postulated as favorable or unfavorable to desired policy outcomes. Monitoring relevant developments worldwide may point to accumulating danger signals as well as moments of opportunity. Study of all the supposed indicators would also suggest whether our theories are correct on the linkages expected between certain goal-oriented policies, underlying conditions, policy outcomes, and optimization of particular values. International social accounting of this kind might reveal unintended or unexpected policy outcomes—whether benign or harmful—correlating with conditions or policies presumed to have the opposite effect. The obstacles to creating a meaningful monitoring system of this kind, of course, are manifold and profound. If we agree on some abstract value such as "social justice," what does this mean in concrete terms? In different societies? What operational indicators will reveal its growth or decline? Can we hope to understand its correlations (if any) with other values, such as ecological balance and economic welfare.

Subjective Requirements

Our efforts at policy planning are complicated further by the fact that, even if we knew the *sine qua non* conditions for preferred outcomes in the past and in the future, these requirements may not take us "all the way." They may be essential or necessary, but not sufficient. The problem is not only that particular vested interests may block rational decisions made in response to overall conditions facing a government and its people. Top leaders may fail to make these decisions because they lack the requisite intelligence, foresight, and moral qualities. Or they may fail to implement such decisions because they are thwarted by associates or citizens' groups who think or feel differently.

Only if a "modernist conception" of arms control is accepted at many levels in national and global society are we likely to obtain the sufficient conditions to contain and reverse the arms race. Our focus until this point has been on the essential objective conditions conducive to arms control. The conditions sufficient to generate and sustain policies in harmony with the objective realities are more subjective. Unless certain values and principles are internalized by the leaders, policy-making elites and wide numbers of ordinary citizens of many countries, the hopes for arms control rationality are slim for the long run.

Principles of a Modernist World View[4]

If we are to move toward a better, rather than a worse, possible world over the next decade, a new way of thinking about arms control problems must be developed. The term "modernist" seems appropriate to characterize this new attitude, because the urgent task is to develop a way of looking at problems that accords with the imperatives of the present and—still more—of the future. If we look at the field of nation-building, a modernist approach denotes a syndrome of policies directed to enhancing economic growth and national unity. These objectives commonly lead to policies aimed at better planning of resource utilization, the cultivation of personal and community incentives, improved education, increased living standards, and broader participation in decision-making.

Similar objectives and means are appropriate to a modernist arms control mentality, except that *world* rather than *national* community must be the criterion shaping the total constellation of policy. While the arms race itself leads to feelings of insecurity, the fact remains that the only way to throttle the roots of arms competition is to build a deeper sense of human community and global security. It would be unrealistic to assume that the underlying sources of international tension can be eliminated in the near or intermediate future, but we can specify minimum characteristics of a modernist arms control approach which are within reach.

Though we cannot hope, in the foreseeable future, to fully eradicate the basic causes of competition in arms, we can still outline the kind of philosophy needed to contain and control it. This outlook would build upon a basic insight which was not widely accepted until the late 1950s: the principle that arms control, like defense policy, should be a means of enhancing national security. Though this principle suggested the need for cooperation among adversaries, and proved useful in providing the rationale for such agreements as the limited test ban, its stress on self-interest may be inadequate for the challenging problems of the 1970s. The outlook necessary for dealing with these problems must contain a broader sense of the common dangers and opportunities facing all mankind— including of course one's own particular country. Some aspects of what we call a modernist approach have been propounded by arms controllers and other political analysts for some time, but the thrust of the total package is different in attempting to bring into focus the roles of political realism and idealism, national and world interests, the contributions of the large and smaller powers.

A modernist philosophy of arms control will include and build upon five principles:

1. Adversaries usually share some interests in common. Their security and economic goals will probably be enhanced in the long run if they can jointly develop the positive sum aspects of their relationship.
2. Preventive arms control is much more feasible than corrective therapy.
3. Power should entail responsibility.
4. The "worth of nations" must be defined more in moral than in military and other material terms.
5. Holistic, long-term planning should guide all decisions on arms and arms control.

The first principle affirms that adversaries usually have interests in common which could be enhanced despite their interests in conflict; the former, in time, could come to overshadow or supplant the latter. Both Soviet and American leaders have espoused this concept and acted on it to some extent. Its rationale has been elaborated in the game theory models of non-zero sum competition and in the ideological position that "peaceful coexistence has elements of cooperation as well as conflict." But while U.S. and Soviet leaders have done much to recognize and build on these insights, much more can be done to convert them into a *modus operandi* rooted not in cold war suspicion but in affirmation of *de facto* interdependence. Even the theory has gained little support from other sets of adversaries, such as Israel and the Arabs or black vs. white Africans. The example of the superpowers, however, has been partially reflected in improved relations between the governments of divided Korea and divided Germany. The possible benefits of mutual cooperation have also been affirmed by the once intransigently hostile governments of President Nixon and Mao Tse-tung/Chou En-lai.

In the long run, it appears, the primordial interests of all political actors would be enhanced if they could base their policies toward each other on the assumption of a positive sum relationship, one in which both could profit if they cooperated over time and shunned the temptation of quick rewards from cheating or other unilateral actions. As the biologist and social philosopher Petr Kropotkin put it, mutual aid—not individual struggle—has been the key to the survival and flourishing of species and civilizations.[5]

Many problems confound this principle. First, the interests of any individual or organization are difficult to define and to order according to rank, *a fortiori* if we speak of nations or even larger groupings. Nonetheless, we can surely hypothesize survival and physical well-being as *sine qua non* conditions for reaching most other interests—two values which arms control should serve. Second, exploitation may "pay" in the short run or even for many years. In the domain of arms control, however, it seems clear that one-sided agreements are unlikely to be entered voluntarily. If they do not satisfy the overall interests of each side, they are likely to be abrogated. The Versailles limitations on Weimar Germany, for example, were one-sided and provided strong incentives to clandestine violation. Only if the other Versailles signatories had themselves disarmed, in accordance with their pledged word, could there be a long-term possibility to keep Germany disarmed. Like the threshold nuclear-weapons states today, Germany called on other powers to reduce their arms or permit her own to increase.[a]

As the pace of history quickens and the events of one continent are readily felt on another, the time frame in which exploitation may be profitable narrows. More than two thousand years ago Plato saw that the tyrant is the least happy of men, because his policies engender opposition, and he cannot long rely on the types of men who would serve him. Adam Smith (followed by Karl Marx) saw that no society can be healthy if large segments of its population are impoverished. As two survivors of Czechoslovakia's travails from 1938 through 1968 have put it: "As long as there are people who are vanquished, all victory is

---

[a]German violation of the Versailles obligations commenced in 1921-23 on the territory of the other pariah—Soviet Russia; these actions were publicly debated in Germany by 1927, but Germany did not withdraw from the League of Nations disarmament discussions and begin openly to rearm until after Hitler came to power.

self-destructive."[6] Thus, Hitler's gains from deceit and conquest in East Central Europe certainly proved short-lived. We might also wonder what would have been Russia's long-term gains had the policies of Stalin and his successors to this region been premised more on mutual aid than on exploitation.

Theoretical models are difficult to test in the muddied waters of historical experience, but we may compare the results of America's basically exploitative policies toward Cuba with those premised more on mutual aid in Puerto Rico. After profiting *some* Americans for decades, the former led to complete estrangement between the two countries, converting the weaker party into a forward base for Washington's major adversary in world politics. U.S.-Puerto Rican relations, though by no means conforming to some ideal standard, have left the majority of Puerto Rican voters content with "Commonwealth" status. If we look for cases in arms control, we find, for example, that the one-sided gamesmanship pursued by Washington and Moscow from 1946 to the mid-1950s netted no accords and some hollow propaganda victories. Only when both sides acted on the premise of non-zero sum interests could they begin to contain their competition to mutual advantage.

The potential value of the second modernist principle is implicit in the saying "An ounce of prevention is worth a pound of cure"; the principle is applied in preventive medicine programs pioneered abroad and recently begun in the United States.

The wisdom and value of preventive action have been intuitively or implicitly accepted by many statesmen of the past and present. As military technology grows more powerful, and as nations' destinies become more interdependent, however, it is of utmost importance that the preventive arms control approach become an explicit and clearly formulated aspect of the policy-making process in every country.

It is one thing to regulate a weapons system already extant or in production; it is another thing to prevent its creation or deployment in the first place. Both logic and the historical record suggest that preventive measures are more feasible than steps taken *after* some weapons system has been developed or deployed. The earlier the development of some weapons system can be averted, the easier the task of assuring that it will not be perfected, produced, and prepared for use in war or in coercive diplomacy.

The importance of the preventive approach is underscored by the fact that virtually every arms limitation since World War II has been preventive in character. Following the imposition of disarmament upon the defeated belligerents after the war, there is only one case when nations voluntarily agreed to dismantle and destroy military facilities and instrumentalities: the convention on the prohibition of the development, production, and stockpiling of bacteriological (biological) and toxin weapons and their destruction, which entered into force in 1972. Washington and London initiated this measure, the USSR and others agreed, in part because biological weapons could prove counterproductive in peace as well as war.[7]

The preventive measures agreed to since 1945 have sought to prohibit the production, deployment, or use of certain military forces *before* these actions have occurred. For example: the demilitarization of Antarctica and partial demilitarization of outer space and the seabed; the prohibition of further nuclear testing in certain environments; the non-transfer and nonacquisition provisions of the nuclear nonproliferation treaty; and the treaty prohibiting nuclear weapons in Latin America. As suggested below in Appendix C, "A Typology of Preventive Arms Controls," many preventive measures have proved feasible (if not always useful) since the Hague Peace Conferences called by Tsar Nicholas failed to produce disarmament but did approve elementary machinery for war prevention and tightened codes on the laws of war. From the Washington Naval Conference to SALT the preventive approach has yielded limitations on both qualitative and quantitative aspects of weaponry; affecting all states or particular regions; sometimes banning war itself as well as certain other military activities. This typology illustrates the wide variety of preventive measures which could be utilized in the future. A detailed analysis of this history would also suggest the conditions in which certain preventive measures endured and proved meaningful while others (such as bans on aerial bombardment and submarine mines adopted at The Hague) were soon violated.

Without elaborating this history here, we should note that U.S.-Soviet negotiations in the early 1970s produced a number of preventive controls, some of which attempted to cope with the greatest theoretical and practical problems for the preventive approach: how to deal with research and development (R & D) on weapons already limited or which nations might one day want to limit. This problem is seen even in the 1972 biological disarmament convention, for it does not prohibit research aimed at production of the specified agents or at development of new warfare agents not banned. Nor are its prohibitions absolutely comprehensive, for they apply only to types and quantities of agents and toxins "that have no justification for prophylactic, protective, or other peaceful purposes."

Most scientific research can have both military and non-military applications. How to ban the former while permitting the other? How can any ban be inspected? Nations might close down one military laboratory in public while opening another in secret. They may also wish to sustain intensive R & D if only to keep abreast of knowledge which the adversary may decide to exploit. If the treaty should be abrogated for any reason, all parties may wish to be ready to resume the once-banned activities. They may also wish to keep some of their best minds employed in military R & D, and may even justify this as a kind of substitute for a real arms race.

Even with relatively benign intentions on both sides, continued R & D can be unsettling to arms controls already agreed to. Both Washington and Moscow agreed in May 1972 to supplement their ABM treaty with a statement that:

in the event ABM systems based on other physical principles and including components capable of substituting for ABM interceptor missiles, ABM launchers, or ABM radars are created in the future, specific limitations on such systems . . . would be subject to discussion in accordance with the ABM treaty's Articles XIII and XIV.[8]

This provision presumably aims at coping with the possibility of "exotic" ABM systems, such as lasers, whose physical characteristics could not be precisely defined at the time of the SALT I accords. As it now stands, the agreed interpretation quoted above is read by some in the U.S. government—particularly in the U.S. Arms Control and Disarmament Agency—as a ban on the deployment of exotic ABMs. But others in Washington interpret the statement less restrictively. They note that the U.S. delegation to SALT I proposed somewhat stricter language for the joint statement which was rejected by the Soviet team. The existing language suggests that if new ABM systems are "created," they may be deployed—subject only to "discussion." Surely their deployment would be allowed if, in practice, both sides agreed. But even if one side objected, it is arguable that—legally speaking—the other signatory might proceed to convert or supplement old ABM systems with those based on newer physical principles, so long as this had been "discussed."

The U.S. and probably the Soviet military R & D establishments continue to investigate ABMs based on new physical principles if only to keep abreast of what the other side might learn from clandestine research. "Civilian" investigations on lasers also proceed apace. Were new ABM systems to become feasible, both sides would probably wish to review their options. How can a government be sure it wants to prohibit some new weapon until something is known about its cost and effectiveness? Those who emphasize this question are challenged by others who demand that politics lead, not follow military R & D.

Despite the difficulty in curbing basic research in any area, the United States and USSR in their 1972 treaty agreed not to "develop, test, or deploy ABM systems or components which are sea-based, air-based, space-based, or mobile land-based . . . [or] ABM launchers for launching more than one ABM interceptor missile at a time . . . [or] systems for rapid reload of ABM launchers." They undertook not to test other types of missiles or radars "in an ABM mode," and to limit the number of ABM launchers at test ranges to fifteen. (None of these limitations, however, need apply to laser research—for ABM or related weapons, such as SAMs.)

Other preventive measures in the ABM treaty were recounted by the Chairman of the Joint Chiefs of Staff in early 1973:

Each Party is limited to no more than 200 ABM missiles and 200 ABM launchers—100 of each for the defense of the national capital, and 100 of each for the defense of an ICBM area.

No more than six ABM radar complexes (excluding, in the case of the USSR, the existing mechanical scan ABM radar complexes) may be deployed for the defense of the national capital, and no more than two large phased-array ABM radars and eighteen smaller ABM radars may be deployed for the defense of the ICBM area; and the center points of the two defended areas must be at least 1,300 kilometers apart. . . .

SAM systems may not be upgraded to ABM capability.

ABM systems and components may not be deployed outside the national territory of each Party and may not be transferred to other states.

In addition, there are various limitations on the capacity of ABM radars, the deployment of early warning radars, the radius or diameter of the defended areas, etc.[9]

The 1972 interim agreement set limits on the numbers and size of strategic offensive weapons each superpower may deploy. The U.S. interpretation holds even that silos may be expanded only in one dimension, and that deployment of mobile ICBMs would violate the spirit of the accord. Neither side, however, seems to have made a serious attempt in SALT I to forestall MIRV. The Americans, for their part, never proposed a MIRV ban without (fatally) linking it with on-site inspection, while the Russians never proposed a ban on flight testing of MIRV—a step that could have given assurance to both sides that these weapons had not been perfected to the point where they could be deployed. As John Newhouse puts it, "The time to have stopped MIRV was August, 1968, before either side had started testing it. After that, it was probably too late. Thus, the invasion of Czechoslovakia, by retarding SALT, may have erased whatever chance there ever was of blocking MIRV deployment."[10]

The 1971-73 negotiations between Moscow and Washington also yielded some measures of crisis control and war prevention: They agreed to

1. modernize the 1963 hot line;
2. prevent incidents at sea;
3. prevent accidental war;
4. avoid actions that could lead to nuclear confrontations between their countries or with third nations.

Spheres of abstention may have also been discussed, just as spheres of influence were considered in earlier talks, e.g., between Stalin and Churchill in 1944. Agreements outlawing the use of force to settle disputes have been concluded between Bonn and many members of the Warsaw Pact, including the USSR.

Except for the accord to eliminate biological weapons, the great powers have reached no measure of disarmament or even arms reduction. What of the future? The vast numbers of strategic delivery systems available to Moscow and Washington make it possible for the superpowers to contemplate their reduction. Even the 1972 interim agreement looked forward to phasing out some weapons (and replacing them with more modern ones). Subsequent rounds of negotiations can and should go at least some distance toward force reductions, if only of obsolete or redundant systems. The more than 7,000 tactical nuclear weapons under U.S. control in Europe could be drastically reduced without impairment to European security. If Moscow reciprocated by cutting the forces in which the USSR is particularly strong, a downward spiral could get underway.[12] Conversely, a new generation of tactical nuclear weapons for NATO will put pressure on the Kremlin to respond in kind.

Even if preventive measures are agreed to on a timely basis, they will be difficult to sustain if one of the parties feels itself to be "have-not," unfairly or unnecessarily discriminated against. Preventive measures may be thwarted not only by explicit repudiation, but by technological innovation or by escape clauses permitting "modernization" of obsolete or worn-out equipment.[13]

Despite these drawbacks, preventive arms control remains one of the most hopeful and important ways for the superpowers and others to curb their competition to mutual advantage. As in the case of the treaty governing outer space, an accord may reassure each side that it need not deploy weapons in some new arena simply to maintain symmetry. Such accords also help to build and maintain a climate conducive to further-reaching measures. Finally, the grim lesson of history is that the most awesome weapons developed are likely to be produced and deployed unless curbed in advance by joint agreement.

The third modernist principle holds that the worth—indeed, the wealth—of nations must be defined more in moral than in military and other material terms. If we measure grandeur in terms of assured destruction capability, our long-term fate will be like that of lemmings marching to collective suicide. The dignity of nations will rather be found in moral equivalents to war, e.g., scientific and cultural discovery; providing models of economic development consistent with ecological well-being; and steering men from egotistical materialism to a broader identification with the global human community and with other beings in the chain of life. Military power does not ensure omnipotence, as Moscow and Washington have learned in Albania, Vietnam, and elsewhere.

It goes without saying that the realization of any national or transnational value is dependent upon the physical survival and wellbeing of the population. Our values also demand that each people be free to choose its own course, free from external dictation (unless their activities infringe on the basic rights of others, e.g., by nuclear tests that contaminate the world's resources). Assuming that basic physical necessities have been assured, however, the modernist conceptions of worth and wealth anticipate a world in which peoples will be proud of themselves—not because they have exploded atomic bombs and wedded them to delivery systems—but because of their achievements in the humanities, sciences, in upgrading their own and others' living and cultural standards.

The giants have feet of clay in many respects. The changing essence of usable power means that both material objectives and national influence are increasingly realizable through economic and moral growth rather than through stockpiling the tools of warfare.[14] Thus, idealistic appeals are to some extent reinforced by realistic appraisals of the world environment.

So long as governments and peoples believe their prestige and influence depend primarily upon military—especially nuclear—power, the chances are low for limiting the spread of nuclear arms. Thus, the French and British Governments seem to believe that their participation in world affairs depends upon keeping up nuclear forces, even if at a substantially lower level than those of the superpowers. Put another way, some Indians have stated that their country needs an atomic bomb—not so much for defense—but to energize a divided and lethargic nation, and to renew its confidence that its capabilities are not inferior to those of its most powerful rival, Communist China.

The fact that the nuclear powers themselves—Washington no less than Peking—reaffirm on occasion the political and strategic importance of their atomic weapons makes the lack of such arms more sorely felt in the threshold states. Nevertheless, the prospects are not totally bleak. We have the example of Canada, a nation that has deliberately refrained from developing nuclear weapons, though she long has had the capability. Sweden and Switzerland have conducted their industrial development so as to keep open an option to go nuclear, but have not yet exercised it. French political leaders such as Mitterand and numerous voices in the left wing of the British Labour Party have called for opting out of the nuclear arms race.

The most hopeful attitudes, however, have been articulated in West Germany and Japan, where strong voices have risen suggesting that national pride and influence should be sought by political and economic development rather than military. To be sure, some influential German and Japanese leaders and intellectuals believe that their countries will never play a world political role proportionate to their economic strength unless they acquire nuclear arms. But others argue that there is no point attempting to compete militarily with the superpowers, and that the limited resources of middle powers such as Germany and Japan should rather be expended in economic and technological enterprises, the product of which will net greater political influence than costly maintenance of miniature nuclear forces. Happily for the proponents of such arguments, technological ventures such as Japan's space program and West Germany's atomic energy program keep alive the industrial capabilites that can be converted to advanced military purposes if alliances and collective security fail.

Fourth, power connotes responsibility. This should not be read as a claim for some broad privileges or the premise that "might makes right." Still less should it support hoary notions of a "civilizing" (or "revolutionary") mission that might justify forceful interventions abroad. Whether power is actively used or kept at home, however, its existence ineluctably affects the fortunes of others in an interdependent world. The modernist conception therefore argues that it should be used responsibly, in accordance with the other four principles.

This principle, like that which calls for redefinition of the worth of nations, helps to confront the crucial question of which party will take the first steps needed to break a vicious circle or prevent one from evolving. No matter what area of arms competition we examine, we find a dynamism fed by many factors. The balance of power is rarely acceptable to all sides, so that agreement to freeze the situation requires a degree of sacrifice for one or more participants. On occasion, a few nations may take an initiative to stabilize a situation acceptable to them but not to others, e.g., the U.S.-U.K.-Soviet accord on nuclear testing. Frequently, however, the major adversaries find themselves at odds regarding the opportune moment to stifle some aspect of their competition. Examples abound. Will the U.S. acquiesce in Soviet strategic parity or renew its drive to maintain a vast superiority? Will India or Japan acquiesce in a nonproliferation accord that denies them nuclear weapons but permits them to China? What recipient of arms in the Middle East will be the first to say, "We have enough"? What supplier of arms to that troubled area will say, "We will ship no more arms and call on other suppliers to follow our example"?

If absolute power and wealth are the only variables, it seems clear that the stronger nations should take the lead in initiatives for peace, since they have the margin of security and the means to rebuild their power if a particular first step proves abortive. Thus, for example, the more affluent suppliers of arms—whatever their balance of payments dilemmas—should take the lead in cutting sales to the Middle East. But other variables do exist and they complicate the problem considerably. Power, for example, is relative to commitments. Different levels of power may be needed to defend rather than attack, etc. Nevertheless, since all states can claim various kinds of extenuating circumstances, it is still the responsibility of the most powerful—and enlightened—governments to mobilize their resources and creativity to identify and take the first steps for peace.

Mindful of the perception problems and interaction cycles that exacerbate international relations, psychologist Charles E. Osgood has suggested that nations deliberately embark on a strategy of graduated reciprocation in tension-reduction (GRIT). Though either side may initiate such a policy, the party with greater wealth and power may do so with less risk. The initiating party should announce to the other side that it seeks to de-escalate their tensions and is commencing with steps to demonstrate its goodwill; if these are reciprocated, even larger initiatives for peace will be undertaken.[15] Many problems can confound a program of this kind. It may be difficult to rally domestic support; to find initatives which will not weaken one's own vital interests but which still persuade the adversary of one's good intentions; to sustain the program while the other side contemplates how to respond; to maintain momentum in the face of crises in the Third World; to avoid the temptation to abuse concessions by the other side so as to gain the upper hand, at least temporarily. Despite all these problems, many aspects of the GRIT strategy appear to have been helpful in easing U.S.-Soviet tensions in 1962-63 and in 1972-73. In both instances, arms control measures formed part of the larger ensemble of moves toward de-escalation. Coining a term less onerous than "unilateral disarmament" or "GRIT," Khrushchev called for "disarmament by mutual example."

Though the moves of each side must be reciprocated in order to gather momentum, we are left with a need for someone to take the initial steps, and to help steady the boat if the waves begin to rock it. Hence the requirement of responsibility implied in power.

There is also a narrower domain in which this principle applies: Whichever nation appears to lead in some field of military technology should take the initiative in formulating rules of preventive arms control. Usually, the opposite has been the case. Thus, Washington called in the mid-1950s for a ban on the deployment of mass destruction weapons (ICBMs) that would fly through outer space. Moscow agreed with this sentiment, but killed it with the demand that the United States disband her foreign bases. Similarly, the Soviets opposed any ban on ABMs so long as their lead was exclusive and well established. When U.S. technology overtook Soviet, and Washington played its bargaining chip, negotiations on ABM commenced in earnest. U.S. restraint in the ABM case was quite helpful; Washington's headlong rush into MIRV deployment made serious negotiations impossible. Power should connote restraint as well as enlightened initiative.

The fifth modernist principle is implicit in the others: the need for holistic, long-term planning in all decisions affecting arms and arms control. Each decision of this kind is more than the sum of its parts (costs, resources, etc.) and affects the entire climate and structure of world affairs, including the physical ecology.

The arms race is but one example of modern technological developments that threaten the wellbeing of every country and people inhabiting spaceship earth. It is the cutting edge of an ecological crisis that threatens to overtake the world unless all nations—rich and poor—concert their efforts to cope with its dangers. In arms control, as in other ecological problems, we must adopt a preventive approach as well as look for therapies for existing problems.[16]

A holistic, long-range approach to policy planning would help nations to pass up the quick-fix or exploitative gain that serves them for a time, but which may boomerang in the long run. Looking to the future, statesmen will see common interests—not merely in survival but in the optimal use of resources—outweighing disagreements over ideology, boundaries, and spheres of influence; they will act today to thwart the development and deployment of arms that will raise that cost and danger of weapons competition tomorrow. Looking to the future, the governments that are the most powerful and those (large and small) which are the most noble will commit more of their energy and prestige to the initiatives necessary to build a safer and more prosperous world.

More generally, however, the call for a futurist orientation denotes the basic thrust appropriate for a modernist approach to arms control. This approach assumes that traditional ways of thinking and traditional institutions must be efficiently adapted if not profoundly revised just to keep pace with the dangers as well as the opportunities inherent in the ongoing revolutions in technology and society.

Many observers have pointed to the role of "worst case" assumptions in fueling the arms race, despite the fact that, as Marshall D. Shulman has noted, "the 'worst case analysis' has rarely, perhaps never been borne out." One root of the problem is the difficulty of anticipating the adversary's arms plans over a five or seven year period, i.e., the lead time required to move from weapons design to production. Though planners prefer to err on the side of caution, could we "not learn something from experience of the range of reasonable projections," since the extreme interpretation of prudence has often "served to decrease rather than increase our security?" Furthermore, recognizing the destabilizing effect of weapons innovations, could we not better control the innovation process rather than accepting it as inevitable?[17]

Holistic planning also implies a caveat: The principles of the modernist approach may not be applicable in all times and places. If either party will seize upon any concession and strive to turn it to his own advantage, graduated reciprocation in tension-reduction or peace-building is impossible. Positive sum characteristics of relationships cannot be cultivated if one party emphasizes the negative sum aspects.

Prudence, in these circumstances, may call for limiting one's vulnerabilities. Economic factors, at times, may dictate policies based on self-sufficiency. The prospects of technological breakthroughs or other "x" factors likely to unsettle bonds of collaboration must also be considered. Alternatively, if nations put their greatest value on expressive release and gratification of national sentiments rather than on pragmatic or instrumental results, they too might better go it alone. Statesmanship, in sum, requires a judgment as to whether the tenor of the times makes the modernist approach feasible and desirable in terms of national objectives. Given the difficulty in assessing the dangers and opportunities of specific moments, U.S. relations with the Soviet Union should be understood and maintained as "multidimensional in order that we may oppose where necessary and collaborate where possible, having always in mind a longer-term sense of direction toward the moderation of conflict."[18]

From Arms Control to Interdependence

Wherever feasible, the principles of the modernist approach should be expanded from the realm of arms and arms control to form guidelines for the conduct of foreign policy in general. Indeed, it is unlikely that they can be applied with any consistency in the sensitive area of arms competition unless parallel policies are conducted in other domains of domestic and foreign affairs. Pursued in a number of vital policy arenas, the approach would probably gain the benefits of a multiplier effect. On the other hand, if quite contrary policies were applied, say, in economic relations to less developed countries, their consequences would tend to subvert modernist efforts in arms control.

The chances that the modernist approach to arms control will achieve positive results in relations among nation-states will be greatly enhanced if complementary policies are pursued at other levels of world politics: from the individual to the global environment. Indeed, all change in world affairs is contingent upon the degree to which individuals accept the modernist or any other world view. Governments' official policies affecting war and peace will be conditioned—perhaps overwhelmed—by domestic factors such as succession crises or scandals as well as by transnational movements of people, ideas, resources. As a team of Soviet experts have written, "international relations" is the entire complex of "economic, political, ideological, legal, diplomatic, and military connections and mutual relations among peoples, among states and systems of states, among the basic social, economic, political forces and organizations, operating in the world arena."[19]

But we must also bear in mind that policies are to serve people—individual human beings—and not vice versa. As Lincoln P. Bloomfield has put it, "neither states nor ideology nor things but people [should] represent the highest value for American policy."[20]

Bloomfield also advocates a "final litmus-paper test for policy," one that underscores the linkages among the many dimensions of policy, and relates them to the individual:

After we ask "Is it strategically important"?—which we must—and after we ask "Is it politically feasible or viable"?—which we must—and after we ask "Is it cost-effective"?—which we should—perhaps the greatest lesson of Vietnam for the United States is that we should also ask *"Is it humane"?* This is not a substitute for the other questions. But only with this additional question, or so it seems to me, can we cure the sickness that has crept into the veins of American foreign policy.[21]

Each country and every individual suffers from comparable sicknesses, to one degree or another. Wherever we live and whatever our position, we might heed another maxim: "Heal thyself." For the superpowers and others, part of the treatment entails curbing the arms race. Some of our ills can be treated locally, but some need regional or worldwide projects of control and cooperation.

As basic elements of foreign policy generally, the modernist axioms would be helpful not only in limiting arms competition but in transforming the cold war relationship of Moscow and Washington into a mutually beneficial network of interdependence.[22] The cold war has been fueled not only by the dynamics of the arms race, but by ideological, political, economic, and cultural conflicts, all exacerbated by misperception and accumulated habits of distrust and disbelief.

Arms control can be an instrument not only for maintaining communications and relaxing tensions but for moving from détente toward entente.

An expanded recognition of Soviet and American interdependence at many levels does not require the political systems of each country to "converge" toward some common model. Historical and cultural factors make it likely that public ownership of the means of production and a predominantly one-party system will continue in the USSR for the foreseeable future, just as private enterprise and competitive parties appear likely to endure in the United States. The negative aspects of each system can be tempered without destroying its foundations. And each system can be adjusted in ways that make it possible to expand the realms of cooperative interaction. Some domains will be more resistant to change than others; e.g., the Soviets are sensitive to free exchanges of cultural and political information. But such rigidities have not prevented the growth of bilateral programs in significant areas of science, medicine, trade, etc. Positive experiences in a variety of fields, nurtured over years, will probably exert a cumulative effect enhancing the prospects for cooperation in other domains.[b]

Will the development of bilateral Soviet-American relations harm the interests of third parties? Will the superpowers act in tandem to exploit weaker countries and curb the growth of all challengers? These contingencies are theoretically possible, but highly unlikely in the 1970s and beyond. First of all, the non-zero sum consciousness required for the evolution of interdependent action programs can hardly be confined to two countries. Were it to stop short of embracing all mankind, it would more likely be confined to groupings which already have more in common culturally and economically than the two military superpowers. In practice, both the Soviet Union and the United States depend too much on other countries to mount coordinated action programs against them. Nor do they have the will for such adventures. Despite their use of the carrot and the stick, the superpowers have been unable to persuade Israel, India, and some other potential nuclear-weapons countries to adhere to the nonproliferation treaty. Their means for imposing any kind of regimen on Europe, China, or Japan are still more limited. The trade and other ties linking the United States with Canada, Western Europe, and Japan are incomparably stronger than any that can be conceived with the USSR in the middle-range future. These industrialized nations are also allied militarily with Washington. Their mutual interdependence is a fact of long standing.[23] It need not be jeopardized by an

---

[b]The agreements signed during Brezhnev's visit to the United States in June 1973 covered cooperation in developing peaceful uses of atomic energy; in oceanography; in transportation, with emphasis on research into cold-weather operations; in agricultural research, including "the regular exchange" of information on long-term estimates of production; and on income taxes paid by each country's citizens living in the other country.

Brezhnev urged development of large-scale, long-term trade, involving billions of dollars and agreements for up to 15 years.

"We want the further development of our relations to become a maximally stable process," he said, "and what is more, an irreversible one."

expansion of U.S. ties with the Soviet Union. As the military component in world affairs becomes less salient and usable, the non-military assets of the other great powers will exert a weightier influence than they did in the pre-SALT era.

Does the shift from relatively tight bipolarity to multipolar politics signify that the future of world peace is becoming increasingly dependent on the good will of all nations? Does implementation of a modernist approach to arms control and other issues by the superpowers depend upon reciprocal behavior by all other political entities, large and small? Can U.S.-Soviet détente be derailed by third parties as readily as Black September upset the Israel-Arab dialogue in 1971-72? Would a U.S.-Soviet entente be as vulnerable to third party action as the 1972-73 Paris accords on Indochina were to unilateral actions by Saigon? If the superpowers moved to convert the United Nations into an effective instrument of international cooperation and collective security, would their handiwork be as fragile as the League of Nations confronted by the aggression of a Mussolini or a Hitler?

The answer to most of these questions is, "Not necessarily." The impact of refractory behavior by other parties could limit the *scope* of U.S. and Soviet actions affecting world peace. But there are many realms where those nations who choose to cooperate may do so, despite objections by others. To begin with, military power remains concentrated in the two superpowers. Few experts expect Europe or China to close the gap between their nuclear arsenals and those of the superpowers in the 1970s. If Washington and Moscow wish to regulate their own arms competition in accord with the principles of the modernist approach, they have the means to do so.

The behavior of China and the European nuclear states can make it easier or more difficult for the superpowers to reach bilateral accommodations. But it is in the interest of the lesser nuclear powers not to provoke the USSR or the United States into building massive ABM systems or other weapons that would downgrade the smaller arsenals maintained in China and Europe. Few experts expect the Chinese to behave less rationally or responsibly than the leaders of other nuclear powers.[24] One might rather anticipate that the influence of a nuclear China may make it less likely that the superpowers would engage in nuclear brinkmanship vis-à-vis each other or intervene with conventional forces in the domestic affairs of other states. China and the European nuclear states, in turn, have a vested interest in freezing the nuclear-weapons club at its present size.

Going beyond the military sphere, what Adam Smith posited for the domestic health of a single country probably pertains with increasing force to the entire planet: If there are substantial numbers of people anywhere who are impoverished—or feel themselves deprived in other ways—the consequences will be negative for the entire planet. If there is starvation or genocide or cultural oppression anywhere, we can recall John Donne's admonition: "Any man's death diminishes me."

How soon we will recognize and act on these truths is uncertain. For the modernist approach to take hold and become effective, it must be adopted not only by particular governments but by large numbers of their people. Without reciprocity, no government is likely to pursue this approach for long toward others.

Ideally, the policies of all countries will increasingly be premised on the principles of mutual advantage and mutual aid, rather than on suspicion or hopes for unilateral gain. Clearly, years, decades, centuries, perhaps millennia will be needed to make non-zero sum politics a basic feature of global society. While the Chardinist model of world politics remains distant, we can nevertheless plot a path that moves the superpowers and other countries in that direction, along whatever dimensions and at whatever rates prove feasible.

Each of us plays a vital role on one or more levels of world politics. Each individual's conduct helps determine whether we move toward or away from principles like those adhering to the modernist conception. Americans, if only by virtue of their material wealth, can and should assume a leading role in the planning and initiatives necessary to move the world toward implementation of the modernist principles—toward an affirmative interdependence—not just of the superpowers, but of all mankind.

Appendixes

Appendix A

Propositions on Soviet External Conduct

A systematic survey of American writing on Soviet foreign policy by William Welch finds that the leading studies on this subject view the Kremlin's conduct as falling within three categories: ultrahard; hard; or mixed (i.e., neither hard nor soft). Allegorically, these categories correspond to images of a Great Beast; a Mellowing Tiger; and a Neurotic Bear. Though U.S. academic views differ in this way, the survey concludes that there is little dissent on the following propositions:

1. that "Soviet conduct is hardly to be described as peaceable";
2. that "its aims include the spread of communism and expansion of Soviet influence";
3. that "in pursuit of these aims it is active, militant, and not too moral";
4. that "it employs military force and the threat thereof cautiously";
5. and that "it treats its own, namely, other Communist states, no more considerately than the rest of the world."[a]

That this survey, the most systematic ever undertaken of U.S. images of Soviet foreign policy, summarizes the American consensus in this manner is distressing. The first proposition appears to be polemical, aimed perhaps against Soviet characterizations of Moscow's policy. Stated in the negative, it tells us nothing positive. How are we to understand "peaceable"? If Moscow's policy is not peaceable, can we understand this by reference to another country whose policy is peaceable? The ESP data and other surveys show a broad consensus among experts that the United States has, at least in 1969-72, demonstrated a greater propensity to use armed force to achieve her objectives than the USSR.

The second proposition is also imprecise. It holds that Soviet aims *include* certain objectives. But what else do they include? And how important is the "spread of communism" compared with the "expansion of Soviet influence," e.g., toward the Persian Gulf?

Contrary to the thrust of Welch's statement, most Western writing in recent years distinguishes sharply between Moscow's concern for "national interest" and its concern with the "spread of communism," placing the former far above the latter in importance. Further, as Welch's survey also indicates (in another

[a]*American Images of Soviet Foreign Policy: An Inquiry into Recent Appraisals from the Academy Community* (New Haven and London: Yale University Press,1970), p. 26. See also William Welch and Jan F. Triska, "Soviet Foreign Policy Studies and Foreign Policy Models," *World Politics*, XXIII, No. 4 (July 1971), pp. 704-733. See also note 3 to Chapter 1, where the findings of Triska and Finley seem at variance with the dominant images reported by Welch.

place), it is important to distinguish among policies aimed at defending the status quo and those extending one's power still further.

The third proposition lumps activism, militancy, and morality in one grouping (though the author separates them later on), a practice that could only lead to confusion. Welch also seems to ignore here writers, such as Frederick L. Schuman (whom he discusses later as a paradigm proponent of the Neurotic Bear image), who emphasizes the extent to which Soviet conduct has been reactive rather than active.

The fourth proposition strikes this writer as basically sound, though use of the word "cautiously" to describe Soviet use of military force and threat does not seem very helpful. Rather, one would want to know: *In what circumstances* did Moscow behave "cautiously," and when was caution thrown to the winds? A Cuban gambit every decade might end in a global holocaust.

The fifth proposition also seems fairly sound, though its use of the word "considerate" to evaluate Moscow's policy toward its "own" and "others" again intrudes sentiment and imprecision into an analysis that attempts to be scientific.

After surveying American writing on Soviet external behavior, Welch concludes that there is little solid evidence to support the model of the Great Beast of the Apocolypse, but that there is empirical support for the Mellowing Tiger and Neurotic Bear models. He proceeds to underscore, "correlatively," five certain "truths" about Soviet conduct (pp. 172-173). These "truths," I would argue, are much more defensible than the five propositions that Welch ascribes to the American academic consensus, but they are still too weak to support as generalizations. His first point is quite sound: that Soviet conduct has been intermittently rather than continuously expansive, moments of extension (e.g., 1939-41) being interspersed with moments of mere preservation (e.g., 1921-39) and moments of contraction (e.g., 1955-56). The second point is that Soviet behavior has varied in time between high and moderate militancy. As periods of "moderate militancy," Welch cites the early 1920s and the 1950s. What this example suggests is that Welch's whole approach is rather one-dimensional, for it omits the possibility that the USSR at these times was simultaneously pursuing a policy of rapprochement with the West, perhaps even a strategy of interdependence. If aspects of Soviet policy were "militant," other aspects were conciliatory.

Welch makes the third point that Soviet policy has varied between substantial and low addiction to the military instrument, the periods 1946-49 and 1953 on exemplifying these two values. Though Welch's general point seems sound, his historical examples suggest a failure to think through the kind of distinctions made by Thomas Schelling between "compellence" and other uses of military force such as "deterrence" or indirect influence. Fourth, Welch concedes that Soviet conduct is not wholly initiatory, "but at times responsive ... to challenges from environing states...." This is an important point, but—as shown in the work by Triska and Finley cited in note 3 to Chapter 1—the phrase "at times responsive" could well be changed to "often" or even "usually." Fifth, a point on which only the Great Beast theoreticians would take issue: Soviet conduct is not changeless, but has undergone significant change over time. When Welch stresses how Soviet conduct has "especially . . . moderated in the post-Stalin period," however, the thrust of his conclusion is questionable. Surely the Khrushchev and the Brezhnev regimes have carried out some policies much more adventurous (missiles to Cuba; pilots to Egypt, etc.) than those of Stalin in the 1920s and 1930s.

In summary, the major defects of Welch's own propositions are twofold: first, he analyzes Soviet policy mainly along a continuum more or less militant, forgetting that the Kremlin may *simultaneously* be moving toward an orientation of peace and cooperation; second, in stressing factors of change, Welch overlooks elements of continuity or of circularity, elements that see Moscow reverting in the 1950s or 1960s to policies devised and tested—*mutatis mutandis*—in the 1920s and 1930s.

Another kind of imprecision is found in Welch's discussion of basic classifications for individual and state behavior. After analyzing the classificatory schemes of Eric Fromm, Hans Morgenthau, and others, Welch endorses that of his former teacher, Arnold Wolfers, as the most useful: i.e., a distinction based on whether a policy aims at self-extension; self-preservation; or self-abnegation. Still, as Welch points out, even Wolfers' scheme is logically incomplete, because it omits the category of "contraction, retraction, liquidation, or what you will." But there is still another lacuna that Welch himself misses. This gap is his failure to include as a logical possibility a strategy or interdependence, one based on a recognition that politics can be a non-zero sum game. By emphasizing the dichotomy between "egotism" and "altruism," Welch ignores the possiblity that a policy of enlightened self-interest might benefit one's own country and other countries as well) pp. 32-34).[b]

This theoretical shortcoming may explain Welch's fixation on the military or militant side of Soviet behavior, a focus that overlooks the fact that relations between the USSR and the West can have elements of cooperation simultaneous with elements of conflict.

A more logically complete spectrum of Soviet policies (or those of any state) would proceed from the basic distinctions noted by Arnold Wolfers—self-preser-

[b]Not by accident, perhaps, Welch lists only one non-traditional international relations text to see whether it offers images that would be more useful than those developed by Morgenthau, Wolfers, et al. (p. 34). This is George Modelski's 1962 study adapting systems analysis to foreign policy. Had Welch gone further in his survey of international relations literature as a whole, surely he would have given greater emphasis to game theory and other approaches that might enrich the discussion of Soviet foreign policy. (He does cite some other works and bibliographies on pp. 181-185, but continues to reemphasize Modelski and one or two other examples of systems analysis. Had Welch not excluded "limited" studies of aspects of Soviet policy, such as those on the military-arms control dimension or on foreign aid, he might have found other fruitful approaches in Western literature on the USSR.)

vation; self-extension; self-abnegation—and by Professor Welch: contraction or retraction. But it would add what we call a strategy of interdependence.

The Welch-Wolfers terminology is revised and put forward in the present book as follows:

Self-Preservation = Status Quo Policy

This may be in regard to territorial frontiers or social systems operative therein or great power spheres of influence. The status quo policy may be pursued militantly (as in Czechoslovakia 1968) or supportively (as in propping the Polish economy 1970-71).

Self-Extension = Forward Strategy

This may be pursued by leftist, direct means, or by an indirect advance, using rightist tactics in an indirect advance.

Self-Abnegation

Omitted in the present book because there is little historical basis for including it, though Bukharin sought to rest Soviet survival in 1918 on the success of a revolutionary war against Germany.

Contraction = Isolationism or partial withdrawal from all or some foreign involvements.

Strategy of Interdependence

This may be carried out with regard to other Communist states; the West; or the Third World. As applied to the developing countries, it could be manifested in a development orientation, carried out in cooperation or in competition with the West.

Some of these orientations can coexist simultaneously, even in a single part of the world, but one or some can come to the fore, universally, regionally, or vis-à-vis particular countries.

Whatever its shortcomings, Welch's *American Images of Soviet Foreign Policy* is an important and seminal book that should move Western students of the USSR to be more self-conscious and systematic in their work, whether they adhere more to a traditionalist or behavioral persuasion.

Appendix B

The Arms Control Spectrum
in Soviet Thinking

The three stages in Lenin's view of disarmament outlined in Chapter 2 correspond in part with a six-part typology of Soviet arms policy outlined by Franklyn Griffiths,[a] adapting language originally used by Robert A. Levine to analyze the arms debate among U.S. strategists: I. Anti-imperialism: (a) systemic and (b) marginalist; II. Middle marginalism: (a) activist and (b) analytic; and III. Antiwar views: (a) marginalist and (b) systemic.

The analysis presented here and that of Griffiths concur that the early Lenin was a systemic anti-imperialist, dedicated to eliminating the capitalist system as the *sine qua non* for achieving a world without war. As the Soviet Government entered arms control negotiations in the early 1920s, however, the Comintern assumed a "marginalist anti-imperialist" posture, because it was willing to use the negotiations as a means of promoting world revolution through politics of exposure. A similar attitude was taken by Stalin even as Litvinov put forward the Soviet proposals for general or partial disarmament from 1927 to 1933. This view continued to be held by Molotov, Kaganovich, and other opponents of Khrushchev in the mid-1950s. (Griffiths places Defense Minister Malinovsky and his successor, Marshal Grechko, among the marginalist anti-imperialists, together with some commentators in the military press. This placement is probably justified by the public record of their speeches and writings. It seems doubtful, however, that their dedication to revolution has been dogmatically strong, or even that they have favored a forward strategy in foreign policy. The anti-imperialist flavor of their public statements is probably due more to a concern to maintain or increase the budget for defense.)

The middle position along Griffiths' spectrum seeks both to promote anti-imperialism *and* to reduce the danger of war. In its activist variant this view emphasizes arms control policies likely to promote revolution from below, an aim sometimes mentioned by Stalin in the late 1920s and by Khrushchev in 1956. A second variant, labeled "analytical middle marginalism," seeks to exploit the presence of both a hawkish and a sober tendency among Western elites. For Griffiths, both the Lenin of 1922 and Khrushchev of the early 1960s fit this model. But while both men sought to manipulate contradictions in the West, it would seem that Lenin (in this second stage) seemed to view disarmament basically as a tactic, while Khrushchev (developing a third stage only adumbrated by Lenin) saw disarmament as a viable and desirable objective.

[a]See his "Inner Tensions in the Soviet Approach to 'Disarmament'," *International Journal*, XXII, No. 4 (Autumn 1967), pp. 593-617. Portions of that analysis are further extended in Griffiths' "Genoa plus 51: Changing Soviet Objectives in Europe," *Wellesley Paper* 4 (June 1973) (Toronto: Canadian Institute of International Affairs).

This objective may also have been shared in 1954 by Malenkov, who after being attacked by Khrushchev (in temporary alliance with Molotov) later saw his arms control position carried on by the man who defeated him. Disarmament as a strategic goal may have helped to motivate the work of Chicherin and Litvinov, but among professional Soviet Foreign Ministers only Gromyko lived to see the achievement of far-reaching arms control agreements between the Soviet Union and the Western governments.

To the right of the middle marginalists are those who are more concerned with eliminating war than with overcoming imperialism. If we could modify Griffiths' scheme, this group should probably include the Stage III Leninists who believe that technology and other factors can or should make war obsolete. The priority of state interests over revolutionary ones certainly helps to explain Khrushchev's willingness to break with Peking over the nuclear test ban and other issues in the early 1960s. Griffiths, however, puts no government officials or Party leaders in this category. Instead, he lists a number of international lawyers, historians, economists, and a retired general as "anti-war marginalists." The extreme position of "anti-war systematism" is reserved only for the "Soviet people." Griffiths would presumably agree, however, that only *some* Soviet people occupy this position, for many have displayed a xenophobic and aggressive attitude on such occasions as the Ussuri River boundary dispute with China in 1969.

Appendix C

A Typology of Preventive Arms Controls

A basic distinction must be made between quantitative and qualitative measures of preventive arms control. Both types of measures, however, must be analyzed according to their degree of generality:

1. all actors or some subset (e.g., non-nuclear weapons states);
2. all weapons systems or some subset (e.g., germ warfare);
3. all specified weapons or some subset (e.g., a percentage ratio of existing levels).

Quantitative Restrictions

1. Weapons Systems. One set of quantitative measures pertains to existing or planned weapons systems. A classic example of this approach was the decision of the Washington Naval Conference (1921-22) to limit the capital ships of the United States, Britain, Japan, France, and Italy according to ratios of 5, 5, 3, 1.75, 1.75. The tonnage ratios adopted meant that the United States could increase her capital ships from 16 to 18, while Britain had to decrease hers from 32 to 20, while Japan's fleet remained stable at ten capital ships. (France and Italy were to lay down new tonnage at later, specified dates.) Thus, the conference illustrated the point that arms control may result in an increase, a decrease, or a freeze in the number of existing armaments.

The Washington Conference also showed that arms controls are easier to achieve in areas deemed to be militarily insignificant or where technological uncertainties have been largely removed. Battleships were deemed to be obsolete and not cost-effective by many observers in the early 1920s. Significantly, the conference placed no limit on the number of auxiliary ships or submarines, not to speak of air and land forces generally, though it did set an upper limit for aircraft carrier construction. A convention sought by the United States and Britain to restrict submarine warfare was resisted by France and failed for her lack of ratification. On the other hand, the United States, Britain, and Japan agreed to maintain the status quo with regard to fortification on specific Pacific island possessions. There were also accords reached on the withdrawal of foreign troops from China and Siberia. Nevertheless, the point remains that the Washington conferees failed to achieve the most meaningful kind of preventive arms controls, i.e., they failed to come to terms with the most salient dangers of the future.

The 1972 SALT accords have been criticized on similar grounds. They permitted each superpower to retain or build up to the quantitative levels already planned for 1972-77, while failing to grapple with multiple warheads and other technological innovations expected to be most significant in the future. In June 1973, however, both superpowers pledged not to rest on the record and to continue with efforts to reduce their strategic forces and curb their qualitative as well as quantitative features.

2. The Number of States. A second type of quantitative measure is concerned with the number of states possessing certain kinds and levels of armaments. The Washington naval agreements, for example, bound only the five contracting parties, because no other states were then in a position to consider building large numbers of capital ships. In a different vein, the treaties ending World War I imposed severe disarmament measures on Germany, Austria, Hungary, and Bulgaria, but this was done—at least in theory—"in order to render possible the initiation of a general limitation of the armaments of all nations." Similarly, following World War II, arms limitations were imposed on Germany, Japan, and other defeated belligerent states, though these have since been revised upward. Even at the time when Federal Germany joined the West European Union and NATO, however, she did so on the understanding that she would not produce atomic, chemical, or biological weapons; long-range missiles; strategic bombers; or certain conventional armaments on her territory.

This type of restriction illuminates the issue of "haves vs. have-nots." The Baruch Plan proposed that the U.S. retain her atomic monopoly until such time that Washington considered the international atomic energy authority to be functional. Inspired by a concern to maintain China and Germany in their non-nuclear weapons status, Moscow advocated nuclear-free zones for Central Europe and Asia as well as for other parts of Eurasia.

The nuclear nonproliferation treaty (signed in 1968 and entered into force March 1970) offers a major example of preventive arms control concerned with limiting manufacture and ownership of specified weapons systems to particular states. It calls on the existing nuclear-weapons states not to transfer their weapons to other states, and it obligates the non-nuclear weapons countries not to produce or otherwise obtain such weapons. Even if the treaty is formally accepted—or observed—by such key threshold states as India, Japan, and Israel, it is clear that great foresight and effort will be necessary from all sides to make the treaty endure. Preventive arms controls, even if implemented for the moment, require continuous support if they are to remain viable.

Qualitative Restrictions

1. Types of Weapons. We have already seen that the Washington Naval Conference and the peace treaties following the two world wars set limits on the kinds of weapons that various nations could produce or acquire. Had the Baruch Plan been accepted and implemented, it would probably have removed one kind of armament—nuclear weaponry—from the arsenals of any nation-state.

A prime example of a successful preventive arms control treaty in this domain is the 1925 Protocol on Asphyxiating, Poisonous, and other Gases, and Bacteriological Warfare, signed and ratified by most nations earlier and endorsed in 1969 by President Nixon. Especially if the United States ratifies the 1925 Protocol, its ambiguities should be eliminated (e.g., whether tear gas is also prescribed) and its gaps corrected (especially the need to include biological and radiation warfare).

Qualitative as well as quantitative restrictions of strategic arms are being considered by Soviet and U.S. representatives in SALT II. The importance of qualitative characteristics was underscored earlier, of course, by the transition in the 1950s from nuclear to thermonuclear warheads, and it was emphasized again in 1961 when the Soviet Union began testing of warheads over twice the size of those ever tested by the United States. The first proposals to emphasize the interdependence between offensive and defensive systems were put forward by President Johnson in January 1964 in his call for exploration of "a verified freeze on the number and characteristics of strategic nuclear offensive and defensive vehicles."

2. Geographical Restrictions. The use of some geographical principle has been common to efforts to maintain peace, whether through support for some regional balance of power or establishment of arms control on a territorial basis. Thus, even the revolutionary regime of Soviet Russia welcomed demilitarized zones and areas of arms limitation in her treaties with neighboring states in the turbulent years 1918-1921. Later, Stalin worked with Roosevelt and Churchill to plan a postwar world security system based on demilitarization and disarmament of Germany. Though Germany turned out to be divided and rearmed, Austria proclaimed her neutrality in 1955, suggesting to many analysts and leaders a model that might be applied to other states facing both to East and West.

Regional schemes for atom-free zones have been proposed not only for Europe and Asia, as noted earlier, but also for Africa, Latin America, and the Middle East. Though many of the purposes of the atom-free zone proposals would be accomplished by the nonproliferation treaty (NPT), the former are more radical: they would prevent deployment of nuclear weapons by nuclear powers on the territory of all states in the region, whereas the nonproliferation treaty prohibits only the transfer of such weapons to non-nuclear weapons states. The NPT, for example, leaves the Soviet Union and the United States free to deploy nuclear weapons in Germany, a step proscribed by the various suggestions for an atom-free Central Europe. On the other hand, an atom-free Asia is now a physical impossibility, since China has joined the nuclear weapons club, and U.S. nuclear weapons remain in the area; hence, the furthest-reaching nuclear arms controls available for Asia are those laid down by the NPT. In other parts of the world, however—Africa, Latin America, and the Middle East—there is still time to take preventive action to assure that each region remains entirely void of nuclear weapons. A regional treaty to that effect has been signed and ratified by most states of Latin America.

Less glamorous than proposals for atom-free zones, important suggestions have also been made to limit the levels of conventional arms on a regional basis. Various Congressmen have called on the United States to curtail her shipments of arms to Latin America because the area has become saturated with arms and is engaged in an economically disastrous course of action. Similar problems abound in every part of the world, the most explosive being the Middle East, where outside suppliers and regional actors have combined to create an unstable situation in which no side believes it can ever have "enough." A great power embargo on arms shipments to the area would help to cut the upward spiral. Such an accord seems remote, however, not only because of the difficulty in determining a moment when the existing balance is adequate for the defensive needs of the parties in the area, but because regional as well as exogenous powers still hope to increase their influence by the arms buildup and possibly by force of arms. There is the further asymmetry that the arms industry of one side, Israel, is becoming more self-sufficient than that of the Arab states.

An interesting model of another kind was created in 1959 when the twelve concerned powers agreed to keep Antarctica demilitarized; to declare it off bounds for military maneuvers, nuclear and other weapons tests; to prohibit any new territorial claims to the area; and to open all their installations there to international visits and observation. The Antarctic analogy was used by legal analysts in Moscow as well as in Washington when they drafted the 1967 treaty governing the peaceful uses of outer space. But the 1967 treaty also differs from that of 1959 in several respects, one of them being that it prohibits only weapons of mass destruction in outer space; it thereby permits not only military observation and communication satellites but also the stationing in space of weapons not capable of "mass destruction." On the moon and other celestial bodies, however, all military installations, tests, and maneuvers are prohibited. The outer space treaty, in turn, helped provide a model for the agreement of May 18, 1972 to prohibit the stationing of mass destruction weapons or the seabed. Analogous to the permissive attitude of the earlier treaty toward reconnaissance satellites, the seabed treaty permits various detection devices to be deployed on the ocean floor. Further, whereas the space treaty would permit missile carriers to pass *through* outer space *en route* to their target, the seabed treaty would not prevent missile-carrying submarines from travelling through the seas or even from resting on the ocean bottom.

Finally, we should note how a kind of geographical principle has been used to limit certain kinds of military testing and development. We have already noted that Antarctica and outer space have been declared off limits to military tests and maneuvers. No less interesting, the 1963 "Moscow Treaty" prohibited the testing of nuclear weapons in three environments—in the atmosphere, in outer space, and under water—but not underground. Nuclear tests in this fourth environment have continued without violation of the treaty, except to the extent that many have "vented" and carried radio-active debris beyond the territory of the country involved. Though this treaty appeared to be a useful measure of preventive arms control when it was signed, the possibility of testing underground has allowed the more advanced nuclear powers to continue refinement of ABM and other systems which, some hoped, would be thwarted by the three-environment ban. The less sophisticated nuclear powers, France and China, have not been restrained since they refused to sign the test ban and have continued atmospheric testing. The fifth nuclear power, Great Britain, has signed the treaty and stopped nuclear testing, but has become even more dependent on the United States as a result. Many ingenious schemes have been suggested to allow the USSR and United States to bridge their differences on verification of an underground test ban.

In another sense, the test ban treaty has served as a quasi nonproliferation treaty. If the non-nuclear weapon signatories of the Moscow Treaty wished to begin nuclear testing, they would have to denounce the treaty unless they chose the expensive and difficult route of commencing their atomic test program underground.

General Restrictions. Apart from these examples of quantitative and qualitative measures, other preventive arms controls strike at the general problem of arms buildups, the use of the military arm, and the relationship between tension and armaments. The League of Nations and the United Nations were inspired in part by a desire to prevent a felt need for upgrading and increasing national armaments. Since the League of Nations Covenant permitted a resort to war under certain circumstances, however, many nations sought to plug its loopholes through other means, one of them being the 1928 Kellogg-Briand Pact on the Renunciation of War as an instrument of national policy, an accord endorsed by Moscow through the so-called Litvinov Protocol.

Although the Kellogg-Briand Pact remains in force, at least theoretically, and though the United Nations Charter permits military action only in self-defense or as part of a U.N. action, various countries continue to propose special accords outlawing the resort to war. Chairman Khrushchev proposed in December 1963 an agreement affirming that war would not be used to alter existing state frontiers. Because the Soviet proposal seemed to approve military force in certain circumstances (wars of national liberation and wars to regain territory allegedly occupied by alien powers, such as Taiwan), President Johnson, in January 1964, proposed a comprehensive ban on the use or threat of force, which Moscow rejected. In a more limited sphere, West Germany has signed with her eastern neighbors treaties renouncing the use of force in their mutual relations.

The Chinese People's Republic, for her part, has put forward several proposals for nuclear disarmament, beginning with a ban on the use of nuclear weapons. Proposals for general and complete disarmament have also been tabled by most of the great powers since the late 1950s, programs that would involve disarmament but which would also stipulate preventive measures to ensure against future arms buildups.

More modestly, but more realistically, unilateral steps have been taken to ensure that existing arms are not used by accident, by the decision of a madman, or in violation of national policy. We know more about U.S. policies in this regard than about the policies of other nuclear powers. American weapons are generally placed under a series of electronic locks that cannot be opened except after approval by several levels of authority reaching all the way to the White House. Bombers of the Strategic Air Command have their "fail-safe" system. Tactical nuclear weapons in Europe cannot be used by NATO allies until a two-key system is opened by authority of the local as well as the U.S. government.

Advanced as these various techniques may be, however, some near-catastrophic accidents have taken place. Radar screens cannot always detect the difference between flying geese and an incoming enemy rocket. Communications between the mainland and submarines at sea are complicated, and would be more so in time of a crisis or war. The whole issue of command and control remains a vital issue of arms control, one that may prove still more problematic if the number of weapons and nuclear-weapons countries mounts.

The hot-line agreement between Washington and Moscow in 1963 offered a testimony to the anxieties both sides felt in the 1962 Cuban missile crisis over their difficulties at direct communication. This kind of link has gone on to serve as a model for communications networks between other sets of countries and was updated between the USSR and United States in 1971-72. This kind of preventive measure warrants further study and elaboration in the future, including attention to ways of limiting its abuse by irresponsible parties.

The general approach that is most applicable in a wide range of circumstances may be what Soviet spokesmen have termed "disarmament by mutual example." Even if arms are not actually reduced or eliminated, they may be controlled to mutual advantage by the tacit agreement of the concerned parties.

Unilateral actions and tacit agreements may be used to promote "disarmament by mutual example," as in cuts of military spending (by Moscow and Washington in late 1963) and reductions in production of fissionable materials—announced by unilateral declarations by London, Moscow, and Washington in 1964.

Of course the most important area for preventive action lies in creating conditions in which nations feel no need to maintain arms races or threaten their neighbors. This is the problem of "peaceful change," discussed by John W. Burton (*Peace Theory: Preconditions of Disarmament* [New York: Knopf, 1962]) and earlier by E.H. Carr. Prescriptive lessons from case studies have been put together by Lincoln P. Bloomfield and Amelia C. Leiss (*Controlling Small Wars* [New York: Knopf, 1969]) for policies that would help to avoid, control, and settle such crises. A strong role for the United Nations in preventive diplomacy has been laid out in the works of Inis Claude.

Lessons for the Future

This typology points to many cases where nation-states have decided, unilaterally or jointly, to limit the extension of military technology in particular realms of technology or in certain geographical areas. The examples given to illustrate the typology are not comprehensive, though they do seem to be typical.

Most accords on preventive arms control have taken place in domains which the competing powers wanted for ulterior motives to remove from the scene of arms competition. Missiles on the moon, for example, do not add to the deterrent force of Moscow or Washington, but would be highly costly, inefficient, and accident-prone.

On the other hand, the cases enumerated here show not only that the great powers have sometimes refrained from exploiting military technology to the hilt, but that they are developing a certain frame of mind that could lead to more significant results in the future, e.g., in the SALT negotiations. Even the "easiest" victories in preventive arms control to date, such as Antarctica and outer space, are important for several reasons beyond their objective content. First, such accords have helped affirm the signatories' interest in the principle of preventive arms control. Second, they have offered symbolic assurance that arms control agreements were possible between adversaries. Third, each treaty helped to generate and perpetuate some momentum toward détente and further arms control. The outer space treaty in 1967, for instance, helped to signify the willingness of Moscow and Washington to progress on other matters even while the Vietnamese war continued, and, in the process, helped to facilitate the more difficult movement toward the non-proliferation treaty. Fourth, these treaties helped to assure the superpowers that neither needed to exploit a facet of military technology just because the other was likely to do so. In this way, these accords helped to interrupt the interaction process that so often has led to upward spirals in the arms race.

An essential task for the decades to come will lie in preserving and extending the principle of preventive arms control to other domains of military technology. It will be difficult to maintain the principle even in those areas where it has already been applied, but it will be still more difficult to secure its application in areas that seem militarily more promising or in which the adversary is believed to have a significant head start.

As argued in Chapter 5, however, many of the U.S.-Soviet accords of the early 1970s went some distance toward coping with the most difficult problems of all for preventive arms control: limiting the development, testing, and modernization of new weapons.

Notes

Notes

Introduction

1. For a definition of the cold war and an assertion as to its inevitability, see Jack C. Plano and Roy Olton, *The International Relations Dictionary* (New York: Holt, Rinehart and Winston, Inc., 1969), p. 54. A defense of Western "orthodox" interpretations may be found in Arthur Schlesinger, Jr., "Origins of the Cold War," *Foreign Affairs*, Vol. 46, No. 1 (October 1967), pp. 22-52. A critique of "revisionist" writing by Robert James Maddox, *The New Left and the Origins of the Cold War* (Princeton, N.J.: Princeton University Press, 1973) is reviewed and challenged by several authors in *The New York Times Book Review*, June 17, 1973, pp. 6-10.

The evolution of Western images of Soviet foreign policy from an essentialist/Manichean model to a cybernetic view combining stimulus-response plus learning capacities is put forward by William Zimmerman, "Soviet Foreign Policy—A New Perspective," *Survey*, XIX, No. 2 (Spring 1973), pp. 188-198. For reviews of William Welch's *American Images of Soviet Foreign Policy*, see *Newsletter on Comparative Studies in Communism*, VI, No. 2 (February 1973), pp. 2-40, also Appendix A. While this ferment continues in the West, an official orthodoxy persists in Soviet writing, senior historians such as A.A. Gromyko and Viktor Israelian allowing no hint that subjective factors such as "misunderstanding" might have helped account for the cold war. On the brighter side, Soviet as well as Western sources are used abundantly in works such as V.M. Kulish, *Istoriia Vtorogo Fronta* (Moscow: Nauka, 1971).

2. Louis Halle, *The Cold War as History* (New York: Harper & Row, 1967), p. xiii. See also the author's " 'Misperception' versus 'Realism' in Superpower Relations: A Problem for Statesman and Scholars," *Journal of International Affairs*, XXVI, No. 1 (1972), pp. 106-112.

3. See John G. Stoessinger, *Nations in Darkness: China, Russia, America* (New York: Random House, 1971).

4. For definitions and bibliographic citations, see Colin S. Gray, "The Arms Race Phenomenon," *World Politics*, XXIXV, No. 1 (October 1971), pp. 39-79; and his "Social Science and the Arms Race," *Bulletin of the Atomic Scientists,* XXIX, No. 6 (June 1973), pp. 23-26.

5. Jan F. Triska and David D. Finley, *Soviet Foreign Policy* (New York: Macmillan, 1968), pp. 284-309.

6. For a survey of the literature reporting different views on the dating of the cold war, see Paul Seabury, *The Rise and Decline of the Cold War* (New York: Basic Books, 1967), pp. 6-10.

7. See *The Private Papers of Senator Vandenberg*, ed. by Arthur H. Vandenberg, Jr. (Boston: Houghton-Mifflin Co., 1952), pp. 136-138, 399-420;

James F. Byrnes, *Speaking Frankly* (New York: Harper and Brothers, 1947), pp. 171 *passim.*; Gerhard Wettig, *Entmilitarisierung und Wiederbewaffnung in Deutschland, 1943-1955* (Munich: R. Oldenbourg Verlag, 1967), pp. 140-148.

8. V.M. Molotov, *Problems of Foreign Policy* (Moscow: Foreign Languages Publishing House, 1949), pp. 46, 55-69, 443-448, 601-608. For a report on Stalin's meeting with Secretary of State Marshall in April 1947, see Walter Bedell Smith, *My Three Years in Moscow* (Philadelphia: J.B. Lippincott Co., 1950), p. 221-225. See also Adam Ulam, *Expansion and Coexistence* (New York: Praeger, 1968), pp. 445-447.

9. Dwight D. Eisenhower, *Mandate for Change, 1953-1956* (Garden City, N.Y.: Doubleday, 1963), p. 527. The open skies proposal had been updated and recommended to the President in June 1955 by a panel headed by Nelson D. Rockefeller, the President's Special Adviser for Cold War Strategy. See Robert J. Donovan, *Eisenhower: The Inside Story* (New York: Harper & Row, 1956), pp. 345 ff.

10. Lincoln P. Bloomfield, Walter C. Clemens, Jr., Franklyn Griffiths, *Khrushchev and the Arms Race* (Cambridge, Mass.: The M.I.T. Press, 1966), pp. 21-27.

11. On the crucial role of Averell Harriman, see Robert F. Kennedy's foreword to *Toward a Strategy of Peace*, ed. Walter C. Clemens, Jr. (Chicago: Random House, 1966), pp. xiii-xiv.

12. Joseph I. Lieberman, *The Scorpion and the Tarantula: The Struggle to Control Atomic Weapons 1945-1949* (Boston: Houghton Mifflin, 1970), p. ix.

13. Comments on SALT in *Survey*, XIX, No. 2 (Spring 1973), pp. 175-182 at p. 182.

14. Iklé cites Winston Churchill as noting that "the deterrent does not cover the case of lunatics or dictators in the mood of Hitler when he found himself in his final dugout. This is a blank." Iklé contends that "the most disturbing defect, today, in the prevalent thinking is the cavalier disregard for this blank." See Fred Charles Iklé, "Can Nuclear Deterrence Last Out the Century?" *Foreign Affairs*, LI, No. 2 (January 1973), pp. 267-285 at p. 269.

15. On this and other game theory concepts referred to in the text, see Anatol Rapoport, *Two-Person Game Theory* (Ann Arbor: University of Michigan Press, 1966); also Anatol Rapoport and Albert M. Chammah, *Prisoner's Dilemma* (Ann Arbor: University of Michigan Press, 1965).

Chapter 1
Can the USSR Live With Stability?;
The United States With "Sufficiency"?

1. "International Negotiation," *Hearings Before the Subcommittee on National Security and International Operations of the Committee on Govern-*

ment Operations, United States Senate, Ninety-second Congress, Second Session, Part 7, with William R. Van Cleave, July 25, 1972 (Washington: U.S. Government Printing Office, 1972), pp. 240-243.

2. Thomas W. Wolfe, "Soviet Interests in SALT," in William R. Kinter and Robert L. Pfaltzgraff, Jr., eds., *SALT: Implications for Arms Control in the 1970s* (Pittsburgh: University of Pittsburgh Press, 1973), pp. 21-23.

3. Portions of the following analysis were first published in *Worldview Magazine*, XVI, No. 2 (February 1973), pp. 40-47.

The findings of Triska and Finley are especially germane to Proposition I. They note that "Soviet troops have not been normally employed except in crises within the Communist party-states system; . . . the USSR has appeared more sensitive to crises in the Communist party-states in Eastern Europe than anywhere else in the world; increasingly it appears more important for the USSR to contain the influence of its opponents in the Communist party-states systems than to expand and advance its own interests. . . . " See Jan F. Triska and David D. Finley, *Soviet Foreign Policy* (New York: Macmillan Co., 1968), pp. 313, 316, 317.

Triska and Finley report that "the majority of Western writers on the subject perceive the USSR as past- and present- (rather than future-) oriented; with Soviet decision-makers viewing the horizon as relatively limited (rather than wide open); with greater reliance on national and interstate (rather than ideological, party, and movement) ties; where restraint is perceived as prudence (rather than fear); where slow persuasion and agreement is preferred to rapid and risky force; and where in fact both tactics and goals (rather than tactics only) change over time."

The Triska-Finley findings are basically consonant with the ESP data reported in Chapter 1. The Welch study discussed in Appendix A, however, gives a somewhat different picture of the consensus among sovietologists.

4. The difficulty in using Soviet declaratory policy as a means of inferring policy priorities is illustrated by the May Day slogans of the CPSU Central Committee published in *Pravda* on April 18, 1971. The first three slogans contain general references to international proletarian solidarity. Slogans #4 through #41 have to do mainly with domestic tasks and institutions of Soviet society (#21 saluting Soviet servicemen "always ready to rebuff any aggression") (#37 saluting scientists and workers conquering outer space). Most of the remaining slogans (in a total of sixty) deal with foreign affairs: saluting peoples of socialist countries; the working class of capitalist countries; the peoples of newly independent and still oppressed colonial countries. The peoples of Indochina and the Arab peoples receive special attention, ranked just above those of Europe, who are encouraged (slogan 56) to "advocate more actively the transformation of Europe into a continent of stable peace and peaceful cooperation between states." (They are also told to be "vigilant toward the intrigues of the forces of reaction and revanchism. . . . ") Matters of arms control

are put off until slogan 57: "Peoples of the world: Demand the prohibition of all types of nuclear, chemical, and bacteriological weapons! Struggle for universal and complete disarmament, for the strengthening of international security!" The next two slogans also refer to the peace policies of the USSR.

These slogans can be interpreted in a way that makes them consistent with the hierarchy of Soviet foreign policy goals suggested here, but Soviet actions and statements in other fora must be examined for a fuller view. A major study of May Day slogans from 1917 to 1943, however, supports the main lines of the goals hypothesized here: "Taken as a whole, the May First slogans are in the last analysis mainly variations on a single theme. That leitmotif is the security of the Soviet regime. Even the interest Moscow takes, or pretends to take, in revolutionary activities abroad is subordinated to this main concern. The blending of international with patriotic slogans and the changes, in the course of years, in their mutual relationship are also primarily dependent upon survival considerations." (Sergius Yakobson and Harold D. Lasswell, "Trend: May Day Slogans in Soviet Russia, 1918-1943," in Harold D. Lasswell, Nathan Leites, and Associates, *Language of Politics* (Cambridge, Mass.: The M.I.T. Press, 1965), pp. 233-297 at p. 284.)

5. A more extreme statement of this argument, one that seems to exaggerate the role of external provocations giving rise to military actions by the USSR is presented in Frederick L. Schuman, *The Cold War: Retrospect and Prospect* (2d ed.; Baton Rouge: Louisiana State University Press, 1967). Schuman also seems to give undue weight to the similarities between Tsarist and Soviet policy, without taking adequate account of the differences. For an evaluation which, in turn, seems unduly critical, see William Welch, *American Images of Soviet Foreign Policy* (New Haven and London: Yale University Press, 1970), pp. 157-165.

6. A point often ignored is the fact that Western influence in Iran could be expected to endure, even after British and U.S. troops departed (on schedule) because of British and American oil interests. The departure of Soviet troops would leave the country under predominantly British (and U.S.) influence, contrary to the agreements of World War II. The issue of Iran was one of several on which no accord was reached at the 1945 Yalta Conference. See Diane S. Clemens, *Yalta* (New York: Oxford University Press, 1970), pp. 224-246. 255-258.

Iranian politics and diplomacy, aided by Western intelligence operations, helped to foil the Kremlin again in 1950 when Moscow thought that it had oil leases in its pocket.

Stalin's personal interest in creating a Soviet Republic in northern Iran dated from 1920-1921, when his efforts were undermined with the approval of Lenin and the Soviet ambassador in Teheran. This information was provided by Chicherin to Louis Fischer in 1929. See Louis Fischer, *The Soviets in World Affairs, 1917-1929* (2d ed.; 2 vols.; Princeton, N.J.: Princeton University Press),

I, xvi. The most comprehensive book is George Lenczowski, *Russia and the West in Iran, 1918-1948: A Study in Big-Power Rivalry* (Ithaca, New York: Cornell University Press, 1949).

For a provocative comparison, see C. Bailey, "America and the Soviet Involvement in Azerbaijan in 1946: Some Parallels for 1970," *International Problems* (Tel Aviv), IX, No. 3-4 (November 1970), pp. 20-24. As Bailey points out, Molotov urged Germany in November 1940 to recognize "the area south of Batum and Baku, in the general direction of the Persian Gulf, as the center of the aspirations of the Soviet Union."

7. According to the memoirs attributed to Khrushchev (riddled with many inaccuracies even if they are his reminiscences), Kim Il-sung came to Stalin in 1949-1950 to obtain Soviet approval to initiate the war. Soon, however, Stalin withdrew Soviet advisers (against Khrushchev's recommendations). China's entry into the war took place after consultations between Stalin and Chou En-lai. See *Khrushchev Remembers* (Boston: Little, Brown and Company, 1970), pp. 367-373.

8. I.F. Stone, *The Hidden History of the Korean War* (New York: Monthly Review Press, 1952).

9. See Uri Ra'anan, *The USSR Arms the Third World: Case Studies in Soviet Foreign Policy* (Cambridge, Mass.: The M.I.T. Press, 1969), pp. 14 ff.

10. Immediately after the outbreak of the Suez War in 1956, Soviet pilots flew their planes out of Egypt and away from the combat zone. See J.M. Mackintosh, *Strategy and Tactics of Soviet Foreign Policy* (New York: Oxford University Press, 1962), p. 186. Soviet caution was also reflected in the statement attributed to Stalin, explaining why he withdrew Soviet advisers from Korea: "It's too dangerous to keep our advisors [*sic*] there. They might be taken prisoners. We don't want there to be evidence for accusing us of taking part in this business. It's Kim Il-sung's affair." (*Khrushchev Remembers*, p. 370.)

11. Stewart Alsop quoted the President as saying that "in some cases we might have to take the initiative" in using nuclear weapons. "Kennedy's Grand Strategy," *Saturday Evening Post*, March 31, 1962, at p. 11. *Krasnaya Zvezda* (May 11, 1962) cited the interview as proof for the view that the United States was caught up in a "preventive war" strategy. Khrushchev also lamented the President's statement in speeches reported in *Pravda*, May 20, 1962 and June 20, 1962.

For Robert S. McNamara's June 16, 1962, address endorsing a doctrine of counterforce, see *Survival*, September-October 1962.

12. See Frank Gibney's introduction to Oleg Penkovskiy, *The Penkovskiy Papers* (Garden City, N.Y.: Doubleday and Co., Inc., 1965), p. 17. See also remarks of the then C.I.A. Director Richard Helms in *The New York Times*, April 15, 1971, pp. 1, 30.

13. On "jokers" in arms control proposals, see John W. Spanier and Joseph L. Nogee, *The Politics of Disarmament: A Study in Soviet-American Gamesmanship* (New York: Praeger, 1962), esp. Chapters 1 and 2.

14. See Walter C. Clemens, Jr., "Lenin on Disarmament," *Slavic Review*, XXIII, No. 3 (September 1964), pp. 504-525.

15. See Jules Moch, *Histoire du réarmement allemand depuis 1950* (Paris: Robert Laffont, 1965), pp. 330-331.

16. This change in the sequence of the Soviet plan for general disarmament came after the collapse of the Paris summit conference, which may have led Khrushchev to believe that there was no further point in courting the United States until a new president had been elected. See his message to the governments of all countries and revised Soviet proposals on disarmament of June 2, 1960, in *Documents on Disarmament, 1960* (Washington, D.C.: U.S. Government Printing Office, 1961), pp. 98-111, esp. 107.

17. See Lincoln P. Bloomfield, Walter C. Clemens, Jr., Franklyn Griffiths, *Khrushchev and the Arms Race: Soviet Interests in Arms Control and Disarmament, 1954-1964* (Cambridge, Mass.: The M.I.T. Press, 1966), p. 186. Moscow also modified its general disarmament proposal to allow for a nuclear umbrella on September 21, 1962. See ibid., p. 187.

18. Robert F. Kennedy, *Thirteen Days* (New York: W.W. Norton, 1969), pp. 25-27, 39-42, 66. In the same vein, it has been reported that Khrushchev told Western negotiators several months before the USSR resumed nuclear testing in September 1961 that Moscow would never be the first to break the moratorium on nuclear testing that had existed since 1958.

19. *World Armaments and Disarmament: SIPRI Yearbook, 1973* (New York: Humanities Press, 1973), pp. 234-235.

Firm inferences from the Soviet data are the more difficult in that they may also be interpreted as a mere reaction—for the official record or in fact—to the ups and downs in American defense spending (conditioned mainly by the rise and fall of U.S. involvement in Indochina). The lockstep pattern is seen in the average percent changes per year of U.S. and Soviet defense spending (respectively):

					Budgeted change in	Budgeted change in
1966-67	1967-68	1968-69	1969-70	1970-71	1972	1973
+15.4	+ 2.6	−4.2	−9.8	−7.8	+3.0	−4.0
+ 8.0	+15.5	+5.9	+1.1	±0	±0	±0

The magnitude of change in the Soviet budget is thus smaller than that for U.S. defense spending, but the trends are in the same direction. See ibid., pp. 213-215. Also, *World Armaments and Disarmament: SIPRI Yearbook, 1972* (New York: Humanities Press, 1972), p. 53. American spending has decreased as a percent of GNP and as a fraction of government expenditures since about 1969; the same is probably not true of Soviet defense spending. See data in *Statement of Secretary of Defense Elliot L. Richardson Before the Senate*

Armed Services Committee on the FY 1974-1978 Program, Wednesday, March 28, 1973 (Washington: U.S. Government Printing Office, 1973), p. 41.

20. Summarized in Walter C. Clemens, Jr., *The Arms Race and Sino-Soviet Relations* (Stanford, Calif.: The Hoover Institution, 1968), p. 208.

21. Text on display at the Lyndon B. Johnson Presidential Library in Austin, Texas, *Cf. The New York Times*, April 11, 1971, p. 1.

22. Welch, op. cit., pp. 210-261.

23. See Chapters 1 and 2 of the author's *The Arms Race and Sino-Soviet Relations*.

24. George F. Kennan, "A Proposal for Western Survival," *New Leader*, XLII, No. 41 (November 16, 1959), pp. 14-15. The quotation cited, of course, runs contrary to other passages in Kennan's works where he argues there was little the West could have done to persuade Lenin and his comrades to perceive the West more benignly and act accordingly.

25. See the chain of psychological variables suggested by Etzioni: Hostility→ psychological blocks→rigidity→repression of fear→stereotyping→and paranoia. Even in its milder forms paranoia could lead either Soviet or Western leaders to write off the other side's proposals (even if offered in good faith) as a trick.

See Amitai Etzioni, "The Kennedy Experiment," *Western Political Quarterly*, XX, No. 2. Part 1 (June 1967), pp. 361-380 at p. 362.

26. For documentation, see Bloomfield et al., op. cit., pp. 22-27.

27. Ibid., pp. 147-151.

28. See Bernhard G. Bechoefer, *Postwar Negotiations for Arms Control* (Washington, D.C.: The Brookings Institution, 1961), pp. 490-512.

29. For related developments, see Bloomfield et al., op. cit., pp. 155-156.

30. Norman Cousins, "Notes on a 1963 Visit with Khrushchev," *Saturday Review*, November 7, 1964, pp. 16-21, 58-60 at pp. 20, 21. For the sequence of events (and misperceptions?) on which Khrushchev's views rested, see Harold K. Jacobson and Eric Stein, *Diplomats, Scientists and Politicians: The United States and the Nuclear Test Ban Negotiations* (Ann Arbor, Michigan: University of Michigan Press, 1966), pp. 430-435.

31. Wilson's memoirs, in *Life*, LXX, No. 19 (May 21, 1971), pp. 54B-66, corroborated by Lyndon Baines Johnson, *The Vantage Point* (New York: Holt, Rinehart and Winston, 1971), pp. 253-254.

32. Quoted in *The New York Times*, June 9, 1971, p. 2.

33. *The New York Times*, April 20, 1972, p. 17; ibid., April 22, 1972, pp. 1, 11.

34. Johnson, op. cit., pp. 514-520.

35. See Neil Sheehan in *The New York Times*, April 20, 1972.

36. See Terence Smith, ibid., September 24, 1971, p. 8.

37. See *Strategic Survey 1970* (London: International Institute for Strategic Studies, 1971), pp. 43-44, 90-91. Other sources used in the following analysis include Le Monde, Facts on File, Mizan, and various digests of the world press.

U.S. and Egyptian officials have been interviewed in Washington, Cairo, and other Middle Eastern capitals.

38. From this assertion and from Gromyko's 1962 denial that Moscow was placing offensive weapons in Cuba, Morgenthau concluded that, "it is peculiar to the Soviet approach to negotiated settlements to enter sometimes into such settlements with the intention not to honor them." See Hans J. Morgenthau, "Changes and Chances in American-Soviet Relations," *Foreign Affairs*, Vol. 49, No. 3 (April 1971), pp. 429-441 at pp. 440-441. Professor Morgenthau made the equally irresponsible assertion that the West German-Soviet treaty of 1970 was a first step toward "another understanding between Germany and the Soviet Union after the model of the Rapallo Treaty of 1922. . . . " (Ibid., p. 438).

39. See George H. Quester, "Missiles in Cuba, 1970," *Foreign Affairs*, XXXIX, No. 3 (April 1971), pp. 493-506.

As regards the understanding on Cuba in 1962, it should be noted that—as phrased by President Kennedy—the accord could be (and has been) interpreted as being conditional upon removal of the Soviet missiles under U.N. observation and with safeguards against reintroduction of such weapons to Cuba. See statement by the President on October 27, 1962 and also by Chairman Khrushchev the next day. Documents, e.g., in Robert F. Kennedy, *Thirteen Days*, pp. 202-207.

In late 1970 this understanding was apparently updated in talks between Presidential aide Henry A. Kissinger and Soviet diplomats. The American interpretation was that the United States agreed not to seek the overthrow of Premier Castro's regime, while the USSR agreed not to service nuclear-armed Soviet vessels "in or from" Cuban ports. The closest that Soviet publications came to expressing the Kremlin's accord was in a statement issued by TASS on October 13, 1970, denying that the USSR was building "its own military base" in Cuba. In 1970 and 1971 fleets of Soviet vessels visited Cuban waters in what some American officials saw as a test of U.S. endurance and determination. In March 1971, for example, a Soviet guided-missile cruiser, accompanied by an oil-supply ship arrived in Havana harbor, while a 9,000 ton tender used to service nuclear submarines was 100 miles south of Cienfuegos, on Cuba's southern coast. Some reports indicated that the tender was accompanied by an N-class Soviet submarine, a vessel propelled by nuclear power and carrying 21-inch torpedoes. U.S. officials were unsure whether the guided-missile cruiser carried nuclear warheads, but tended to believe that it did. They agreed that the N-class submarine was not technically a violation of the alleged understanding, but thought that it and the submarine tender aimed at testing the United States. See *The New York Times*, February 14, 1971, p. 2.

40. *SIPRI Yearbook of World Armaments and Disarmament, 1969/70* (New York: Humanities Press, 1970), see esp. Part III: Reference material, pp. 259-387.

41. Texts of the agreements in *Arms Control and Disarmament Agreements,*

1959-1972 (Washington: U.S. Arms Control and Disarmament Agency, 1972), pp. 108-118 and insertions. The following analysis is based in part on interpretations on the accords by Henry A. Kissinger and Gerard C. Smith, in *Weekly Compilation of Presidential Documents*, VIII, No. 23 (June 5, 1972), pp. 929-936, 956-963.

42. Admiral Thomas H. Moorer, *United States Military Posture for FY 1974*, Statement Before the Senate Armed Services Committee on 28 March 1973, pp. 16-17.

43. *Strategic Survey 1972* (London: International Institute for Strategic Studies, 1973), p. 17.

44. *The Military Balance, 1972-1973* (London: International Institute for Strategic Studies, 1972), p. 85.

45. Moorer, op. cit., pp. 11-13.

46. *Statement of Secretary of Defense Elliot L. Richardson Before the Armed Services Committee on the FY 1974 Defense Budget and FY 1974-1978 Program March 28, 1973* (Washington: U.S. Government Printing Office, 1973), pp. 14, 27, 29, 51.

47. *The Military Balance, 1972-1973*, pp. 70, 71. Soviet sensitivity to the effects of coordinating the strengths of the Atlantic Community is seen, e.g., in I.M. Ivanova, *Kontseptsiia "Atlanticheskogo Soobshchestva" vo vneshnei politike SShA* (Moscow: Nauka, 1973).

48. For a survey based on CIA as well as academic analyses, see Herbert E. Meyer, "Why the Russians Are Shopping in the U.S.," *Fortune*, February 1973, pp. 66 ff.

49. *The Military Balance, 1972-1973*, p. 86.

Chapter 2
Nicholas II to SALT II:
Logic Versus the Organization(s)

1. See Alexander George, *Propaganda Analysis: A Study of Inferences Made from Nazi Propaganda in World War II* (Evanston, Ill.: Row, Peterson, 1959), pp. 58-61. For an attempt to analyze Soviet policy toward China in terms of strategic logic and a variety of more behavioral explanations, see the author's *The Arms Race and Sino-Soviet Relations* (Stanford, Calif.: The Hoover Institution, 1968), Chapters 1 and 2.

2. See also Paul Hollander, *Soviet and American Society: A Comparison* (New York: Oxford University Press, 1973).

3. See Graham T. Allison, *The Essence of Decision: Explaining the Cuban Missile Crisis* (Boston: Little, Brown, 1971). For a critique of attempts to apply methods of analysis designed to fit American decision-making to the Soviet Union, see Matthew P. Gallagher and Karl F. Spielmann, Jr., *Soviet Decision-*

Making for Defense: A Critique of U.S. Perspectives on the Arms Race (New York: Praeger, 1972).

4. For a discussion of this framework in the Soviet and Chinese contexts, see *The Arms Race and Sino-Soviet Relations*, Chapter 14.

5. Pioneering works by Kenneth N. Waltz, J. David Singer, John Spanier, and others have usually focused on three levels of analysis, thereby minimizing the importance of others, such as the national and global environment, included in this listing. The list, of course, could be greatly expanded by including, e.g., regional, transnational, and other levels.

6. Portions of the following analysis first appeared in *International Affairs* (London), XLIX, No. 3 (July 1973), pp. 385-401.

7. For documentation on Tsarist policy in 1899, see L. Teleshevskoi, ed., "K istorii pervoi Gaagakoi konferentsii 1899 g.," *Krasnyi arkhiv*, L -LI (Moscow, 1932), 64-96, and "Novye materialy o Gaagskoi mirnoi konferentsii 1899 g.," *Krasnyi arkhiv*, LIV-LV (Moscow, 1932), 49-70. For documentation on the conferences, see *Actes et documents relatifs au programme de la conférence de la paix publies d'ordre du gouvernement par Jhr. van Dachne van Varick* (The Hague: Martinus Nijhoff, 1899); *The Proceedings of the Hague Peace Conferences: The Conference of 1899*. Translated and edited under the direction of James B. Scott (New York: Oxford University Press, 1920); *The Proceedings of the Hague Peace Conferences: The Conference of 1907*. Translated and edited under the direction of James B. Scott (New York: Oxford University Press, 11921-1922), Vol. I and II. On the initial economic considerations for the Tsar's proposal, see Count S.Y. Witte, *Vospominaniia: Tsarstvovanie Nikolaia II* (Berlin, "Slovo," 1922), I, pp. 143-146. See also Jean de Bloch [Ivan Bliokh], *La guerre: traduction de l'ouvrage russe: La guerre future, aux points de vue technique, économique et politique* (6 vols.; Paris, 1898-1900, reprinted in New York by Garland Publishing Co., 1971).

A Soviet writer in 1922 condemned Tsarist policy for proposing mainly to freeze the arms race instead of calling for complete disarmament. He also condemned British policy (1906) and President Harding's (1921) for seeking merely to limit arms spending until such time as conditions again favored investing heavily in armaments. M. Pavlovich writing in *Ot Vashingtona do Genui* (Moscow: Vysshii voeennyi redaktsionnyi sovet, 1922), pp. 5-11. His essay could easily be used by Peking commentators to criticize Moscow's position in the SALT negotiations.

8. For historical analyses of recent Soviet participation in efforts to contain the arms race, see Thomas B. Larson, *Disarmament and Soviet Policy, 1964-1968* (Englewood Cliffs, N.J.: Prentice-Hall, Inc., 1969), pp. 139-183; Roman Kolkowicz and Others, *The Soviet Union and Arms Control: A Superpower Dilemma* (Baltimore: The John Hopkins Press, 1970); Thomas W. Wolfe, "Soviet Approaches to SALT," *Problems of Communism*, XIX, No. 5 (September-October 1970), pp. 1-10; Lawrence T. Caldwell, "Soviet Attitudes to SALT," *Adelphi Papers* (London), No. 75 (February 1971).

9. See Nikolai Notovitch, *La Pacification de l'Europe et Nicolas II* (Paris: P. Ollendorf, 1899). For a study of Stalin's use of the peace movement as an adjunct to Soviet policy, see Marshall D. Shulman, *Stalin's Foreign Policy Reappraised* (Cambridge, Mass.: Harvard University Press, 1963).

10. Sovietologists have probably exaggerated the degree to which various parts of the Soviet policy apparatus have worked in concert. For a collection of essays that challenge the old orthodoxy, see H. Gordon Skilling and Franklyn Griffiths, *Interest Groups in Soviet Politics* (Princeton, N.J.: Princeton University Press, 1971). Of particular relevance to the concerns of this book, see the essay by Franklyn Griffiths (discussed later in this chapter), "Inner Tensions in the Soviet Approach to 'Disarmament'," *International Journal*, XXII, No. 4 (Autumn 1967), pp. 593-617; also Kolkowicz and Others, op. cit., 9-17.

The earlier emphasis on monolithic interpretations of Soviet foreign policy might have reflected more on the *Pravda* cartoon showing Chicherin's frustrations arising from Zinoviev's passionate speeches, included in Louis Fischer, *The Soviets in World Affairs, 1917-1929* (2 vols.; 2nd ed.; Princeton, N.J.: Princeton University Press, 1951), II, p. 471. The introduction to the second edition also contains material derived from interviews on the differences between Litvinov, Chicherin, and Trotsky. See ibid., I, p. xii-xvi.

11. This thesis does not ring true for A.A. Gromyko, but it is implicitly supported in the recollections of I.M. Maisky, "Diplomats of the Lenin School: Georgi Chicherin," *New Times*, No. 44 (November 1, 1967), pp. 10-13. See also A. Leonidov, "Socialism's First Diplomats," *New Times*, No. 28 (July 12, 1967), pp. 12-16.

Chicherin joined the Tsarist Foreign Ministry in 1898, just as preparations began for the First Hague Conference.

For detailed studies of Chicherin and Litvinov, see the essays by Theodore H. von Laue and Henry L. Roberts in Gordon A. Craig and Felix Gilbert, eds., *The Diplomats, 1919-1939* (Princeton, N.J.: Princeton University Press, 1953).

See also the analytical survey by Robert M. Slusser, "The Role of the Foreign Ministry," in Ivo J. Lederer, ed., *Russian Foreign Policy* (New Haven, Conn.: Yale University Press, 1962), pp. 197-242, esp. the discussion of Litvinov's place in the power struggles of the 1930s, at pp. 215-230. Many other essays in the Lederer book are relevant to the problems of continuity and change discussed here.

12. From 1917 until 1973 there have been only seven Soviet Foreign Ministers: Trotsky (November 1917-April 1918); Chicherin (1918-1929); Litvinov (1929-1939); Molotov (1939-1949 and 1953-1956); Vyshinsky (1949-1953); Shepilov during 1956); Gromyko (1957-   ). That Gromyko's term has been the longest, extending through the regime of Brezhnev as well as Khrushchev, is a commentary on the role of the specialist. The perquisites of professional status were also suggested in 1971 when Gromyko's son, Anatoly, toured the United States, accompanied by the Deputy Permanent Representative of the USSR at the United Nations. Though Gromyko's son is associated with a

research institute in Moscow, Soviet Ambassador Israelian deferred to him in matters of protocol and speaking privileges.

The first two professionals—Chicherin and Litvinov—became members of the Party Central Committee only late in their careers. Gromyko attained this status in 1956. Trotsky and Molotov were the only Foreign Ministers to become full members in the Party Politburo until Gromyko did in 1973. Vyshinsky and Shepilov were alternate members of the Politburo (or Presidium) during their incumbency.

As Aspaturian has noted, the Party leaders have historically preferred "a low-ranking Party member as Foreign Minister rather than one of first rank, except under critical circumstances, since it enhances the flexibility of Soviet diplomacy while hampering that of other countries, who are forced to accommodate their diplomacy to the bureaucratic channels of the Soviet Foreign Office." When the Foreign Minister is of top rank, "he participates in the decisions he is asked to execute, and in at least two cases (Molotov and Shepilov), has actually flouted the will of the decision-makers in favor of executing a foreign policy of his own choosing." See Vernon V. Aspaturian, "Soviet Foreign Policy," in Roy C. Macridis, ed., *Foreign Policy in World Politics* (2d ed.; Englewood Cliffs, N.J.: Prentice-Hall, Inc., 1962), pp. 133-199 at p. 176.

13. The following analysis is based on Franklyn Griffiths, "Origins of Peaceful Coexistence: A Historical Note," *Survey*, No. 50 (January 1964), pp. 195-201.

14. Ibid., p. 201.

15. Walter C. Clemens, Jr., "Lenin on Disarmament," *Slavic Review*, XXIII, No. 3 (September 1964), pp. 504-525.

16. M. Trush, "Lenin's Foreign Policy Activity (April-July 1922)," *International Affairs* (Moscow), No. 1 (January 1970), pp. 63-66 at p. 64.

17. George Modelski, "The Foreign Ministers as a World Elite," *Peace Research Society (International), Papers*, XIV, 1970 (The Ann Arbor Conference, 1969), pp. 31-46. See also Barry R. Farrell, "Foreign Policies of Open and Closed Political Societies," in Farrell, ed., *Approaches to Comparative and International Politics* (Chicago: Northwestern University Press, 1966), pp. 167-208.

18. See, e.g., L. Trotskii, *Kak vooruzhalas' revoliutsiia: na voennoi rabote* (3 vols.; Moscow: Vysshii voennyi redaktsionnyi sovet, 1923-1925). On Trotsky's project of "militarization of labor," see Isaac Deutscher, *The Prophet Armed, Trotsky: 1879-1921* (New York and London: Oxford University Press, 1954), pp. 487-503. Trotsky did, however, argue for a reduction of Soviet military personnel and their transfer to civilian production in 1920. See Walter C. Clemens, Jr., "Soviet Disarmament Proposals and the Cadre-Territorial Army," *Orbis*, VII, No. 4 (Winter 1964), notes 14 and 15. In exile in 1935, on the other hand, Trotsky castigated the Second and the Third Internationals for day-dreaming about disarmament and the League of Nations. See *Trotsky's Diary in Exile*

(Cambridge, Mass.: Harvard University Press, 1958), pp. 113-114. For a minor spat between Trotsky and Lenin in 1921 liquidation of a coast guard department, see the author's "Lenin on Disarmament," loc. cit., note 66.

19. Frunze would have preferred to forestall the transition to a mixed cadre-territorial army. See his *Sobranie sochinenii* (3 vols.; Moscow: Gosudarstvennoe izdatel'stvo, 1926-1929), II, p. 8. Also his *Izbrannye proizvedeniia* (2 vols.; Moscow: Voennoe izdatel'stvo, 1957), II, p. 20. See also the author's "Soviet Disarmament Proposals and the Cadre-Territorial Army," loc. cit., note 16. Frunze continued in the mid-1920s the sharp formulations made by Lenin in the years of War Communism about the inevitability of an armed struggle between the capitalist and communist systems. See Frunze, *Sobranie sochinenii*, III, 104.

Military colonies combining farming and soldiering were set up under Tsar Alexander I. On these and other military practices having latter-day analogues in Soviet times, see John S. Curtiss, "The Peasant and the Army," *The Peasant in Nineteenth-Century Russia*, ed. by Wayne S. Vucinich (Stanford, Calif.: Stanford University Press, 1968), pp. 108-132.

20. See, e.g., K.E. Voroshilov, *Oborona SSSR* (3rd ed.; Moscow: Voennyi vestnik, 1928), pp. 28-36, 89, 160-170; *K.E. Voroshilov: stat'i i rechi* (Moscow: Partizdat TsK VKP (b), 1937), pp. 513, 540.

21. See, e.g., Roman Kolkowicz, *The Soviet Military and the Communist Party* (Princeton, N.J.: Princeton University Press, 1967), pp. 153-165. See also the materials attributed to Oleg Penkovskiy, *The Penkovskiy Papers* (Garden City, N.Y.: Doubleday & Co., Inc., 1965), pp. 231-260.

22. Frunze, *Sobranie sochinenii*, II, p. 134.

23. For corroborating documentation, see *The Nuclear Revolution in Soviet Military Affairs*, trans. and ed. by William R. Kintner and Harriet Fast Scott (Norman, Oklahoma: University of Oklahoma Press, 1968). The apparent alarm in the Soviet Defense Ministry regarding the consequences of any SALT accord was manifested for example, in "A Policy of Active Resistance to Aggression," *Krasnaia Zvezda*, June 1, 1971: "Our preparedness to support real measures for disarmament must match and does match our preparedness for any turn of events." The evolution from 1968 through 1972 is traced in Thomas W. Wolfe, "Soviet Interests in SALT," in William R. Kintner and Robert L. Pfaltzgraff, Jr., eds., *SALT: Implications for Arms Control in the 1970s* (Pittsburgh: University of Pittsburgh Press, 1973), pp. 34-41.

24. "Military Men in the Higher Organs of the CPSU," *Radio Liberty Dispatch*, April 20, 1971.

25. For documentation, see, e.g., Walter C. Clemens, Jr., *Outer Space and Arms Control* (Cambridge, Mass.: The M.I.T. Center for Space Research, 1966/processed/), pp. 44-47.

26. See the author's "Lenin on Disarmament," loc. cit.

27. On Stalin's personal participation and oversight of programs during

World War II aimed at improving Soviet technology in ways that would overtake the West, e.g., in range of fighter planes, see the memoirs of a leading Soviet engineer and designer: A. Iakovlev, *Tsel' zhizni (zapiski aviakonstruktora)* (2d and enlarged edition; Moscow: Politizdat, 1969), esp. pp. 336-351.

28. Even in the 1920s and 1930s, however, there were Soviet writers and diplomats who took an "analytical middle marginalist" or "marginalist anti-war" approach to disarmament talks. Some of them, such as E.A. Korovin, continued this line despite criticism from powerful foes. Litvinov and his secretary at the League negotiations, Boris Shtein (the present author's mentor at Moscow University in 1958), seemed also to belong to this non-ideological grouping. For references, see Griffiths, "Inner Tensions in the Soviet Approach to 'Disarmament'," loc. cit., pp. 600-602.

29. See Marshall D. Shulman, *Stalin's Foreign Policy Reappraised* (Cambridge, Mass.: Harvard University Press, 1963).

30. See Lincoln P. Bloomfield, Walter C. Clemens, Jr., Franklyn Griffiths, *Khrushchev and the Arms Race* (Cambridge, Mass.: The M.I.T. Press, 1966).

31. "Open Letter" of the CPSU Central Committee "To All Party Organizations and All Communists of the Soviet Union," *Pravda*, July 14, 1963.

32. See George H. Quester, "On the Identification of Real and Pretended Communist Military Doctrine," *Journal of Conflict Resolution*, X, No. 2 (June 1966), pp. 172-179.

Reduced to its simplest outlines, Quester's model says that a government's declaratory policy will either deprecate or exaggerate the role of nuclear weapons in the following manner:

| | PHASES* | | | |
	I	II	III	IV
military decisiveness	–	–	+	+
pain-inflicting capabilities	–	+	+	–

*(– to deprecate   + to exaggerate)

If we apply this model to Soviet responses to environmental change, outlined above, there appears to be a rough fit. Phase I applied from 1945 to the early 1950s. Once Stalin passed from the scene, however, monolithic doctrine became a thing of the past. In the years since 1953, therefore, we see a struggle going on between political leaders (e.g., between Malenkov and Khrushchev); between military strategists (e.g., missile-minded "modernists" and "conservatives" for balanced forces); and between political and military factions—each with allies in the others' camp. Nevertheless, Phase II of Quester's model seemed to apply generally from 1954 until Sputnik I and the first Soviet ICBM test. From 1957 to 1961 Soviet doctrine moved between Phases III and IV, in part because it was unclear in the West whether the USSR had obtained rough parity or superiority or neither. As the missile gap myth was exploded in the early 1960s, the USSR moved back to doctrines ranging between Phase II and III. In the late 1960s, however, the increase in Soviet ICBM capabilities led to doctrinal claims ranging again between Phases III and IV.

33. See the author's "Ideology in Soviet Disarmament Policy," *Journal of Conflict Resolution*, VIII, No. 1 (March 1964), pp. 7-22.

Chapter 3
The Conditions for Arms Control:
Cuba to SALT II

1. For a fuller discussion of the pros and cons, see Chapter 4.

2. The tone of this technical approach was ably set in Donald G. Brennan, ed., *Arms Control, Disarmament, and National Security* (New York: George Brazziler, 1961) and has been continued in the more partisan collections on the pros and cons of ABM defense. A broader gauged study is David V. Edwards, *Arms Control in International Politics* (New York: Holt, Rinehart and Winston, Inc., 1969). For a critical review, see Davis Bobrow in the *American Political Science Review*, LX, No. 4 (December 1969), pp. 1339-1340.

3. League of Nations, *Official Journal, Special Supplement*, No. 9 (1922), p. 27.

4. *Conférence de Moscou pour la limitation des armements* (Moscow: Commissariat du Peuple aux Affaires Etrangères, 1923).

5. See E.A. Korovin and V.V. Egor'ev, *Razoruzhenie* (Moscow: Gosizdat, 1930), pp. 151-154.

6. From a speech by K.T. Mazurov at the Kremlin Palace of Congress on the anniversary of the Bolshevik Revolution. See *Pravda*, November 7, 1972, p. 2. Telegrams of congratulation reprinted that day came from the following countries (in order): Bulgaria, Hungary, North Vietnam, East Germany, Outer Mongolia, Poland, Czechoslovakia, Yugoslavia, India, Iraq and—in much briefer messages—from the Presidents of Italy and the United States and the Emperor of Japan! The omissions, of course, are even more ironic than the inclusions.

7. Iu. Kostko, "Voennaia konfrontatsiia i problema bezopasnosti v Evrope," *Mirovaia Ekonomika i Mezhdunarodnye Otnosheniia*, No. 9 (September 1972), pp. 17-25 at 24. See also his argument in ibid., No. 6 (June 1972), pp. 87-89.

8. *Peking Review*, November 3, 1972, pp. 22-23. For background, see the author's "The Sino-Soviet Dispute—Dogma and Dialectics on Disarmament," *International Affairs* (London), Vol. 41, No. 2 (April 1965), pp. 204-222.

9. "Parity" means equivalence—not precise equality—of opposing forces, such that each side can accomplish comparable results, e.g., destruction of a certain percentage of civilian or military targets in a second strike. Soviet writers

use a similar but more ambiguous term when they assert that the 1972 SALT accords were based on foundations of "equal security [*odinokavaia bezopasnost'*]."

10. See also Roman Kolkowicz et al., *The Soviet Union and Arms Control: A Superpower Dilemma* (Baltimore: Johns Hopkins Press, 1970), pp. 34-38.

11. For negotiations in the mid-1960s, see, e.g., the author's *The Arms Race and Sino-Soviet Relations* (Stanford: The Hoover Institution, 1968).

12. For a number of options considered and put forward by the U.S. in SALT I, see John Newhouse, *Cold Dawn* (New York: Holt, Rinehart and Winston, 1973), pp. 170-186.

13. Colin S. Gray has argued that the 1972 SALT accords were based not on "parity" but upon "presently balanced asymmetries." His major thesis, however, is that they enshrined an arms control package "asymmetrical in ways that could promote 'instability' for the rest of this decade and beyond." See his "The Arms Race is About Politics," *Foreign Policy*, No. 9 (Winter 1972-73), pp. 117, 125.

14. For background, see John W. Spanier and Joseph L. Nogee, *The Politics of Disarmament: A Study in Soviet-American Gamesmanship* (New York: Praeger, 1962).

15. See Roger Fisher, *International Conflict for Beginners* (New York: Harper & Row, 1969), pp. 15-26.

16. *De facto* Soviet capital city defenses but no ICBM defenses, U.S. missile defenses but no capital defenses; *de jure* equal rights in each type.

17. W.K.H. Panofsky, "From SALT I to SALT II," *Survey*, XIX, No. 2 (Spring 1973), pp. 160-174 at p. 160. Recognition of linkages between the global superpower confrontation and superpower interests in the Middle East helped in one political-military exercise to resolve an Arab-Israeli crisis. See the author's "How the U.S.S.R. Brought Peace to the Middle East in 1972," *War/Peace Report*, X, No. 6 (June/July 1970), pp. 14-23.

18. Marshall D. Shulman in *Survey*, XIX, No. 2 (Spring 1973), p. 181.

19. Panofsky, loc. cit., p. 164.

20. *Statement of Secretary of Defense Elliot L. Richardson Before the Senate Armed Services Committee on the FY 1974 Defense Budget and FY 1974-1978 Program, March 28, 1973* (Washington: U.S. Government Printing Office, 1973), pp. 55-56.

21. Shulman, loc. cit., p. 181.

22. Charles E. Osgood, *An Alternative to War or Surrender* (Urbana: University of Illinois Press, 1962).

23. For references, see Walter C. Clemens, Jr., *Soviet Disarmament Policy, 1917-1963: An Annotated Bibliography of Soviet and Western Sources* (Stanford: Hoover Institution, 1965), pp. 78-86, 104, 125.

24. Estimates by the Stockholm International Peace Research Institute on defense expenditures for Warsaw Pact and NATO countries are given in *SIPRI*

Yearbook of World Armaments and Disarmament, 1969/70 (New York: Humanities Press, 1971), pp. 28-30.

25. Washington's sanguine hopes may reflect the more positive experiences gained from leverage enjoyed in Europe between the two world wars.

26. Historical studies of these periods are provided, e.g., in the SIPRI *Yearbook* for 1968-69, 1969/70 and for 1972 (New York: Humanities Press, 1970, 1971, 1972); in the *Annual Report* to Congress of the U.S. Arms Control and Disarmament Agency; and in *Strategic Survey*, issued annually by the International Institute for Strategic Studies in London.

27. These evaluations are meant (a) to refer only to *the forces affected by the agreement* and not to the overall military balance; and (b) to describe the *objective* situation *following* implementation of the accord. We further assume, however, that in these cases where much time and energy goes into consideration of the pros and cons of the agreement, both governments would perceive the objective realities in much the same way. Estimates regarding "sufficiency" and "other trade-offs," of course, require us to read the minds of political leaders much more than do evaluations of "symmetry" or "parity." Though there is certainly room for disagreement and divergent interpretation in particular cases, these rankings have been generally corroborated in validity checks by independent specialists with experience both in academia and in the government (Soviet as well as U.S.).

For definitions of symmetry, and the other terms used in these rankings, see above, note 9, and the accompanying text, pp. 58-61.

N.A.= non-applicable.

A fuller analysis of the conditions for arms control would have to inquire also into the periods when both sides appeared to come *close* to accords, or when they took positions that facilitated agreements several years later (e.g., Moscow's refusal to supply more nuclear know-how or material to China in 1959). Our list omits the moratorium on nuclear testing observed by London, Washington, and Moscow in 1958-61 and the first formal arms control treaty signed by the superpowers and others after World War II, the 1959 Antarctica Treaty.

28. The notion that Kennedy struck Khrushchev as "soft" at Vienna in 1961 may derive from a myth. At any rate it receives no support from *Khrushchev Remembers* (Boston: Little, Brown, 1970), p. 458. In the event, Kennedy took a series of resolute steps in 1961 (some of them noted in ibid., pp. 458-459) that should have disabused Khrushchev of any illusions about the President's capacity for determined action well before Moscow embarked on its Cuban missile gambit.

29. These themes are manifest, e.g., in I. Biriukov, "Fruitful Results, Great Tasks," *Pravda*, June 3, 1972, p. 4; a positive report from Bonn, and from the UN in *Izvestiia*, June 4, 1972, p. 1; in Viktor Mayevskii, "In the Interests of All Peoples," *Pravda*, June 8, 1972, p. 4; "In the Cause of Peace and Socialism,"

Pravda, June 8, 1972, pp. 3-4; a roundtable discussion on Moscow Domestic Service in Russian 0900 GMT June 11, 1972; a major article by N. Inozemtsev, "The Principle-Mindedness and Effectiveness of Soviet Foreign Policy," *Pravda*, June 9, 1972, pp. 4-5; "Yesterday's Men," *Literaturnaia Gazeta*," June 7, 1972; N. Arkadyev in *Novoe Vremia*, No. 23 (June 2, 1972), pp. 4-5; and V. Matveev in *Izvestiia*, June 10, 1972, p. 4. Even *Krasnaya Zvezda* published four letters supporting the SALT accords written by military personnel (June 3, 1972, p. 1), though an article the previous day ("Improving the Quality of Political Studies") spoke of the necessity "to unmask more convincingly and specifically the aggressive essence of imperialism. . . . " Lenin's approach to arms limitation was discussed in still another article on "Genoa" (1922) in the May issue of *International Affairs* and in the Inozemstev article cited above.

While the Soviet press downplayed Nixon's assurances to Congress that the U.S. would not be weaker than the USSR, *Pravda* (June 4, 1972) quoted *Morning Star* reports from England on U.S. conservatives accusing Nixon of "selling out" in a deal that would assure Soviet superiority in the years to come.

Soviet press surveys of events in other parts of the world emphasized the role of negotiations in settling difficulties: in Indochina, in the Middle East, and in Europe. See, e.g., *Izvestiia*, June 7, 1972, p. 2.

For comparable material in 1963, see *Khrushchev and the Arms Race*, especially pp. 183-200.

30. The emphasis in 1963 seemed to be more revolutionary than in 1972. Thus, Soviet apologists in the earlier period stressed the importance of the "socialist camp led by the USSR" in the campaign against capitalist imperialism (more important than the front of oppressed peoples which China aspired to lead). The 1972 material seemed to stress more the importance of great power stability: Thus, Academician Inozemtsev wrote in *Pravda* (June 9): "The normalization of relations between the Soviet Union—the most powerful socialist state and the first to embark on the path of building communism—and the United States—the biggest contemporary capitalist state—is a matter of paramount importance. The international political climate largely depends upon the direction in which Soviet-American relations will develop." He then quoted Lenin on the importance of knowing how to compromise while remaining true to revolutionary principles.

Chapter 4
The Arms Control Road to Peace:
Pros and Cons

1. This chapter is adapted from essays appearing in *World Affairs*, LXXXV, No. 3 (Winter 1972), pp. 197-219 and in Rudolf Weiler and Valentin Zsifkovits, eds., *Unterwegs zum Frieden* (Vienna, Freiburg, Basel: Herder, 1973), pp. 369-390.

2. See, e.g., Peter A. Corning, "The Biological Bases of Behavior and Some Implications for Political Science," *World Politics*, XXIII, No. 3 (April 1971), pp. 321-370. Lionel Tiger and Robin Fox, *The Imperial Animal* (New York: Holt, Rinehart and Winston, 1971). See also the essay review of Ernest Becker, "Biological Imperialism," *Society*, IX, No. 5 (March 1972), pp. 40-43.

3. On the limited value of disarmament as a direct approach to peace, see Inis L. Claude, Jr., *Swords Into Plowshares: The Problems and Progress of International Organization* (4th ed.; New York: Random House, 1971), pp. 286-311. For a survey of the literature on Soviet policy during the time when Moscow tended to emphasize the value of general disarmament rather than "mere" arms limitations, see Walter C. Clemens, Jr., *Soviet Disarmament Policy, 1917-1963: An Annotated Bibliography of Soviet and Western Sources* (Stanford, Calif.: The Hoover Institution, 1965).

4. See John W. Spanier and Joseph L. Nogee, *The Politics of Disarmament: A Study in Soviet-American Gamesmanship* (New York: Praeger, 1962).

5. On the political uses of disarmament negotiations by the Soviet leadership, see Lincoln P. Bloomfield, Walter C. Clemens, Jr., Franklyn Griffiths, *Khrushchev and the Arms Race: Soviet Interests in Arms Control and Disarmament, 1954-1964* (Cambridge, Mass.: The M.I.T. Press, 1966), esp. pp. 59-76, 271-276.

6. On "Stage II Leninism," see above, Chapter 2.

7. On these distinctions, see Edward Hallett Carr, *The Twenty Years Crisis 1919-1923* (London: Macmillan, 1939), Chapter II.

8. W.K.H. Panofsky, "From SALT I to SALT II," *Survey*, XIX, No. 2 (Spring 1973), p. 162. On the first three goals, see Morton H. Halperin, *Contemporary Military Strategy* (Boston: Little, Brown, 1967).

9. A radical critique of both disarmament and arms control as ways to peace was presented by Johan Galtung at the International Studies Association annual meeting, Dallas, in March 1972. He argued that arms control may be seen merely as a way of perfecting the mechanisms of the deterrence system. Arms control "is to the power-market what governmental safeguards against trusts, etc., are to the economic market: a projection of free competition. Both systems operate under the same basic assumption: if all parties try to be rich/secure, the total system will be rich/secure. At best, both propositions are true to a limited extent only. Beyond that, the competitive effort to become rich leads to public poverty through depletion and pollution, and the competitive effort to become secure leads to the burden of arms races and the insecurity accompanying it—in addition to depletion and pollution." Galtung further argues that emphasis on "balanced" controls reinforces deterrence-type thinking, while a focus on "control" serves as a "stimulus to develop a new military technology that will escape any control efforts." His conclusion is that "so long as a peace structure does not exist, a new crisis, almost certain to be produced within a non-peace structure, will only lead to rearmament...." See Johan Galtung, "Europe: Bipolar, Bicentric or Cooperative?" (pp. 4-5).

10. See the author's "Ecology and International Relations," *International Journal*, XXVIII, No. 1 (Winter 1972-3), pp. 1-27.

11. See the author's, "The Ecology of Weaponry," *Bulletin of the Atomic Scientists*, XXVI, No. 7 (September 1970), pp. 27-31.

12. On preventive diplomacy, see Claude, op. cit., pp. 312-333.

13. See Richard A. Falk, *This Endangered Planet: Prospects and Proposals for Human Survival* (New York: Random House, 1971); Harold and Margaret Sprout, *Toward a Politics of the Planet Earth* (New York: Van Nostrand Reinhold Co., 1971).

14. See Kenneth N. Waltz, *Man, The State and War: A Theoretical Analysis* (New York: Columbia University Press, 1965); also, J. David Singer, "The Level-of-Analysis Problem in International Relations," reprinted in James N. Rosenau, ed., *International Politics and Foreign Policy* (Rev. ed.; New York: The Free Press, 1969), pp. 20-29. See also above, Chapter 2, pp. 38-39.

15. See, e.g., Adam Ulam, *The Rivals: America and Russia Since World War II* (New York: Viking, 1971).

16. As noted in Chapter 2, these modes of explanation are utilized in Graham T. Allison, *Essence of Decision: Explaining the Cuban Missile Crisis* (Boston: Little, Brown, 1971).

17. Malraux reports Mao as saying in 1965: "All I want are six atom bombs. With those bombs I know neither side will attack me. With those bombs I can guarantee the peace of the world." (*The New York Times*, February 9, 1972, p. 4.)

18. Allison, op. cit., pp. 131-132, p. 206.

19. See above, p. 12.

20. *U.S. Foreign Policy for the 1970s: The Emerging Structure of Peace. A Report to the Congress by Richard Nixon, President of the United States, February 9, 1972* (Washington: U.S. Government Printing Office, 1972), p. 29.

21. See Charles E. Osgood, *An Alternative to War or Surrender* (Urbana, Ill.: University of Illinois Press, 1962).

22. Robert Jervis, "Hypotheses on Misperception," reprinted in Rosenau, op. cit., pp. 239-254.

23. See ESP data reported in Chapter 1, Proposition IX.

24. See Walter C. Clemens, Jr., "A Propositional Analysis of the International Relations Theory in Temper—A Computer Simulation of Cold War Conflict," in William D. Coplin, ed., *Simulation in the Study of Politics* (Chicago: Markham, 1968), pp. 59-101, at 68-73.

25. Michael J. Brenner, "Strategic Interdependence and the Politics of Inertia: Paradoxes of European Defense Cooperation," *World Politics*, XXIII, No. 4 (July 1971), pp. 635-664.

26. Samuel P. Huntington, "Arms Races: Prerequisites and Results," reprinted in George H. Quester, ed., *Power, Action and Interaction: Readings on International Politics* (Boston: Little, Brown, 1971), pp. 499-541 at 500.

27. See above, Chapter 2.

28. See Walter C. Clemens, Jr., "Maintaining the Status Quo in East Central Europe: the 1930s and the 1960s," *World Affairs*, Vol. 133, No. 2 (September 1970), pp. 98-105.

29. Data on most of these problems and those enumerated in the following paragraph may be found in the annual yearbook of the Stockholm International Peace Research Institute, *World Armaments and Disarmament* (New York: Humanities Press [title varies], 1969-   ).

30. Studies by the U.S. government indicate that worldwide military expenditures rose steeply from 1964 to 1969, roughly along the same slope as world gross national product, GNP per capita falling steadily as world population grew faster than economic production. From 1968 to 1970, however, world GNP shot ahead of world military expenditures, which decreased in 1970. This movement was spearheaded by the developed countries, which account for the largest share of GNP as well as military expenditures. For the developing countries, however, military expenditures continued to run ahead of GNP in 1969-70, though both curves rose sharply. See *United States Foreign Policy, 1971: A Report of the Secretary of State* (Washington: U.S. Government Printing Office, 1972), p. 257.

Chapter 5
A Modernist Approach to Arms Control:
Toward Interdependence

1. Presidential address of Alexander L. George, "Some Thoughts on an Agenda for International Studies," *Newsletter of the International Studies Association*, No. 3 (June 1973), pp. 8-12.

2. These interdependencies are explored in the World Order Project, directed by Saul H. Mendlovitz for the Institute for World Order. Similar problems are analyzed in Andrei D. Sakharov, *Progress, Coexistence, and Intellectual Freedom* (New York: W.W. Norton, 1968), p. 108. For discussion, see the author's "Sakharov: A Man for Our Times," *Bulletin of the Atomic Scientists*, XXVII, No. 10 (December 1971), pp. 4-6, 51-56.

3. The dynamics of the arms race are discussed in more detail, e.g., in Steven Rosen, ed., *Testing the Theory of the Military-Industrial Complex* (Lexington, Mass.: D.C. Heath, 1973); the author's "Ecology of Weaponry," *Bulletin of the Atomic Scientists*, XXVI, No. 7 (September 1970), pp. 27-31; and in an East-West symposium sponsored by the International Institute for Peace in Vienna, edited by Walter Hollitscher, *Aggressionstrieb und Krieg* (Stuttgart: Deutsche Verlags-Anstalt, 1973).

4. An earlier version of these principles appeared in the author's "Arms Control in 1975—the Utility of a Modernist Approach," *Review of International*

Affairs (Belgrade), No. 418 (September 5, 1967), pp. 19-20 and No. 419 (September 20, 1967), pp. 16-19.

5. *Mutual Aid* (Boston: Porter Sargent [n.d.]), first published 1902.

6. Heda Kovály and Erazim Kohák, *The Victors and the Vanquished* (New York: Horizon Press, 1973), p. 8.

7. See the author's "Toward a Theory of Preventive Arms Control," in *Challenges from the Future*, Proceedings of the International Future Research Conference (Tokyo: Kosanda, Ltd., 1971), III, 405-420. For a critique of the biological convention, see *World Armaments and Disarmament, SIPRI Yearbook 1972* (New York: Humanities Press, 1972), pp. 502 ff.

8. From the text of statements agreed upon and initialed by the Heads of Delegations on May 26, 1972, in *Arms Control Report: 12th Annual Report to Congress*, U.S. Arms Control and Disarmament Agency, January 1–December 31, 1972 (Washington, D.C.: U.S. Government Printing Office, 1973), pp. 50-53.

9. Admiral Thomas H. Moorer, *United States Military Posture for FY 1974*, Statement Before the Senate Armed Services Committee on 28 March 1973, pp. 19-20.

10. *Cold Dawn: The Story of SALT* (New York: Holt, Rinehart and Winston, 1973), pp. 181-182.

12. See the author's "European Arms Control: How, What, and When?" *International Journal*, XXVII, No. 1 (Winter 1971-72), pp. 45-72.

13. For an argument that U.S. technological superiority is being lost to the USSR and needs to be regained, see General George S. Brown, USAF, "Technology: The Mold for Future Strategy," *Strategic Review* (Washington: United States Strategic Institute, Spring 1973), pp. 23-28. Such arguments seem unfounded when read in the critical light of the SIPRI yearbooks on world armament and disarmament, cited in earlier chapters.

14. See, e.g., Seyom Brown, "The Changing Essence of Power," *Foreign Affairs*, LI, No. 2 (January 1973), pp. 286-299.

15. Charles E. Osgood, *An Alternative to War or Surrender* (Urbana, Ill.: University of Illinois Press, 1962). For applications in other areas, see the author's "GRIT at Panmunjom: Conflict and Cooperation in Divided Korea," *Asian Survey*, XIII, No. 6 (June 1973), pp. 531-559, especially notes 22 and 28.

16. See the author's "Ecology and International Relations," *International Journal*, XVIII, No. 1 (Winter 1972-3), pp. 1-27.

17. *Survey*, XIX, No. 2 (Spring 1973), p. 180.

18. Marshall D. Shulman, *Beyond the Cold War* (New Haven, Conn.: Yale University Press, 1966), p. 110.

19. *Mezhdunarodnye otnosheniia posle vtoroi mirovoi voiny* (Moscow: Institut Mirovoi Ekonomiki i Mezhdunarodnykh Otnoshenii, 1962), I, xxiv.

20. "Foreign Policy for Disillusioned Liberals," *Foreign Policy*, No. 9 (Winter 1972-73), pp. 55-68 at p. 63.

21. Ibid., p. 68.

22. See the pioneering work of Vincent P. Rock, *A Strategy of Interdependence* (New York: Scribner's, 1964); also the anthology based around President Kennedy's American University speech, *Toward a Strategy of Peace*, ed. Walter C. Clemens, Jr. (Chicago: Rand McNally, 1965).

23. As Zbigniew Brzezinski has noted, "What we now have, and are likely to have for some time, is a combination of a bipolar power world with a multiple state interplay." There are two overlapping triangles, one of them basically competitive and embracing America-China-Russia, and a basically cooperative one involving America-Europe-Japan. See his "The Balance of Power Delusion," *Foreign Policy*, No. 7 (Summer 1972), pp. 54-59 at p. 57. Brzezinski describes the nuclear balance as "2-$1/2 + y + z$." (Ibid., p. 54.)

24. Only 3 percent of the experts polled in the ESP study thought it likely that Chinese leaders would use their nuclear power less "rationally" or "responsibly" than other nuclear powers. But 61 percent saw China moving vigorously to develop nuclear forces more powerful than those of France or Britain at their present levels of development. A small plurality expected China to possess a significant "second-strike" force poised against the USSR in the period 1973-77.

Bibliography Note

For texts of most of the arms control measures mentioned in this book, see *Disarmament and Security: A Collection of Documents, 1919-55* (Washington: U.S. Government Printing Office, 1956) or the series *Documents on Disarmament*, covering the years 1945-1959 in two volumes and in annual publications for 1961 through the present, published also by the U.S. Government Printing Office, commencing in 1960.

Analysis of arms control matters also requires a reading of the proposals and discussions recorded in the documents of the Conference of the Disarmament Committee, the United Nations General Assembly, and other negotiating forums. For a useful guide, see *The United Nations and Disarmament, 1945-1970* (United Nations: Department of Political and Security Council Affairs, 1970). See also the documentary collection compiled by V.M. Khaitsman, *50 let bor"by SSSR za razoruzhenie* (Moscow: Nauka, 1967).

The notes to this study also provide a general guide to the sources, as well as an indication of the sources of the particular information cited. A complete bibliography would necessarily list literature from many fields of study, as reviewed, for example, in *To End War* by Robert Pickus and Robert Woito (Berkeley, Calif: World Without War Council [Perennial Library], 1971) or *Arms Control and Disarmament; A Quarterly Bibliography with Abstracts and Annotations*, prepared for the U.S. Arms Control and Disarmament Agency, published by the Library of Congress (for which government funding stopped with Volume IX, No. 2 [December 1973]). Important bibliographies as well as original research have been published also by research centers in Canada, the Federal Republic of Germany, Norway, Sweden, the United States and other countries. Information on these and many other sources may be found in Blanche Wiesen Cook, ed., *Bibliography on Peace Research in History* (Santa Barbara, Calif.: Clio Press, 1969); Byron Dexter, ed., *The Foreign Affairs 50-Year Bibliography* (New York: R.R. Bowker Co., 1972); also the author's *Soviet Disarmament Policy, 1917-1963; An Annotated Bibliography of Soviet and Western Sources* (Stanford, Calif.: The Hoover Institution, 1965). Methodological problems are discussed in the introduction to that work and in the section "On Analyzing Soviet Disarmament Policy" in Lincoln P. Bloomfield, Walter C. Clemens, Jr., Franklyn Griffiths, *Khrushchev and the Arms Race: Soviet Interests in Arms Control and Disarmament, 1954-1964* (Cambridge, Mass.: The M.I.T. Press, 1966), the bibliography of which adds to that in *Soviet Disarmament Policy*. Further discussion of the methodological problems in *Khrushchev and the Arms Race* and in the present study may be found in the author's "Underlying Factors in Soviet Disarmament Policy: Problems of Systematic Analysis," *Papers, Peace Research Society (International)*, Vienna Conference (1966).

Index

About the Author

Walter C. Clemens, Jr. is Professor of Political Science at Boston University and Associate of the Russian Research Center, Harvard University. He received the Ph.D. (1961), M.A., and Certificate of the Russian Institute (1957) from Columbia University and the A.B., *Magna Cum Laude*, from Notre Dame University (1955). He has studied for a year in Austria and in the USSR. He has served on the faculties of the University of California, M.I.T., the Salzburg Seminar in American Studies, and lectured extensively in Europe and Asia.

Dr. Clemens served in 1965 as Executive Officer, Arms Control and Disarmament Committee, White House Conference on International Cooperation and in 1972-73 as President, New England Region, International Studies Association. He belongs to the International Institute for Strategic Studies and the Joint Harvard-MIT Arms Control Seminar. He has been a consultant to the Institute for Defense Analyses, the Washington Center of Foreign Policy Research, the Simulmatics Corporation, the National Science Foundation and the Educational Testing Service.

He is the author or coauthor of seven books and numerous articles on international relations, arms control, simulation, ecology, the USSR, Eastern Europe and China.